BANGKOK

Cities of the Imagination

BANGKOK

A cultural and literary history

Maryvelma O'Neil

Signal Books
Oxford

First published in 2008 by
Signal Books Limited
36 Minster Road
Oxford OX4 1LY
www.signalbooks.co.uk

A catalogue record for this book is available from the British Library

ISBN 978-1-904955-39-9 Paper

Cover Design: Baseline Arts
Production: Devdan Sen
All images courtesy Maryvelma O'Neil, except All images courtesy Maryvelma O'Neil, except: p.i Gina Smith/istockphoto; p.43 Mary Lane/istockphoto; pp.55, 114 kevinmillerphoto.com; p.58 Artith Voraphiboonpongse/ istockphoto; p.75 Urban Images/istockphoto; p.92 Vera Bogaerts/istockphoto; p.104 Tourism Authority of Thailand; p.111 Frank van den Bergh/istockphoto; p.189 C W Lawrence Photography/istockphoto; pp.211, 214, 217 Sander Kamp/istockphoto; p.233 Edward Karaa/istockphoto

Cover images: www.kevinmillerphoto.com; Kate Shephard/istockphoto; Richard Stamper/istockphoto; Robert Adrian Hillman/istockphoto

Printed in India

Contents

To my husband Mike, *khun pen khon jai dii lew koo mii nam jai mak mak.*

Foreword

The names of Siam, Ayudhya and then Bangkok evoke a special romance for Europeans that began in the sixteenth century and culminated at the *fin de siècle* when westerners in Bangkok produced numerous written portraits of the incredible floating Siamese capital.

Archives in Europe, especially in Portugal and at the Dutch East India Company, are full of accounts, mostly unread, of Siam. The earliest such description—and one that was read—must be that by Marco Polo, who made Cathay and the Orient the talk of the town in the West. He skirted by a place that was probably Chiang Mai soon after it was founded. Reports started pouring into Europe with the Portuguese capture of Malacca in 1511. Alfonso de Albuquerque, who realized that Malacca was a tributary state of Siam, immediately dispatched an embassy to the Siamese capital, Ayudhya, only to be congratulated by King Ramathibodi II. The Portuguese were then told to keep Malacca on condition that they punished its rebellious sultan on Siam's behalf. Since this is not an academic history book I may have dramatized the episode a little. But all was deadly serious in the 1780s when King Rama I of Bangkok offered Phuket to Captain Francis Light of the British East India Company. Luckily the captain took a wife instead of the island (which is now a major world destination for beach tourism) and asked the Siamese king for Penang instead. So England got Penang and Siam should have received half of Adelaide, since it was founded by Francis Light's Anglo-Siamese son.

The Siamese first burst upon the western scene in 1608 when King Ekathosarat sent Siamese emissaries to Holland. The Siamese were shocked when told that Holland had no king (it was a republic at the time), and the pragmatic Dutch had to make do by placing Prince Maurice of Nassau-Orange, the *stadtholder*, in an elaborate chair on a rostrum to pose as the monarch.

The Siamese developed a taste for the West and followed up with a series of missions to Europe in the 1680s under King Narai the Great. Some of the expeditions, with their exotic cargo of live rhinoceroses, were shipwrecked off Madagascar. But one reached England in 1684, having been chased by Barbary pirates and rescued by the British navy, only to have its gifts, destined for Charles II and Louis XIV, impounded by the Margate customs. Charles, who did not want to lose his presents, sent threatening notes to Parliament, a surprising move given that his father's regicide had taken place not long before. Parliament duly debated, released the diplomatic consignment and the Siamese were treated to some good bitter at a pub in Margate by the local customs officers who then saw them off to France on board the king's personal yacht, the *Charlotte*.

Maryvelma O'Neil picks up this episode in her introduction when she reports, following the (biased) French account, that the Siamese diplomats—there were three in the mission—yawned at the Paris opera. I am not surprised because of the language barrier and because the *Ramakien*, in Siamese eyes, was very much more refined. I am sure westerners would yawn at our *Ramakien* opera, which today is cut down for the benefit of tourists from its entire length of three days.

She then mentions Kosa Pan, the most popular Siamese ambassador to France (1686-87), who did not yawn at anything but thoroughly charmed the French nation, especially at her softest spots. The French *paparazzi* were duly posted outside the gate of the Siamese embassy at 10 Rue Tournon in front of the Luxembourg Palace, and published some juicy accounts in the newspaper of the day, *Le Mercure Gallant*.

Kosa Pan's large embassy was given the grandest audience ever in the Gallery of Mirrors at Versailles and the event was recorded in numerous books and gazettes. It also appeared on a commemorative medallion and the Court almanac, and the ambassador himself left traces behind him including Rue de Siam, the main shopping street in Brest, where he landed to a 21-gun salute in 1686. It is said that Molière's principal Oriental character in *Le Bourgeois Gentilhomme* was actually based on Kosa Pan and that the subsequent vogue of *chinoiserie*, which became the rage of European fashion, was partly due to the Siamese inroad into Europe.

Kosa Pan seems to have been everywhere: he was in the Low Countries to inspect the French conquest; he attended the *levée* of Madame la Dauphine; he witnessed the defence of a thesis, in Latin, by a Siamese student at the Sorbonne; and among over a hundred crates of royal gifts brought from Siam he presented two silver-lined cannons to the Sun King—which were subsequently used to fire on the gates of the Bastille on the fateful date of 14 July 1789.

But what has all this to do with Bangkok, the principal theme of this book?

The same Chao Phraya river runs through Ayudhya and Bangkok, of course. But it is Kosa Pan himself who provides the historical and human link, since he was the direct ancestor of the Chakri kings who built and nurtured Bangkok down the centuries to our time.

When it comes to the Bangkok of the nineteenth and twentieth centuries, I cannot think of any other book that is built upon such a good and complete anthology of western accounts of the Siamese capital—in particular those written by the European visitors and residents at the turn of the nineteenth century, who, reflecting their own *belle époque*, observed the Bangkok phenomenon with refinement, sensitivity and nonchalant humour. The author has retained this *fin-de-siècle* sensitivity and style in her own observations with the child-like first-seen, first-felt, first-smelt and first-heard fascination of Anna in *Anna and the King of Siam*.

For anthropologists of the time, *fin-de-siècle* Bangkok offered fascination in another sense: the water-based or floating city was quickly becoming a land-based city, as its first roads were laid in the 1860s. This metamorphosis was voluntary despite the colonial pressure all around Siam. It was a pressure that demanded an overland mode of transportation and building *parterre*, not a life afloat on water or in amphibious homes.

Rama III, on his deathbed in 1851, counselled his successor to learn from the West but not to become overly fascinated by it. His younger half-brother, Rama IV, then opened up the country to the West. Nothing was new. It was after all in the tradition of King Ekathosarot and King Narai. And it was not due to—although it coincided with—the arrival in Bangkok in 1855 of Sir John Bowing as Queen Victoria's representative, together with gun boats. Rama IV, who learned Latin and English and became a noted mathematician and astronomer, started the English language course in the Royal Palace, expanded the city, built the first streets and sent a dual embassy (there were two embassies at the same time, since his brother, the Second King, also sent a parallel mission) to Queen Victoria and Napoleon III, to their mutual confusion. Rama IV also appointed honorary consuls in Europe, including Sir John Bowring in his retirement, who, in spite of the earlier gun boat diplomacy, became the king's personal friend and Siam's loyal representative in England.

Duality in our history seems to be the national trait of *mai pen rai* or "let it be". We had joint-monarchs, well ahead of William and Mary, at the start of the sixteenth century with King Naresuan and King Ekathosarot. Then today we have two names for the same country: "Thailand" and

"Siam", both official, except that the latter is used only on auspicious occasions. Coexistence of the unlikely is reflected in our two anthems, one republican (or nationalistic); the other monarchist, played on different occasions or even together at diplomatic functions when foreign ambassadors in Bangkok understandably become puzzled. Bangkok today is a flashy modern metropolis overlaying an incorrigible city of the past. It is the epitome of working contradictions.

Sumet Jumsai
Bangkok, July 2007

"When you enter a town where people wink, wink as they do."

– THAI PROVERB

Before jumbo jets shortened the travel time to Bangkok the trip from Europe took about sixteen hours with fuel stops in Dubai and Bombay. During the late 1980s a Red Cross official on a humanitarian mission from Geneva arrived at Chitralada Palace, residence of His Majesty King Bhumibol Adulyadej. After the monarch kindly asked about his journey, the exhausted diplomat replied, "Bangkok is so far!" To which the king quipped in his impeccable French: "Far from what?"

(As related by John de Salis)

Preface and Acknowledgements

This book has its roots in the years I lived and worked in Bangkok: a period that started with a sense of confusion and frustration, but which soon developed into total fascination with the city and its peoples.

Getting to know Bangkok on a deeper level presented a number of real challenges. The first was the sheer difficulty of finding traces of the past in a city that has been radically transformed by urban capitalism, especially in the last fifty years. To try to understand Bangkok is also to engage with contradiction. Conspicuous consumption, widespread materialism and sexual indulgence clash with the governing ethos of Buddhism like Jupiter's thunderbolts. H.M. King Bhumibol Adulyadej, as well as outspoken abbots and secular critics, reiterate the Buddha's core teachings, but such voices are often lost in the constant din.

Looking out from any of Bangkok's skyscrapers today it is hard to locate the glittering temples under the vast modern metropolis. Its new landmarks are towering high-rises that advertise success for the aspirational, gorgeous malls that promote endless shopping and gigantic massage parlours with flashing neon lights that promise orgiastic escape. Add chronic traffic congestion, monsoon flooding, major slums…

This book is not intended as an academic history nor as a conventional guidebook but rather as an attempt to reconstruct the city as it has been imagined and depicted by insiders and outsiders. This imaginary narrative is very different but is in some sense far richer than a straightforward account. It is an evocation of both Old and New Bangkok through the prism of literary and travel writing as well as through my experience.

In delving into the past, one is brought short by the relative sparseness of records. For centuries Siamese* literature was primarily religious and court-sponsored. Texts were inscribed by stylus on specially prepared palm leaves or hand-written on folded manuscripts, but during the destruction of the capital at Ayudhya in 1767 more than nine-tenths of the literature in manuscript form was lost.

The culture and literature of Bangkok was not founded on a Cartesian heritage, as the protagonist of Yukio Mishima's *Temple of the Dawn* (1970) came to see when he visited the city in the late 1960s.

And now Honda realized what was behind the constant smile and the melancholy eyes of the two Siamese princes. It was the feeling of heavy, golden listlessness, of lulling breezes beneath the trees—the constant evasion of any organized logical system; oppressed and languid in the sun. The people of this land of sumptuous temples and flowers and fruits faithfully worshipped the Buddha and believed implicitly in reincarnation.

The *Ramakien*, a rewriting of the famous Indian epic, had an enormous impact on virtually every aspect of Thai culture. In Bangkok, as elsewhere, the performing arts had a predominant cultural role, especially the *khon* masked drama and popular shadow plays.

Siamese prose began to develop during the reign of King Rama IV (1851-68), soon replacing the chanting of poetry as the favoured literary form. The *Royal Gazette*, the earliest periodical dating from 1858 (published by an American missionary), was crucial for the development of modern Thai literature. By mid-century privately owned presses began to churn out a wide variety of works. The fact that Thailand was never colonized meant that, unlike neighbouring countries in Southeast Asia, no western language ever became the official parlance of the country.

By the end of the century we have an idea of the available literature from an account by a French scholar, Lunet de Lajonquière:

Apart from religious texts, which are usually in Pali, literature is negligible, if printed works alone provide a basis for judgment. Up to the present, laws, popular tales, more or less official annals, collections of proverbs, books of fortune telling, plays partly from Chinese sources, translations of Hindu poems and even Arabic tales, and lastly, almanacs and crudely illustrated schoolbooks, have been published. Many of these works are sold in small divisions for a pittance. The printing is bad and mistakes abound.

The professional Thai writer did not appear on the scene until the early 1920s and then the dominant genre of prose fiction was based on tales of mystery and imagination, reflecting popular literature of late Victorian and Edwardian England. A teacher commends a young Thai writer in Kukrit Pramoj's *Many Lives* (1954), then adds, "Once when I was young, I used to like this kind of thing... but writing isn't a real profession in this country."

The course of Thai literature changed dramatically in the 1960s and 1970s when a number of writers took on the dark sides of foreign influence, corruption, dictatorship and rural poverty. Socially conscious authors were prime targets after Field Marshal Sarit Thanarat's coup in 1957. He issued draconian censorship laws, quashed free expression and imprisoned many leftist writers in the name of the international war against communism.

Since 1986 the prestigious SEA Writers' award for Southeast Asian writers has encouraged a new generation of gifted Thai writers. In general, modern urban life in Bangkok is rarely filtered through their works. I have tried to include those who have.

Translations of Thai writing are few and far between and the nation's literature is little known outside the country itself. Herbert P. Phillips published a valuable anthology of modern Thai literature with an ethnographical interpretation (1987). Marcel Barang, a long-time French resident of Bangkok, has translated a select group of modern Thai novels (1994). Susan Fulop Kepner, editor of *The Lioness in Bloom. Modern Thai Fiction about Women* (1996) has rightly noted that "Most Thai literature available in translation reflects the attitudes and objectives of politically active writers, with ties to Western intellectuals."

For all of these reasons I have had to scavenge widely and have drawn upon a varied range of written sources. The works from which I quote include travelogues, novels, memoirs, diaries and reminiscences of westerners who have lived in or visited the city as well as writings by local journalists. More often than not their perceptions of the "other" are coloured by Orientalizing views of social and cultural superiority.

Despite these limitations, many of their responses are highly original and often insightful. They have often genuinely struggled to convey the real sights, sounds and smells that have always been part of Bangkok's great hold on the imagination. Take for example Ernest Young's 1898 description of the giant durian fruit whose entry was forbidden in some local hotels due to its complex and lingering aromas: "a combination of strawberries and cream, nectar and ambrosia, ripe pears and ice cream, but which to the uninitiated suggests more truthfully the presence of exceedingly defective sanitation."

* The name of the nation was changed in 1939 when Siam became Thailand. I have tried to use the former name for the pre-1939 period and Thailand for post-1939 but the two are frequently used interchangeably according to the context. Names of people and places are often spelled in various ways in English transliterations. Official spellings have been used for kings, places and well-known names. Thais are generally called by their given names or nicknames.

You should not surprised if you are presented upon arrival in Bangkok with a *phuang malai*—a delicate floral necklace. The loveliest thread fragrant jasmine petals with accents of colour provided by orchids, marigolds and rosettes at the tips. These spiritual tributes are offered to monks, teachers, parents and friends. Locals make daily visits to the tiny spirit houses that dot the city to leave *malai* for their "residents". Garlands are also worn at many festive events.

This is a fitting occasion to present honorific rings of respect to each of a number of generous and gracious Thais who have significantly enhanced my appreciation of the capital and its varied peoples. I offer deepest gratitude to Her Royal Highness Princess Maha Chakri Sirindhorn for graciously presiding over the inaugural Prince Prisdang Annual Dinner 2007 at the Oriental. Mr. Kurt and Mrs. Penny Wachveitl hosted a magnificent banquet, thanks to the marvellous staff collaboration.

For editorial comments and other support I confer an aromatic *malai* upon my Thai friends: Khun Nid Hinshiranan, Ajarn Kullada Kesboonchoo-Mead, Ajarn Pratoomporn Vajasthira, Khun Nuchan Panna, Khun Yindee Kwangken. Ajarn Chetana Nagavaraja was a true guide and his writings greatly enriched my understanding of Thai culture.

Garlands also go to Samantha Brown, Catherine Butterly, Cynthia Brzak, Jerry Gallagher, Pamela Gerber, Peter J. Henry, Seton Jenkins, Bruce Katz, Brian Martin, Mary Martin, Martha Ritchie, Kate Schrago. Special thanks to Christopher B. Smith who got me to the finish line.

Kateri and Evan O'Neil were the best of company, making *sanuk mak mak.*

Khob khun mak kha to Khun Euyaporn Kerdchouay and Khun Ekkarin Latthasaksiri of the Siam Society, the staff of the National Library, the National Museum Volunteers Library, the Neilson-Hayes Library and the archives of *The Bangkok Post*.

Many thanks go to James Ferguson, a courageous independent publisher who has been immensely patient as well as warmly directive. Hs bird's eye view gave me a lot of creative freedom. Thanks also to Sebastian Ballard for the very useful map. I would also like to acknowledge the constructive comments of Marc Askew.

For Thais the establishment of a debt of gratitude and obligation is called *bun khun*. I am deeply indebted to two gifted readers who shaped this book in so many ways that it seems to have been a collaborative project. My dear friend Caroline Bundy quite brilliantly and elegantly trimmed it. Her veteran editorial skills gave the narrative focus and flow and permitted the authentic voices of past and present to ring clear. Sumet Jumsai brought keen erudition and passion for his native city, setting the record straight on numerous historical points. He is a true sentinel of memory.

Their contributions have hopefully enabled readers to more fully discover Bangkok as an endlessly fascinating city of the imagination.

* Khun, followed by the first name, is the proper form of address in Thailand. I have included surnames as well.

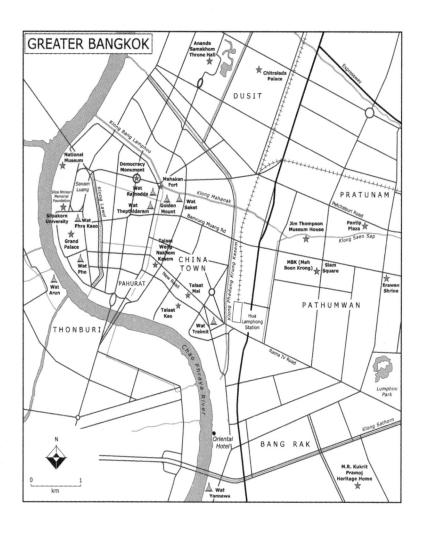

Introduction

FROM FLOATING CITY TO POST-MODERN MEGALOPOLIS

"But where does one begin with Bangkok?" English writer F. K. Exell mused in 1963. "It was a complete mixture of spurious West and inscrutable East. It was dirty. It was clean. It was beautiful. It was ugly. It was ancient. It was modern. It had scented temple flowers and the stench of rotting fish."

For more than a century after Bangkok was founded in 1782 most westerners approached it expecting to find the "Venice of the East", as the former Thai capital at Ayudhya had been called, and would only later discover its unique aspects. Ayudhya had been a prosperous city—like Bangkok built on canals—and one of the greatest maritime ports of Southeast Asia until the Burmese vanquished it in 1767. The Chakri monarchs aimed to replicate the spiritual and physical glory of Ayudhya in the new capital. And they succeeded, to judge from many nineteenth-century-travellers who responded with rapt delight at first view of the astonishing spectacle that appeared just after their steamers rounded the wide bend of the Chao Phraya river. A British traveller reaching Bangkok in 1865 thought he saw a mirage: the city "seemed to have arisen from the waters" right before his eyes. He would have seen the houseboats or huts built on stilts that stretched along the river banks as far as the eye could see. Picture them shaded by tall, slender palm trees. Flame-of-the-forest flowers accent a cerulean sky. Pendulous yellow blossoms—floral chandeliers—overhang impenetrable mangrove swamps.

The king owned all the land—because he is god-like, proclaimed a royal decree. His earthly abode was a fortified palace complex adjacent to the Chao Phraya, the river of kings, coursing through Bangkok before spilling into the Gulf of Siam thirty-five miles downstream. Over the centuries the river became a bustling international emporium with great ships—first junks, then steamers—dwarfing the native dwellings. As the city laid claim to the vast, low-lying deltaic plain of the Chao Phraya valley, traditional amphibious habitats were gradually abandoned. Over the next century the water-world of Old Bangkok was paved over; the last holdouts of the unique floating city were abandoned by government order in the early 1950s.

One of the most destructive factors in the changing nature of the "city in a garden" was undoubtedly the laying down of roads replacing the watery lattice of canals that had been one of the great wonders of Southeast Asia. Rama IV Road, built in 1857, was the first truly public thoroughfare. New Road (Charoen Krung), the earliest macadam street for wheeled vehicles in the burgeoning commercial area next to the port, dates from 1862. The first major boulevard, which slices through the old city, was cut in the late nineteenth century following King Chulalongkorn's visit to Paris.

During the second half of the twentieth century a sprawling, land-based, industrial metropolis began to mushroom on the alluvial plain. The rapid, unplanned and unimpeded expansion in the 1960s was largely due to American development money. Strategic roads led north-east to US military bases on the Thai border. These highways also encouraged an influx of poor peasants who gravitated to the capital, many ending up in sprawling slums.

Although so much has changed in Bangkok over the last century, visitors today experience feelings similar to those recorded in 1963. A sense of bafflement follows the generally conflicting impressions of the place; but few were bored then, and few now. An English visitor remarked that the "continuous and picturesque contrast of splendour and poverty, of fastidious etiquette and informality" kept one on one's toes. The same is true today. Only a few travellers got beyond piquant, Orientalizing contrasts and H. Warington Smyth was one of them. He wrote a lively account of his time as director of the newly created Department of Mines, *Five Years in Siam, from 1891-1896.* He recovered from a poor first impression of the city: "I had yet to learn that there are many Bangkoks." He gives intriguing glimpses of dens of iniquity, of "such thieving as was never dreamt of in their jungle home, of much drinking, of more gambling" and of the great monster: "outrageous all-devouring—officialdom. And truly, I suppose, no place was less easy to fathom," he frankly admits.

This has always been the real challenge for the thoughtful observer: Bangkok teems with paradox. Some sixty years later, Exell's attempt to weave all the loose threads he had assembled into his *Siamese Tapestry* left him feeling somewhat unravelled: "There was a Chinese quarter, an Indian quarter. Pleasant residential areas and the squalor of corrugated-iron huts. There were humble homes that floated by the river bank and lovely princely palaces. Spacious tree-lined boulevards and the noisy chaos of uncontrolled city traffic. Bangkok in the hot season was different from Bangkok in the rains. In other words, I never could describe the place. All one could do was talk about it."

On the one hand Bangkok is a place of great physical presence and complexity. On the other, it is plastic by nature, like other malleable cities. "We mold them in our images," Jonathan Rabin writes, "they, in their turn, shape us by the resistance they offer when we try to impose a personal form on them." Culture comes from this creative interaction of material fact and human subjectivity. But which is the "real" city: the "hard" city of material fact, or the "soft" city of imagination? According to Rabin, "The city as we imagine it, the soft city of illusion, myth, aspiration, and nightmare, is as real, maybe more real, than the hard city one can locate on maps in statistics, in monographs on urban sociology and demography and architecture."

Bangkok makes more sense as an attitude than as a form. This can be seen in the pattern of dense, mixed-use communities where urban life is shaped. On a twenty-minute walk along Sukhumvit from Soi Thong Lor (soi 55) to the Emporium Shopping Centre (soi 24) you will see: Fried Grasshopper Vendor/Barber and Massage Parlour/Car Parts Store/Hainanese Noodle Vendor/Fruit Stand/7-11/Souvenir Shop/Buddhist Emporium/Open-Air Coiffeur/Turkish Baths and Brothel/Chinese Tailor/Art Gallery/School Uniform Store/Antique Dealer. Some of the city's most luxurious hotels, elegant shopping malls, top-notch medical facilities and *haute cuisine* restaurants are wreathed by budget-built shop houses, slums and fetid canals.

The city of Bangkok is made up of a colourful patchwork of individual neighbourhoods, most with a rich and complex social geography. The village-like texture extends into the internally focused lanes (*sois*) and alleys (*troks*), places of relative tranquillity which are extended living and commercial spaces. Most dwellings follow the pattern of shop house on ground floor, bedroom above. A small spirit house in each house compound defines the residents as an imagined community under the protection of a tutelary land god who is well-fed and tended.

The willing foreigner wanders onto a stage set where *cinéma vérité*

plays day and night. Mobile marketers appear on foot, on bicycle, behind rickety motorized carts selling everything: tropical fruit, Thai sweets, dried squid, brooms, brushes, piggy banks and so forth. Most vendors have distinctive jangles and sounds that announce their arrival. The city is a like a gigantic food court with more than 11,000 restaurants and 43,000 street food stalls. Its huge fleshpot entices many hungry men. You name it you got it, but it is rarely how you expected it.

The English writer James Kirkup liked Bangkok's desultory confusion and dishevelment. Though grounded in his native Durham he would have preferred "to live in the East, where I am at home with my sense of disorder."

There are colourful Hindu shrines in Bangkok, *garudas* on royal temples, and Brahman priests preside over royal ceremonies, but the great majority of Thais are adherents of Theravada Buddhism. The "imagined unity of the nation" promotes the myth that most of its sixty million people are ethnically Thai but over one hundred other ethnicities co-exist. The reigning monarch King Rama IX is the focus of state ceremonies and the promoter of orthodox Buddhism. Royal capital and realm are yoked under the official motto: "Nation, Religion, and King". Three distinct marks of Thai national identity are their pride in their independence (they were not colonized), their powers of assimilation and the high degree of tolerance for pluralistic lifestyles within the mixed ethnic pot of their society.

But tolerance has some limits, as Thai statesman-author Kukrit Pramoj wittily advised a gathering of foreigners in the 1960s.

> There are certain institutions which a Thai respects... They are his religion, which is mostly Buddhist, his king and his parents. If you say to a Thai that his politicians are rotten he will kiss you on both cheeks. If you tell him that he is a crook, he will deny it with great good humor and will not take offence. If you call his wife a bitch he will agree with you completely and ask you to have a drink to that. But as for those three institutions which I have already mentioned, I would advise you to leave well enough alone... since according to police statistics, the percentage of premeditated murders in this country is low; most murders are committed in sudden passion.

Victims of nocturnal accidents and violence are under special surveillance by rival groups dubbed "Bangkok's body-snatchers" by the western media, employed by old Chinese benevolent associations, who do brisk business making runs to hospital morgues. Bangkok's bars officially close at 2 a.m. but the *anything goes* nightlife continues in private clubs and hotel rooms. Bangkok "smells of sex," Paul Theroux wrote in the 1970s, "but this sexual aroma is mingled with the sharper whiffs of sex and money."

Today over eleven million people live in the sprawling, densely populated capital that has been named the World's Hottest City by the World Meteorological Organization. Although it is the prime city of Thailand, there is no single commercial centre, no historic downtown per se, and the *ad hoc* urban planning and cryptic zoning have resulted in an unfocused, fragmented city layout that can be utterly bewildering. In diametric contrast to an orderly, well-planned Southeast Asian metropolis such as Singapore, the city of Bangkok is post-modern by default, an agglomeration that has many commercial and entertainment centres. Alistair Shearer dubbed Bangkok *Americasia*, "a hybrid of East and West, the twentieth century come up for air from the ancient swamp of Asia."

Bangkok developed from paddy fields to villages, from small vernacular dwellings to high rise condominiums, from a trading post to the most prosperous city in the country. Although it is decidedly more western today, a rich artistic and cultural heritage exists within the collection of villages that constitute the city. Fragments of extraordinary beauty and sensation abound. Pockets of traditional indigenous life percolate under a lid of modernity. While the "nests of an aquatic race" that Joseph Conrad spotted in 1888 are long gone, the aquatic past flows through the life of the city.

RATTANAKOSIN: ISLAND JEWEL

Rattanakosin lies at the heart of Bangkok. This artificial island (*ko* means island in Thai, the whole means island of Indra's jewel) was created by King Rama I in the eighteenth century to house the royal palace complex which he constructed there. The king, intent on creating a city to compare with the grandeur of the old capital of Ayudhya, summoned experts who could recall details of the old city and replicate what had been destroyed. Because of the need to build Bangkok's new defences quickly with the meagre resources available, rubble from the vanquished site was brought down river and imbedded into fortifications, palace buildings and monasteries. Ayudhya's bricks then became quarry for Bangkok's buildings, much like the antique marbles reused for Renaissance and Baroque Rome. He ordered a second canal to be dug in a concentric arc some 800 yards east of Klong Lawd, which had been dug during King Taksin's reign. Ten thousand Cambodian prisoners of war were set to work on this. Five thousand Laotian captives herded from Vientiane then built a thick crenellated brick and stucco wall around the defensive moat with fourteen watchtowers punctuating it, of which two remain today: Pom Mahakan near the Golden Mount, and Pom Phrasumane on the river at Banglampoo. The total surface area of the royal island was a mere one and a half square miles, far smaller than the former capital.

A comparison of old maps of the two capitals shows how closely Bangkok's general disposition echoed the layout of Ayudhya. The second palace or Wang Na (the Palace of the Front, now National Museum)) was built near the Grand Palace for the king's brother, the deputy-king. Royal temples with the most important Buddhist relics were clustered around the palaces; these served religious, educational and recreational functions. Mandarin households ringed the royal complex; many nobles built family compounds and founded temples on the riverbanks and near major canal junctions. Artisans, merchants and traders often congregated on nearby waterways so as to profit from their patronage.

The royal citadel was to become the seat of the king and the dominion of the gods. Siamese kingship had inherited Hindu traditions of palace and religious life derived from eleventh-century Khmer polity. The *devaraja* (god-king) was a distant and imposing figure; commoners were forbidden to look at him. His city (*muang*), centre of his divine power, had three highly symbolic places: a royal palace for the ruler, a temple housing a Buddha images and relics, and a shrine to the spirit guardian of Siam, Phra Siam Devathiraj.

In 1785, three years after the birth of Bangkok, King Rama I staged a lavish ceremony to consolidate and legitimize the Chakri dynasty and the primacy of Buddhism. This splendid three-day festival at the start of the Siamese New Year was held "in honour of the king, for the well-being of the government, for the happiness of the people". Buddhist monks chanted on the battlements and the festival offered the Thai equivalent of bread and circuses at royal expense. Food was distributed at key points around the city, coins were tossed to the crowds, and *likay* (traditional improvised Thai folk drama that runs in episodes like a TV sit-com) played day and night at theatres erected along the main path from the palace to Chinatown's mall, Sampheng.

A Jesuit envoy to Ayudhya had noted that the Siamese "give pompous names to everything which they honour." In this vein, the king conferred an auspicious title on the new island-citadel that yoked Brahmanic and Buddhist cosmology. A marble plaque in front of Bangkok City Hall spells out the forty-three syllables that constitute this, the longest city name in the world.

> Great city of angels, the supreme repository of divine jewels, the great land unconquerable, the grand and prominent realm, the royal and delightful capital city full of nine noble gems, the highest royal dwelling and grand palace, the divine shelter and living place of reincarnated spirits.

Thais venerate their capital city as Krung Thep—the City of Angels—but the Portuguese called it Bangkok in the sixteenth century and this became its cosmopolitan name.

"It's almost impossible to translate," complained a Japanese interpreter and tour guide in Yukio Mishima's *The Temple of Dawn* (1970). He explains that: "Thai names are like temple decorations, unnecessarily pompous and flowery, ornate for the sake of ornateness... They choose exaggerated and ostentatious nouns and adjectives and string them together like beads on a necklace." Joseph Conrad found it beautiful: "O Bangkok Magic name, blessed name/Mesopotamia (recalling Odysseus) wasn't a patch on it."

Sino-Siamese City

Located at the mouth of the largest river in the kingdom, Bangkok was a thriving port for trans-shipment where goods, people and messages from the interior met those coming from abroad. Its principal resources were a very large concentration of people and the unsurpassed suitability of the Chao Phraya flood plain for wet-rice cultivation. Most of the commodities produced, as well as the proceeds from exports, remained in Bangkok although an important part of the king's income came from trade with China. The capital grew slowly during its first fifty years and enjoyed a relatively long period of unbroken peace and prosperity, largely free from internal strife and foreign influence.

Most of the inhabitants lived on houseboats anchored two or three rows deep along the riverbanks or in ethnic enclaves on the riverbanks; these functioned as identifiable communities that were given over to particular trades. The Chinese were the shopkeepers and merchants; the Siamese were farmers, administrators and court officials. There were sizeable amphibious communities of Mon, Vietnamese, Khmer, Thai and Lao. Daily life for the populace was public, communal, and spent largely outdoors in vernacular thatch houses or on houseboats. Temple festivals were the highlight of social life.

For almost half a century after its founding the right to reside on land was granted by the king almost exclusively to nobles or Buddhist monks. There were two exceptions: the Portuguese (who had long provided guns and mercenaries) were allowed to settle around Santa Cruz church in Thonburi, and the Chinese had a settlement at Sampheng. Descendants of refugees and war captives gradually created amphibious enclaves. A specialized craft or a trading base linked these communities to the city's economy. A few of the most commercially successful later moved inland—the Cham refugees of Ban Krua who revitalized the silk trade, and Makassar Muslims from Indonesia who settled in the Makasan area near the present-day Indra Regent Hotel. Sikhs congregated in the Pratunam area. The river linked the capital to a patchwork of far-flung villages and to key waterways.

Siam had largely turned her back on the West (apart from some ongoing trade with the Dutch) for almost 150 years after the pro-Catholic policy of Constans Phaulkon, a Greek adventurer who was chief minister to King Narai of Ayudhya, in 1688, and the immediate expulsion of the French whose interests he had unwisely promoted. But when western diplomats began to request royal audiences after 1815, King Rama II became uneasy. John Crawfurd, a British diplomat and trader, had an audience with the king in 1822. When asked if he had been sent "with the knowledge of the king of England", Crawfurd handed the monarch an unsatisfactory letter from the Governor-General of India—the king was unimpressed. Moreover, he could not supply modern firearms and the good gunpowder that the king wanted. Crawfurd must have hoped that his luck would change as he stayed on in Bangkok for four months. During this time he kept a diary that contains the earliest glimpses of the city by an English writer and includes a rare plan.

The morning presented to us a very novel spectacle—the capital of Siam, situated on both sides of the Maenam. Numerous temples of Buddha, with tall spires attached to them, frequently glittering with gilding, were conspicuous among the mean huts and hovels of the natives, throughout which were interspersed a profusion of pale, ordinary fruit trees, and the sacred fig (*ficus religiosa*). On each side of the river there was a row of floating habitations, resting on rafts of bamboo, moored to the shore. These appeared the neatest and best descriptions of buildings; they were occupied by good Chinese shops. Close to the aquatic habitations were anchored the largest description of native vessels, among which were many junks of great size, just arrived from China. The face of the river presented a very busy scene, from the number of boats and canoes of every size and description which were passing to and fro. The number struck us as very great at the time, for we were not aware that there were few or no roads at Bangkok, and that the river and canals form the common highways, not only for goods, but for passengers of every description.

Given King Rama II's obduracy to foreigners, Crawfurd relates a curious anecdote. Members of his party were suddenly awakened one night by the arrival of a special messenger sent by the king who brought with him a life-size doll or puppet. The courier conveyed his majesty's wish that the foreigners dress the figure to represent the Emperor Napoleon Bonaparte who had died the previous year. An Indian tailor in their company collaborated with a team of court tailors and shoemakers to turn out "a very fair presentation of the Man of Destiny… greatly to the gratification of the Lord of White Elephants."

Increasing pressure was exerted by the British on the king to loosen trade restrictions, but he refused to negotiate. Rather, trade with the Middle Kingdom became the major economic force thanks to royal privileges extended to Chinese merchants. Continuous immigration made the Chinese the dominant force in the city's economic life. Chinatown, centred on a narrow mile-long strip that ran from Klong Banglampoo to Odeon Circle (near Hua Lamphong train station), was the hub of a widespread network of Chinese commerce. Chinese influence permeated all aspects of the city to such an extent that Bangkok seemed even then a Chinese city with a Siamese veneer. An article in the *Singapore Chronicle* from 3 March 1825 noted that there were a "a great number [of] floating houses, generally neat Chinese shops, moored along the river side, outside the walls, and a good number of the population lives permanently on boats where they have their shops and property." Poor Chinese immigrants provided cheap labour for internal trade and public work projects. Thousands of Chinese coolies constructed the Golden Mount, a giant pagoda built by King Rama III. It crumbled into a brick heap and King Rama IV then converted it into the Golden Mount.

The port of Bangkok at Sampheng was the prime Southeast Asian centre for the junk trade. The above article reported further:

> Bangkok is one of the largest native trading cities in Asia and from March to June the river is crowded with junks not less than 100 of which of all sorts and descriptions, many of them of great size, trade to various port of China and from 50 to 60 to the various ports of the Malayan archipelago. The internal trade is also considerable by the river, its branches and the various creeks and canals which intersect the valley of the Maenam in many directions communicating with the capital. These are crowded with boats conveying salt, cotton, pepper, sugar, and other articles, and with great rafts of teak, sappan, and rose wood.

King Rama III had great enthusiasm for *Chinoisierie*. Mandarin jackets and Chinese slippers were *de rigueur* at court; royal residences were decorated with Chinese silk and porcelain pieces. He even had a temple built in the shape of a junk at Wat Yannawa (on the river near New Road) as a memorial to the vessel that had made the city so prosperous.

There is an old saying in Bangkok that those who built temples were as kindly regarded in the Third Reign as soldiers had been during the reign of Rama I and poets had been for his successor. Nine new temples were constructed by the sovereign; more than sixty more were restored or enlarged during his long and successful reign. Many temples of the Third Reign followed the "Chinese Architectural Royal Model" that wed traditional Thai style to Chinese art. Chinese style stucco gable boards were encrusted with colourful shards of broken porcelain often formed in beautiful floral patterns. Dragons displaced Buddhist *nagas* on the roofline. Monastic grounds were decorated with stone lions and statues of Confucian sages that had served as ballast on rice junks returning from China. Wealthy and ambitious Chinese merchants offered temples to the king to curry favour; some also built colourful shrines on the banks of the Chao Phraya river—a few, largely rebuilt, remain today.

During this temple building spree a single dirt road led from the small royal citadel on Rattanakosin led "through the great bazaar and that was a wretched jumble and tumble of shops on a miserably paved footpath." Many of the poor immigrant Chinese, who were arriving at the rate of 15,000 a year by the end of the Third Reign, had little immunity to river water and fell victim to terrible waves of cholera epidemics. The disease first came from India and claimed many lives as the almanac of 1820 recorded: "On the 7th month, the waxing moon, a little past 9 o'clock in the evening a shining light was seen on the north-west and multitudes of people purged, vomited and died." Later in the century, writer Ernest Young describes little cholera lamps throughout the city swinging aloft at the ends of long slender poles, "telling where the grim fiend has entered in his work of destruction."

CITY IN TRANSITION

The most haunting lady in Bangkok was a legendary young woman known as Mae Naak (Mother Naak) or Nang Naak (Mrs. Naak) who is said to have lived near the once rural rice paddy at the mouth of Klong Phrakhanong during the latter part of the nineteenth century. Popular legend has it that she joined the fearsome ranks of ghosts of women who died during childbirth. By the time her soldier-husband returned home, Mae Naak had already been buried in a nearby cemetery so that her spirit and that of her unborn child would be neutralized underground. But she was a desperate lovesick ghost who stayed on to live with her unknowing husband, disguising herself as human. One day he dropped a lime through the floorboards of their traditional house built on stilts. When she grotesquely stretched an arm fifteen feet below to retrieve it, he realized that something was amiss. In a popular stage play, dating from the reign of King Rama V, she is exorcised by a prominent monk of Wat Rakhang who imprisons her demon in a ceramic pot and drops it in the canal.

During the late nineteenth century the highly placed Prince Damrong conducted a poll at the gates of the Grand Palace and discovered that Bangkokians knew more about the life of Mae Naak than King Rama I. The Mae Naak story has been told in novels, plays, musicals, a mini-series, dozens of films including a blockbuster production *Nang Naak* (1999), and most recently Somtow Sucharitkul's critically acclaimed opera that premiered at the Thai Cultural Center in 2003.

One version of the eerie tale includes Mae Naak's older son who feared that his father would remarry and deprive him of his share of the family assets. To thwart any romance he donned women's clothes to frighten the villagers into believing that his mother's ghost still haunted the place and hired local men to throw stones at people who passed by the cemetery in boats. Although he later confessed, several incarnations of Mae Naak's ghost were still reported to prowl.

"She is horrible yet humane, a murderous ghost yet a motherly goddess," writes KA F. Wong. What is thought to be Mae Naak's burial site (off the On Nut stop of the Skytrain), on the outer edge of the Mahabute Temple, Sukhumvit soi 77/7), is quintessentially Thai. It is surrounded by chicken coops, a menagerie of stray animals, scattered refuse, gauze-encircled *bodhi* trees and little memorial shrines to other victims. People buy birds, turtles, eels and other fish to make merit. Mendicants humbly receive coins from merit makers.

Mae Naak's bust, said to have been made of auspicious soil collected from seven cemeteries, is richly gilded with multiple layers of tissue-paper thin gold leaf squares applied by devotees that lend it a skin-like texture that is enhanced by regular application of oil by her attendants at the shrine. She is dolled-up like a Hollywood starlet from the 1950s and wears a thick black wig, a pink dress and a shiny quartz watch (her outfits change). She is shadowed by a "life-like" portrait. Since she has earned a great reputation for helping petitioners select winning lottery tickets, on

the eve of the draw locals propitiate her ghost for favours with soft drinks, coconuts, orchids, traditional dresses, candles, joss sticks, baby clothes, toys, toiletries, money and jewellery. A donation of twenty baht buys a standard offering kit of incense, a stamp-size piece of gold leaf and a small yellow candle. The two gnarled old takian trees that shade the shrine look almost petrified as worshippers have smoothed yellow wax into it and rubbed it to reveal luck numbers.

Mae Naak's enduring tale is "a fantasy woven into the fabric of myth and superstition," Wong writes while underscoring the prevalence of Thai belief in ghosts. The tsunami of 2004 well-publicized the deeply-rooted fear of ghosts of victims of natural disasters, accidents or other premature deaths. Buddhists are cremated and foreign graveyards cause shudders.

For that reason it has always been a challenge for the wardens of Christ Church (Convent Road) to find local caretakers to tend the Protestant cemetery off New Road (Charoen Krung) that was established by American missionaries in the mid-nineteenth century thanks to a Royal Grant of Land from King Mongkut. Many foreigners in Bangkok died of tropical diseases, including young children among whom the mortality rate was very high. The cemetery is small, sodden and sad but there are a few noteworthy funerary monuments. An obelisk marks the grave of Dr. Dan Beach Bradley (1804-73), an American missionary-physician who arrived in Bangkok in 1835 with his young wife and never left. He made one short-term convert, a Chinese man who abjured after he was ridiculed and accused of "having given up the worship of his Chinese ancestors and embracing the worship of the ancestors of Europeans." Soon after his arrival in Bangkok Dr. Bradley was summoned to treat an ailing prince-monk, Phra Mongkut, for a facial malady that had left his mouth permanently twisted. Thus began a long and mutually rewarding friendship between the two men, though Bradley was too busy to honour his request for English lessons after he became king.

While King Mongkut allowed Protestant missionaries to preach openly in his own royal temple grounds in the mid-nineteenth century, he was (like his predecessor King Narai of Ayudhya) adamant in refusing to be converted to Christianity. One of the western-style murals in the *ubosot* (ordination hall) of Wat Bovornives depicts fashionably dressed Europeans (with all the aplomb of visiting actors on stage) in contemplation of a gigantic pink lotus flower. The painting conveys a royal request, delivered in highly original fashion, for mutual tolerance and respect.

Just before he died in 1851 King Rama III gave warning: "Wars on the Annamese and Burmese fronts have probably ended. But not so with the Farang [westerners]. Beware that you do not play into their hands. Learn from them and emulate what is worthy of their way, but do not become totally subservient to their values." The intense rivalry between Britain and France for supremacy in Indo-China had begun. A letter written the year before the king's death by Sir James Brooke, English soldier, traveller and Raja of Sarawak, reveals Britain's bald ambitions for a puppet leader who would advance their trade interests in Siam.

> As we have delayed for thirty years doing anything, that in the course of this policy we may well wait until the demise of the King brings about a new order of things. Above all, it would be well to prepare for the change, and to place our own king on the throne, and the king of our choice is fortunately the legitimate sovereign. [Who] is now a priest, and a highly accomplished gentleman for a semi-barbarian. He reads and writes English—the latter in the way you may judge of—is instructed in our astronomy and has a very high opinion of our arts, learning and government. This prince we ought to place on the throne, and through him we might, beyond doubt, gain all we desire.

Prior to his coronation in the Grand Palace, an event to which foreigners were for the first time invited, King Mongkut had been a Buddhist monk for twenty-seven years. During this lengthy period he had travelled high and low throughout the country and was intimately aware of the conditions of the Siamese people. The walls of his monastic cell were lined with books on western sciences and history. By contrast to his predecessors, he took a keen interest in world affairs once he became king, thanks largely to scientific journals and reputable newspapers sent by well-placed friends from abroad.

The learned King Mongkut is unfairly known in the West as a kind of Asian noble savage who fell for a plucky young British widow with whom he waltzed under a romantic moonlit sky. Mrs. Anna Leonowens was the Victorian governess who was invited by the king to teach tutor in the royal harem, a position she held for five years. "Bangkok is the most hideous word I have ever heard," she later wrote bitterly. The king's extensive and meticulous diaries contain a single mention of her: "Mem was a great nuisance today." More on Mrs. Leonowens in Part One, but it is pertinent to note here that her books stirred little interest in Thailand until the film version of an adaptation by Margaret Landon, *The King and I*—starring Yul Brynner, who won an Oscar for Best Actor for his part—caused great consternation and Anna's writings were immediately condemned for presenting a highly romanticized and at times almost imaginary portrayal of court life. She was posthumously accused of *lèse-majesté* (at one point she dubbed the king a "withered grasshopper"). Moreover, she had dared to imply that the task of Christian evangelism had made her sexually vulnerable. "How different is the radiant self-portrait she offers when she is on the alert! Here the dedicated woman, whose beauty exposes her to special risks, is seen gently uplifting the barbarians; this self-portrait is nobly conceived and sensitively executed."

Lèse-majesté towards this long-deceased monarch is still a very serious matter. In a recent remake (1999) of the film Anna Leonowens was played by Jodie Foster who was cast as a precocious western feminist. The movie was promptly banned by Thailand's board of censors who decried its disrespectful picture of the monarch. What is more, the king (played by Chow Yun-fat) "wields his sword like a Chinese swordsman," they further complained.

It is true that Anna Leonowens was often exasperated by King Mongkut's fearsome irascibility and was deeply distressed by his large harem, but her final assessment of the monarch was spot on. She reckoned that he was, "in the best sense of the epithet, the most remarkable of the Oriental princes of the present century—unquestionably the most progressive of all the supreme rulers of Siam."

A new era was opened by King Mongkut who had seen the disastrous result of China's attempt to shut out the West. The king's decisive influence on Siam has been likened to that of Emperor Meiji of Japan and later to Kemal Ataturk of Turkey. He was a diminutive man with a scientific and cosmopolitan stamp of mind whose daring aim was, he said, to "shatter the world of his predecessors." During his seventeen-year reign (1851-68) he began to transform the kingdom with a great sense of urgency, recognizing that Siam's progress demanded engagement with the wider world; that national interest required the abandonment of the conservative isolationist policy of old. The main key to this new opening to the world was English, a language he had already taken up in solitary pursuit during his long Buddhist monkhood.

On 2 April 1855 residents of Bangkok were advised that the discharging of gun fire from a foreign ship heralded the imminent arrival of a very important visitor. Sir John Bowring, Governor of Hong Kong, had come at the behest of Queen Victoria to meet the King of Siam. After lengthy deliberation the Anglo-Thai Treaty of Friendship and Commerce (Bowring Treaty) was successfully negotiated. It abolished royal monopolies, equalized the duties on Chinese and western shipping, granted extraterritorial rights to British citizens, and allowed the British to import opium for sale through a government monopoly that would soon become the single largest source of revenue for the crown. Bowring rightly recognized the treaty's signal importance: "The country will be absolutely revolutionized by the change, and in a few years I doubt not there will be an enormous trade."

True to Bowring's prediction, the historic treaty was a watershed as it shifted Siam's trade orientation away from China to the West. A whole new era began when Siam entered into a commercial economy tied to the world trading system led by Britain, thus paving the way for parallel trade agreements with other western powers. The principal export goods were rice, sugar cane, hides and pepper.

King Mongkut hoped that liberalized trade would better protect Siam from the expansionist policies of the French and British. He heaped scorn upon them in a letter sent in 1865 to the Siamese envoy in Paris: "Both the French and the British think of us as animals to gnaw on and carve out; they deceive us into expending our energy as if we were oxen or buffalo. They probably assume that it is not sinful to attack us, kill us and take things away from us because we are not disciples of Jesus." As a precaution against hostile ships he had a huge iron chain forged that stretched across the Chao Phraya river from the east to the west bank. Nine government men-of-war were permanently moored near the royal citadel. But the built

environment of Old Bangkok was not so well-protected and the introduction of a market economy initiated swift changes that dramatically im-
pacted upon the growth and development of Bangkok. It had always been
a cosmopolitan city with lively ethnic areas; it rapidly became a truly international city.

Opening the kingdom to foreign trade led to an expansion of the
economy, increased revenue and ushered in Siam's transition from a traditional Southeast Asian kingdom to a modern administrative state. King
Mongkut decided to develop the area of the city to the east of Rattanakosin
Island in order to accommodate rapid commercial growth, to improve
transport, and to ease overcrowding. A series of forts, accompanied by a
moat or third concentric canal, Klong Phadung Krung Kasem (1851-54),
doubled Bangkok's surface area. A French engineer was commissioned to
cut two long canals through the city running from east to west so that the
water would be sluiced daily by the incoming and outgoing river tides.
The three canals that circled the royal quarter resembled Amsterdam with
its *grachten*.

The nodal points of Old Bangkok were its waterways, temples and
princely palaces; in New Bangkok they would be roads leading to commercial establishments. The king embarked on a road-cum-shop-house
building project to encourage trade and to present a paradigm of modern
commercial urbanism to colonial powers. A major commercial artery
called New Road (Charoen Krung) was developed in response to a petition by westerners who requested a street for exercise and fresh air. This
long road which marked the western boundary of the city followed the
path of an old elephant trail. It extended from the royal citadel through the
Chinese district to the foreign settlements at Bang Kolem and Bang Rak.
The king liked to drive along it in a two-horse buggy to inspect the alterations underway.

Yet for all his reformist ideas and actions King Mongkut upheld the
rigid conservatism of Siamese kingship. He retained his supreme place at
the pinnacle of a pyramid of power that was built upon obeisance to regal
authority and deference to superiors. Rank decided everyone's assigned
place in the pre-ordained scheme of things. Even within the royal family
a child's rank and age determined his or her place in one of the concentric
circles that surrounded the sovereign during the daily afternoon audience
with his children. The royal payroll reflected the scale of the king's com-

mitments. According to an official report published in the *Bangkok Calendar*, in 1860 King Mongkut supported 22,754 people, and this number did not include the scores of princes and princesses, most of them wives and children of King Rama III, who received salaries. About 5,000 Buddhist priests were also provided with a measure of royal sustenance. "Was there ever," the editor of the report openly wondered, "such a city on earth?"

The king ruled Bangkok by edict. These were proclaimed *By Royal Command, Reverberating like the Roar of a Lion* from the Grand Palace: *Concerning People Getting Drunk at the New Year Celebration, Advice on the Inelegant Practice of Throwing Dead Animals into the Waterway* and other memorable civic proclamations.

Contrary to the misogynistic portrayal of the king by Anna Leonowens and those who popularized her story, the king legislated to improve the status of women in the kingdom. Siamese women formerly had no legal rights, even in deciding whether or whom to marry until he ruled in favour of a married woman who had run away with her lover. Women were given the right to choose their husbands, and childless concubines were permitted to resign from the harem, though not without some consequences.

After 1859 King Mongkut moved to a suite of buildings of western design that the architect Prince Krom Khun Rajsrihavikrom Choomsai, head of the Xumsai (also spelled Jumsai) branch of the royal family had built in the Grand Palace (now demolished). The entire royal court honoured the king's every command but he was bound by century-old palatine schedule.

7 a.m.	The King rose from bed.
8 a.m.	He partook of a light breakfast of rice gruel.
9 a.m.	He took his morning meal and went back to bed.
11 a.m.	The ladies of the palace attended him.
1 p.m.	He went out on an excursion.
2 p.m.	He gave audience to his children and members of the royal family.
3 p.m.	He presided over the council of ministers and high officers of the realm and gave his decisions on matters of state.
4 p.m.	He went out on an excursion.

5 p.m.   He went to the Royal Chapel.

6 p.m.   He decided on the affairs of the Palace.

7 p.m.   He studied the Art of War.

8 p.m.   He studied Politics.

9 p.m.   A meal was served to the King. He then went to his personal apartments and immediately his domestic bulletin was issued naming the woman whose presence he desired and also identifying those whose turn it was to be on duty during the night.

10 p.m.   He conferred with astrologers and pundits and discussed religion and philosophy.

12 a.m.   Musicians and singers were brought before the King.

1 a.m.   Storytellers were brought before the King.

2-3 a.m. The King went to bed.

The king was a studious man, relentless in pursuit of knowledge, and disdainful of superstition and intolerance. An American visitor who had an audience with him in 1857 found it "hard to believe that I was in a remote and almost unknown corner of the old world and not in the new. The conversation was such as might take place between two gentlemen in a New York parlour. On every side were evidence of an intelligent and cultivated taste… it seemed to me then, and a subsequent interview with the king confirmed the feeling that I had been in one of the most remarkable palaces, and with one of the most remarkable men in the world." In order to transform Siam's image abroad, the king corresponded with major western leaders—Pope Pius IX, Queen Victoria, Napoleon III, American Presidents Pierce and Buchanan.

King Mongkut, the first Asian monarch-linguist, prided himself on his knowledge of Sanskrit, Pali and modern languages. On several occasions his American missionary tutor was summoned to the Grand Palace in the middle of the night to find the king huddled over Webster's dictionary in search of the correct word for a composition or letter. He once came four miles to help him decide whether "murky" was preferable to "obscure" and "gloomily dark" better than "not clearly apparent." However, the king maintained an idiosyncratic style in English, noted here in a letter accompanying some photographs sent to Queen Victoria: "We on this occasion have liberty to let our native photographers take the likeness of ourselves when we adorned with the watch decked with diamonds and the double-edged sword which were honorary royal gracious gifts from, your majesty, received by us a few years ago and seated ourselves by the tables containing the gift silver inkstand and desk together with the revolving pistol and rifle wholly being royal gracious gift from your majesty."

Two pendant stained glass windows from the late nineteenth-century Immaculate Conception Church (near Krung Thon Bridge and Sam Sen Road) show the king beside the remarkable Bishop Jean-Baptiste Pallegoix, his intellectual companion and language partner; the first taught Pali, the second Latin. Like the king, Pallegoix was a monument of a man. He compiled a huge *Dictionnaire-siamois-latin-français-anglais* in addition to his highly informative two-volume account of Siam. Shortly after the bishop's death in 1862 King Mongkut wrote a letter of condolence to his *confrères*, expressing enormous gratitude for a man "qui a été mon bon, intime et sincère ami pendant vingt-huit ans."

King Mongkut's chief love—modern astronomy—proved to be a fatal attraction. The king was fascinated by the precision of western scientific measurement. His calculations had pinpointed the precise spot to best observe a total eclipse of the sun: a disease-ridden rainforest near Hua Hin on the marshy south-east coast of the Gulf of Siam. He hoped scientific observation of the eclipse would supplant popular belief that the sun was being devoured by a dragon. French astronomers and distinguished foreign diplomats were invited to gather at the purpose-built "town in the jungle" to witness the natural phenomenon. The French captain describes coming upon the scene: "The King of Siam, with all his court, a part of his army and a crowd of Europeans from Bangkok were at sea, with a cortege of a dozen steam boats of the navy, while troops of cattle, elephants and horses were on land." After the sun appeared following the eclipse on 18 August 1868 (just minutes within the time the king had predicted), and the wild excitement had begun to die down, he strode triumphantly into his royal pavilion and jubilantly proclaimed his fellowship with western scientists: "Now will you believe us? Now will you believe the foreigners?"

His satisfaction was regrettably all too brief, for he had contracted malaria on the beach. Although he had been on the throne for seventeen years, the disciplined habits of monkhood remained with him to the very end. As he lay dying, the priestly king asked to be turned on his right side in emulation of Lord Buddha's death. Before he expired he was heard to mutter "This is the correct way to die." The Reverend Bradley sadly commented that the eclipse expedition was "rather a grand outpouring of treasure and of life in the interest of science."

EUROPEAN INFLUENCE

The modernization of Siam along western lines begun by King Mongkut was given greater impetus by his son King Chulalongkorn (Rama V reg. 1868-1910). Civil War General Ulysses S. Grant made a state visit to Siam in 1879 and came away highly impressed by the Siamese sovereign.

> The King is a spare young man, active and nervous in his movement, with a full, clear, almost glittering black eye, which moved about restlessly from one to the other, and while he talked his fingers seems to be keeping unconscious time to the musical measures… Everything about the King betokened a high and quick intelligence, and, although the audience was a formal one, and the conversation did not go beyond words of courtesy and welcome from the King to the General and his party, he gave the impression of a resolute and able man full of resources and quite equal to the cares of his state.

King Chulalongkorn made timely social reforms to the semi-feudal system in Siam; he abolished slavery and forced labour and put an end to the ancient royal custom of prostration. Skilled foreign advisers brought administrative, financial, technical, architectural and artistic skills. In 1882 the Royal Mint replaced cowrie shells, which had been legal tender in Siam, with flat coins. He recruited Europeans to reorganize government services; he revamped education, started a police department trained by English ship captains and allowed the British to install a telegraph line from Burma to Penang (via Bangkok). Foreign consulates, business firms and residences mushroomed up in the loosely scattered, semi-colonial area near the Oriental Hotel.

The king also approved the paving of two modern, western-style trading streets that intersected on Rattanakosin—Bamrung Muang (Nurture the City) and Fuang Nakhon (Prosperous City)—at considerable expense due to the swampy land. Bamrung Muang was later extended east into the interior; it became Rama I Road in the early twentieth century. In the 1930s it was extended into the paddy lands to create Ploenchit and Sukhumvit roads. As more roads were laid, land titles were issued. Shop-houses and western-style villas increasingly fronted streets rather than waterways. Small neighbourhoods called *troks* developed in the interstices created between new streets and roads. A plan of Bangkok from about 1867 shows very dense urban settlement in the eastern area (formerly the Sea of Mud) between New Road and Wat Saket.

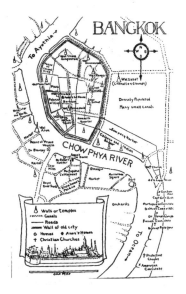

In foreign policy, King Chulalongkorn had the extremely difficult task of sailing the ship of state through the dangerous reefs of imperialism. France had long lusted after Siam, envisaging it as the jewel in the crown of French Indo-China, and in 1893 French gunboats forced passage of two forts at the mouth of the Chao Phraya river and proceeded under fire to their consulate. A period of intense crisis then ensued between Siam and France, which led ultimately to the cession to France of a massive area of Indo-China including Angkor (now Cambodia) that had formerly been regarded as Siamese territory.

During his long, productive, and profitable reign the king masterminded a "revolution from the throne". In order to further maintain Siam's independence from colonial powers on the pounce he made sweeping administrative reforms, adopted new technologies, established government institutions on the western model and imported a great number of European advisers in numerous capacities from jurists to engineers to artists. Their expertise "is like having ready-made textbooks," the monarch affirmed.

The king was the first eastern potentate to make the Grand Tour to Europe in 1897 with a repeat visit in 1907. These journeys were ostensibly to visit his sons studying in England but served as fact-finding missions as well. Moreover, the king wanted to be *seen* in order to prove to the western powers that Siam's regent was a force to be reckoned with as well as to give first-hand account of the process of modernization in his kingdom. He was received by the courts of fourteen countries. All members of the Siamese entourage wore stylish men's wear and conducted themselves following European court etiquette. Thanks to his London haberdasher, the handsome Siamese monarch was on the cutting edge of fashion. *Tailor and Cutter* (1897) deemed his appearance befitting "a typical English gentleman". He was awarded an Hon LL.D. at Cambridge, and his warm reception by Buckingham Palace signalled that he was a bona fide member of the European royal elite. In Paris, he was met by M. Félix Faure, Président de la République, who had an official carriage awaiting him at the Gare du Nord.

Upon his return to Bangkok the king launched a new royal district— a showpiece befitting a thoroughly modern Chakri monarch. Suan Dusit (Heavenly Garden), just north of the Grand Palace, was carved out of thickets and forests at such enormous expense that public work projects, such as the railways, were short on building materials. The god-king of the old Khmer cosmology who formerly inhabited a palace that mirrored Mount Meru now wanted functional architecture more suitable for a westernized sovereign. Royal residences were filled with European paintings, Tiffany vases, Fabergé eggs from St. Petersburg, fine porcelain from Sèvres and fashionable jewellery from Berlin. Nineteen princely mansions surrounded the sovereign's Vimanmek Teak Palace, some with ballrooms and private zoos.

Thanon Rajdamnern (King's Parade), a broad, tree-lined, Siamese version of the Champs-Elysées, which linked the Grand Palace to the Royal Plaza, was conceived as a setting for royal parades. The grand beaux-arts Ananda Samakhom throne hall (used for a time as the National Assembly Hall), built of German copper, Carrara marble, Milanese granite and Viennese ceramics, was commissioned by King Chulalongkorn but only completed after his death in 1910.

Traditional Siamese garden style, with its seamless flow between nature and architecture, was replaced by an ersatz Versailles landscape at Suan Dusit. Canals and rectangular lakes "recalling Le Nôtre's style" and "toy-gardens" for the king's wives prompted appreciative comments from a visiting Frenchman.

> There was a delightful view on one of the lakes, just as we arrived on the bank, six or seven little barges left; filled with Siamese ladies in orange, blue, purple, green dresses... some of them were rowing with long, gra-

cious movements. The water was so close to the brim of the barges that they were scarcely visible. One saw only the young women, seated or squatting, close to each other. As the sun set, the barges glided without any noise, tinting the water with vivid hues. The poetry in it was exquisite and charming.

Architects from Piedmont designed handsome administrative and public buildings at royal command: a customhouse, a treasury, a museum, post and telegraph office, army barracks, hospitals and European-style residences for foreign advisers. The Russian diplomat Andreu D. Kalymkow, who arrived in Bangkok at the end of the nineteenth century, was quite relieved to find the Foreign Office located in a European building, for he was admittedly fearful of being distracted from matters of state "by all this oriental magnificence, and wondered how we could discuss serious matters among such theatrical scenery." Emile Jottrand, Belgian adviser to the Ministry of Justice, found the official buildings faintly reminiscent of "the old palaces of Genoa, with their abandoned look, discoloured but despite everything reflecting an air of nobility." To his considerable surprise the lawn in front of the Palace of Justice had an 18-hole golf course with holes a mere 200 yards apart.

When the golf course was not in use, fashionable cycling parties gathered on the grass. The arrival of nobles and ministers on bicycles—wearing white tunics, colourful *panungs* (a wide loincloth-like garment for men) and military uniforms—created a moving spectacle. Prince Ong Noi, one of the king's most important brothers, hosted a magnificent reception for 230 cyclists in fancy dress at the open field (Sanam Luang) near the Grand Palace.

Spokes, tires, saddles, handlebars, chains, and the cyclists, all are adorned, disfigured, disguised, concealed by exterior forms the nature of which are most comical and gracious. First, there is a frog amidst the roses: a frame of more than one meter surrounds the bicycle which is completely concealed by natural roses. The cyclist, in frog's clothes, is astonishingly realistic, right up to his yellow gloves with webbed fingers. Then, there is a swan, big as an ostrich in real white feathers, and rising a white bicycle. Numerous gray, brown, and white monkeys. A bear, a cat, all in real furs. A threesome of Chinese cyclists, dressed in very rich embroidery. A big locomotive enmeshed with wire and covered with flowers. A house two meters in height, the cyclists head's peeping through the window. Finally, some charming reflections of the imagination: angels with big wings, butterflies, Negroes, Lakkon actors, etc.

Less than fifty years after the Bowring Treaty Bangkok's riverfront resembled an eastern Rotterdam, as a British writer observed somewhat ruefully in 1890. He was unsettled by the incongruities between the imagined exotic city and the booming commercial capital.

> I saw with wonderment the little brown children working their small canoes about the river, and diving into the steamers' wash; saw the pretty lines of betel and cocoanut, the distant perspectives of yellowing *padi*, the snug riverside cottages, the floating houses on their rafts, and at last, before us, Bangkok... But where was the Bangkok I had read of—that Venice of the East, delighting the soul with its gilded palaces and gorgeous temples? Before us lay but an eastern Rotterdam; mud banks, wharfs and jetties, unlovely rice mills belching smoke, houses gaunt on crooked wooden piles, dykes and ditches on either hand, steam launches by the dozen, crowded rows of native rice boats, lines of tall-masted junk-rigged lighters, and last, most imposing, towering even above the ugly chimneys of the mills, British steamers, and Norwegian and Swedish barques and ships...

By that date a new tramline had been installed (the first in Asia) linking the new commercial area to the south of the city at Bang Rak and Bang Kolem. European-style banks, commodious offices and residences rose up along newly paved streets in the area. Rice mills, warehouses and wharves were built along the riverbanks. Business was booming, so much so that an American in the capital during the same period wryly observed that the so-called Venice of the East "is often applied with more irony than seriousness."

MINIATURE DEMOCRACY

The Bangkok Department of Public Works, composed mainly of Italians brought from Piedmont, was charged with readying the city for the coronation of King Vajiravudh (Rama VI) on 2 December 1910. In his memoirs the Florentine artist Galileo Chini describes the "truly dazzling spectacles" with a painterly brush.

> I made an involuntary comparison of the celebration of the feast day of S. Maria del Fiore in front of the façade [of the Duomo] when I was young and confess that the difference was extraordinary. The whole was almost indescribable: the white walls, the golden doors, the mosaic or mother-of-pearl windows, the dusty and gilded roofs, the bronze icons colored with a phosphorescent patina supported by a framework of precious or lacquered wood. Sacred elephants with religious masks; their drivers dressed luxuriously in costumes to represent legendary religious, military or civilian figures are stored forever in my memory. The people of every cast in traditional costumes of various colors, sparkling with gold, and proceeding in a long line impressed upon my mind, though I was unable to absorb the profound significance of these scenes.

This was the first Siamese coronation attended by western princes from fourteen of the great European powers. "For my part, I have never seen a crowned head sustain his dignity better than Maha Vajiravudh," wrote Prince Wilhelm of Sweden.

King Rama VI dutifully completed a number of the civic projects left unfinished at his father's death, but his most original idea was a miniature city that he conceived while making sandcastles at the beach with his royal pages. Dusit Thani (The Heavenly City) comprised a thousand buildings measuring about two or three feet in height (the scale was 1:20) that were leased to personal friends and courtiers for a nominal fee. It was first installed at Suan Dusit Palace and later moved to the gardens of Phayathai Palace, the handsome Victorian complex that became his official residence after 1919. (In 1926 the palace was refurbished as the Phya Thai Hotel and rated as the most luxurious hotel in the Far East. Thai classical dance performances were staged in a Greek pavilion in the spacious gardens. It later served as a hospital. (It is now is a stately home that is well worth a visit.)

Dusit Thani was a highly original experiment—a model city of the future that the king had fashioned to teach courtiers and officials how to govern democratically on a microcosmic level. The government consisted of the municipality and two political parties as well as an electoral system.

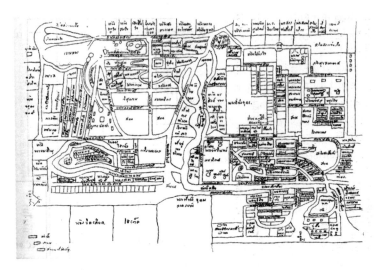

Two daily newspapers provided the latest news and editorial comment on local activities. The king took a keen personal interest in the newspapers; he acted as editor and frequent contributor to a weekly literary magazine.

A rare sketch of the unusual project shows the toyland democracy bisected by a winding river and canals according to a rational plan. It married the traditional Siamese amphibious way of life with a land and road-based system and harmoniously integrated Old and New Bangkok. Each of the six administrative districts had lush gardens; some were interconnected, others had fountains and waterfalls. Gardeners with nail scissors trimmed the exquisite Moghul garden, the little hillock beneath the Swiss chalet and the grounds of the Grand Palace. Royal "residents" spent fabulous sums to create the most beautiful buildings, whether in European, Moorish, Khmer, Indian or Siamese design. The king's beautiful Siamese-style teak palace complex was surrounded by a moat but his weekend escape was an English Tudor mansion framed by imported Japanese dwarf trees in the hilly outskirts. There were schools, markets, shops, water gates, Buddhist temples, bridges, hospitals, civic monuments, banks, hotels, theatres, office buildings, printing presses, a public bath house, a clock tower, a fire brigade, club houses, military barracks and canals. Taxes were collected and budget allocations were made for various parts of the city.

Royal receptions and festive ceremonies were held regularly; miniature boat races were very popular. Dusit Thani must have been utterly enchanting, a magical fairyland when illuminated at night by tiny electric lights. Courtiers could imagine their miniaturized selves in a kind of eastern Lilliputia. A very small portion of the miniature city has been reconstructed on the top floor of the King Vajiravudh Museum next to the National Library on Sam Sen Road.

The king personally drafted a constitution for the model city. Its preamble proclaimed the aim: to promote the concept of self-government among Siamese people. The governing laws laid out the electoral procedures; all citizens, including women, were eligible to vote. Town hall meetings were held at the colonial-style Hotel Métropole that stood behind its miniature version. The plan was to eventually extend the experiment throughout the country. The king wrote plays with a view to teaching politics and democracy and composed a series of reflections on adages. One of them, from the *Merchant of Venice*, captures the dream behind the Dusit Thani project: "If it were as easy to know what were good to do, chapels had been churches and poor men's cottages prince's palaces."

The king was an ardent Anglophile who had been educated entirely in England where he attended Eton and Christ Church, Oxford; he then studied political and military sciences at Sandhurst. No other individual in the realm possessed comparable literary range and command: prose, poetry, dramas, essays, patriotic songs, translations of western writers. He was a major influence in introducing new types of literature into the kingdom and his court became a "salon" where writers, dancers, musicians and poets assembled.

A scholar of Siamese history has captured the king's paradoxical character in a nutshell: "modern by education but traditional by temperament, a perceptive writer but an ineffective politician, a proponent of unity but a constant source of conflict." Given the upheaval that would subsequently occur in 1932, it is a tragic irony that the king ultimately took his absolute power for granted and heeded the advice of counsellors who argued that Siam was unprepared for democracy because of low literacy and a long tradition of authoritarian rule. His pet project had failed to convince them of its seriousness.

At the king's death in 1925 the Chao Phraya river functioned as a major artery for internal trade but it was no longer the great highway to the outside world. New rail lines linked Bangkok with British Malaya, northern Thailand and Indo-China, and a railway bridge was built to cross the river. Within a few years there would be air service to Europe and major cities in Asia.

But Bangkok was not a modern western city laid out in grid plan fashion. It had not developed concentrically from a geographical centre. Houses were built on roads filled in from old waterways but there were no proper access roads. The many narrow streets (*sois*), mostly former footpaths to canals, rarely connected arterial roads.

Last Absolute Monarch on Earth

Memorial Bridge (Phra Buddha Yod Fa), the first to span the Chao Phraya and to link Thonburi and Bangkok, was inaugurated by King Prajadhipok (Rama VII) on 6 April 1932, a hundred and fifty years after the founding of the city. A few months later the bridge came to symbolize the fulfilment of a dark prophecy by King Rama I that the Chakri Dynasty would end on this date.

A few coup attempts had been made between 1912 and 1932 but "fizzled out like damp squibs," a foreign observer reported. The king had inherited a host of grievances, not least the monopoly of royal power and an antiquated administration; at the same time, severe economic problems stemming from the Great Depression coupled with austerity programmes to balance the budget after the profligacy of King Vajiravudh. The Wall Street crash of 1929 had hit Bangkok hard. Salaries of civil servants were cut and the military budget reduced. A disgruntled middle class had already begun to express discontent with the existing order of things in newspapers, magazines, novels, short stories, films and cartoons.

Rumours of a coup began to circulate in Bangkok early in the spring of 1932. According to Gerald Sparrow, a British barrister who was an adviser to the Siamese Ministry of Justice, "They spread like wildfire through the Government offices, through the dense Chinese markets, through the spacious foreign business firms. They even reached the legations and the consulates whose job it was to know such things first." Despite the rumblings, King Rama VII could not be dissuaded from his custom of moving the court to the Hua Hin seaside palace for the hottest months from April to June. In the small hours of 8 June a group of military and civilian *new men* who had studied in France on government scholarships and who had returned home imbued with liberal, meritocratic and egalitarian ideas of western political systems, acted decisively. The bloodless coup of the People's Party dissolved the age-old absolute monarchy and replaced it with a constitutional monarchy on the English model. By mid-morning all but one prince in Bangkok had been arrested and locked in the heavily guarded Throne Hall.

Sparrow was puzzled that the king was retained as a figurehead and asked the Chief Judge of the Bench for an explanation. "Phraya Indra thought a minute; then gave the answer that everyone behaved a little better when the King was there."

But King Rama VII did not agree and went off to London ostensibly for eye surgery. Unable to come to terms with a mission sent to him in London by the People's Party, the king finally abdicated on 2 March 1934 after a nine-year reign. "I was willing to sacrifice my sovereignty to the people," he explained, "but not to a party who used absolute power without listening to the people."

Siam had always been governed by an absolute monarch: its politics consisted largely of palace intrigues. The king was the last man on earth to exercise royal absolutism.

LONG ERA OF THE DICTATORS

Thailand was run by dictators for the next sixty years. Field Marshal Phibulsonggram (Phibul), who dominated Thai politics for most of the period from 1933 to 1957, was supported by a small oligarchy of army and police officers. Phibul was charismatic, highly intelligent, the patriarch of a large family and very handsome (despite the fact that eyes were above the level of his ears which earned him the nickname *Plaeck* or "odd"). He rather easily won over a populace traditionally deferential to authority, and patriotic slogans affirming loyalty to him became mandatory.

Phibul initiated a Speaker's Corner in Sanam Luang, fashioning it after London's soap box institution at Hyde Park but it was quickly outlawed after critical voices spoke out against him. Smouldering dissent could be heard in intellectual circles where it was only safe to speak metaphorically. Veteran Thai journalist Nid Hinshiranan summed up the defiant resignation of intellectuals and activists at the time: "Buffaloes live in a stockade; the grass is very fertile there but they would rather eat somewhere else." During the political purges of 1939 more than fifty people were arrested; eighteen were sentenced to death.

In 1941 the British Prime Minister (then Winston Churchill) asked the Foreign Secretary, "Why is Siam buried under the name of Thailand?" The reply was that Phibul had newly minted Siam as Prathet Thai (Thailand). This radical recasting was aptly described as a "marketing device" for nationalism; and in the name of national unity the populace was recast as a single ethnic entity known as "the Thai". This policy was in sharp contrast to the Siamese kings who had long prided themselves as being rulers of an ethnic and religiously tolerant kingdom consisting of Thai, Chinese, Lao, Shan, Mon, Northerners, Southerners and Muslim people.

The invention of Thailand was also an undisguised hegemonic assertion, as Gerald Sparrow later underscored in 1955: "After the overthrow of the absolute monarch in 1932, which led to the overt development of Thai nationalism, the Thai name… was officially adopted… This was both a patriotic gesture as well as a political one… As a great many Thai people live outside the present borders of Thailand, it served to show that certain claims to frontier adjustments had not been entirely abandoned."

Field Marshal Phibul was a skilful political broker who wanted to leave his mark on the city through grandiose modernization projects. These were meant to illustrate a heroic narrative of Thai history and the martial ethos that underpinned it. He greatly admired Napoleon and kept a signed portrait of Mussolini on the wall above his desk. The Democracy Monument on Rajdamnern Avenue exudes a distinctly fascist chill.

Between 1938 and 1944 Phibul's government promulgated a series of regulations in an effort to "modernize" civil society and "to make Thai people truly Thai." National culture was broadly defined: flourishing development, good order as well as harmonious progress of the nation and good public morals. Cultural "progress" was interpreted almost exclusively as westernization. Mandates prohibited Thai people appearing in public within the municipality "wearing only underpants, pyjamas or other bedroom garments" and declared western-style hats and trousers *de rigueur* to replace the traditional *panung*. A local English-language paper summarized a decree promulgated against "disorderly conduct in public such as making unnecessary noise, offensive remarks or pushing or shoving in crowded places, in the boarding of public vehicles or in the buying of tickets at entertainment places, and bathing in public thoroughfares." *Sawasdee* (the Thai hail and farewell) was imported from India to replace the traditional peasant greeting, *pai nai* (where are you going?). Betel chewing was banned.

Writer Seinee Saowaphon nostalgically recalled Old Bangkok in his short story *Ghosts* (1953). "Gone were the days of silk robes and chintzes and lose bodices and simple cloth wrapped around the waist or tied at the back; now it was all trousers for men and skirts for women. Gone also were the days of powder and turmeric and beeswax, replaced by creams and lipsticks and hair lotions."

Royal Tragedy

When King Rama VII abdicated in 1934 the next in line to the throne was Prince Ananda Mahidol. Since Ananda was at that time a ten-year-old schoolboy in Switzerland, powerless regents took over and the monarchy was reduced to a symbolic shell until his return in 1945 to a joyous populace.

On the morning of 9 June 1946 Ananda was found shot dead in his bedroom of the Grand Palace. A small bullet had pierced his forehead. The official version was accidental death but three palace employees were executed. A thick shroud of mystery covers the tragedy and the truth may never be known.

Alexander MacDonald, an American attached to the Office of Strategic Security during the Second World War, became a household name after the death of the young Prince Ananda. He had loaned the Colt .45 revolver that was found beside the prince, though he was never implicated. MacDonald stayed on in Bangkok to found a new English-language newspaper *The Bangkok Post* but had other reasons as well.

> I had learned to like this exotic little kingdom and its people, all eighteen million of them. Especially did I like this incredible city! Here three-quarters of a million people had been brought together in what was meant to be a modern community; but nowhere else in the world had it been gone about so artlessly. Bangkok was an imposing clutter of old and new, East and West. As a community, it tried on the things of modern civilization—electric power, fast automobiles, telephones, and public health campaigns—like a woman trying on hats, oftentimes giggled at their absurdity and discarded them, relaxing to more informal ways of life. Bangkok was a wily yet guileless city, always ready with new surprises. It was deeply devoted to the arts of pleasure. If nothing else, this would have been enough for me.

AMERICAN PLANS

Post-war, the Americans brought a taste for jazz clubs, jitterbug music, chewing gum and foreign aid. Westernization accelerated under Prime Minister Phibul who embarked upon an anti-communist, pro-American policy. The influx of dollars resulted in rapid urban growth: office blocks, hotels, department stores and cinemas went up all over the city without any coherent urban development strategy.

The first master plan for the development of Bangkok undertaken by an American firm of urban planners in 1960 noted the lack of clearly defined areas. The city was characterized as a complex patchwork of "intimate" neighbourhood settlements that had grown organically without urban planning. The *sois* (or lanes) that branched out from the major traffic arteries (formerly paths to major canals) formed a distinctive and characteristic ecological feature of the city. Markets, shops and schools and a wide variety of habitations formed close-knit neighbourhoods. A few canals still hosted lively communities with their own post offices, police stations, noodle shops and convenience stores. Sometimes the congestion required "policemen climbing on the roofs of larger craft and directing traffic, waving their arms about and blowing their whistles with the same impatient gestures used for keeping traffic moving in the city's streets," a local writer reported.

National development plans devised with American expertise during the military-dominated era from 1963 to 1982 dramatically altered the traditional ways of life, further divorcing city residents from the natural habitat. As a result Bangkok became "the rather confused child of several marriages of convenience", as one writer commented. The US military built six bases, radar stations, and arsenals in north-eastern Thailand across the border from Vietnam. Arguably the most negative long-term impact of American involvement in Bangkok was the unfortunate project to transform it into the Los Angeles of the Orient by building super-highways. In 1979 a Chekhovian tragedy occurred when two hundred beautiful old mango and mahogany trees lining both sides of Sathorn Road were felled to build parallel bridges for vehicular traffic across the Chao Phraya.

Traffic snarls had already begun by the mid-1950s when a jaded young resident advised Australian writer Norman Bartlett, "When you've been here as long as I have, you'll find it much like any other city. Except for the traffic! You've never seen such chaos." Every year more and bigger American, European and Australian cars poured onto narrow, inadequate secondary roads with minimal infrastructure. Field Marshal Sarit Thanarat banned pedal-powered *samlors* to make way for the motorized three-wheel *tuk tuks* that "buzz through the streets like angry hornets," in the words of a man-on-the-street.

The American Trappist monk Thomas Merton (who had a self-proclaimed duty to bear witness to contemplative values) may have been the only visitor who actually enjoyed the traffic. In his journals he describes a number of rollicking rides during a visit in 1968. (Bear in mind that this was his first extended trip after spending twenty-seven cloistered years at Gethsemane Abbey in Kentucky.) "Bangkok was the worst place for traffic I ever saw; no light, you just step on the gas and race five hundred other cars to the crossing. The main rule of Asia driving seems to be: never use the brake, just lean on the horn. It is wildly exciting."

But traffic could also be lethal. The writer Suwanee Sukhontha, who was at the height of her fame, was stabbed to death in 1984 while stuck in a traffic jam. She had a great impact on contemporary's women's writing in Thailand and her murder sent shock waves through the entire Thai literary community. Ironically, one of her finest stories features a wealthy Thai society woman caught in the middle of a traffic jam who emerges from her chauffer-driven car to see why traffic has stalled. As she raises her arm to protect her eyes from the glaring sun, her large diamond ring glimmers in the bright light. A thief suddenly dashes out from a nearby alley, grabs her arm and chops off her finger to get the jewel.

A team from MIT concluded in the early 1990s that Bangkok had "possibly the worst traffic congestion of any city of similar size in the world". The elevated mass transit Skytrain inaugurated in December 1999 and the new subway line opened at the auspicious time of 7:14 p.m. on 3 July 2004 have not really dented the economic cost of gridlock and the nightmarish traffic—wasted fuel, expensive car maintenance and loss of productivity. Forty thousand new cars are purchased every month and the average commuter spends forty-four days a year in transit.

All sorts of diversions—cell phones, distance learning classes, karaoke in the car—make traffic somewhat more bearable. Sila Komchai, former political activist turned social satirist, won a SEA Writers prize for his collection of short stories. In *A Traffic-Wise Family* the driver becomes a father-to-be as he tells a friend.

Hurray! My wife is pregnant! She's become pregnant on the road!... I think of the little one, who is going to make our family life wonderfully complete. I think of the new car, which will be spacious enough for father, mother and child as well as all the accessories family life requires... A car is indeed an absolute priority for a happy life along the streets of the City of Angels.

But these are the values that drive the affluent. Wanich Jarunggidana's short story *The Capital* (1985) is a grim diary of the daily ordeals of the less fortunate who ride dilapidated public transport.

I was really exhausted today, running around town on errands for my boss. I nearly lost my senses while crossing the road at the Rajaprasong intersection. I was standing on the island in the middle of the road, being gassed on the exhaust pipes from the cars accelerating past. I tried to hold my breath so as not to inhale the poisonous gases, only to breathe in a lungful of fumes belched in my face. Thanks to that experience, I discovered that exhaust fumes contain no oxygen at all. In my asphyxiated state, I choked, my ears blocked, and I felt faint.

Deaf Sim, a poor old Chinese woman in Prabhassorn Sevikul's short story by the same title (1984) is a roadside victim. She had married late to an "ugly old" Chinese man who "believed that deaf women had stronger and more unusual sexual desires than normal women." Now she spends her days like many other roadside workers on a very congested street.

Occasionally, she would raise her head and look off down the busy road. Cars sped by continually; crowds of people filled the sidewalks from early morning until late at night. It was a busy, noisy world, but there was no noise in it for her.

Because she was deaf, it was as though she observed the life of the street from a secret place. She removed her spectacles and laid them on the lid of the bamboo sewing basket, which was her means of livelihood and also her best friend. The old woman raised her hands to her eyes and rubbed them hard; they hurt from hours of work.

Since her eyes had begun to worsen, the pain also had worsened. But if she ever gave in, closed her eyes, and let her head droop forward, in a moment she would be jolted from her repose with a start to begin work again. Fear kept her eyes open. Fear that the customers would walk by, afraid to disturb her. Fear that she would not be able to call out to them in time, that another woman would get the work—for she was not alone on her small square bench at the curbside, beside her bamboo basket full of needles and thread, darning eggs, and scraps of fabric. There were other women on other small square benches, any of whom would eagerly snatch away her regular customers if the opportunity appeared. No, she had no choice. Nor did they.

THAITANIC

During the construction boom of the 1980s and 1990s driven by the *arriviste* money of the private sector, quality in design and construction was often in short supply. Bureaucratic conflicts and inertia resulted in crass monumentality. Many private developers put up buildings that look like "decorated sheds" from Las Vegas but their sole semiotic function was pure ostentation.

In *Bangkok Mood* (1995) poet Paiwirin Khao Ngam derides this building boom.

> O Bangkok, city of mundane folks
> Aspiring angels in seven heavens
> Instant abodes, hazy smokes
> Worshipping material existence.

When the Asian economy came to a shuddering halt in 1997 triggering a drastic devaluation of the Thai *baht*, some financial pundits dubbed it the Thaitanic. The disastrous effects of the crisis were felt all over the kingdom. Construction on nearly 300 high rises suddenly ground to a halt after 56 investment and securities companies collapsed taking thousands of businesses with them. Bangkok photo-journalist Manit Sriwanichpoom snapped the casualties in his series of black-and-white prints called *Dream Interrruptus*. Skyline skeletons resembled buildings in a war zone. These unfinished or abandoned construction projects were read by social critics as metaphors for the greed of the economic elite and as punishment for their hubris.

As far back as 1927 the challenges facing structural engineers in erecting large buildings and wharves on a mud bed were being noted in the *Bangkok Times Weekly Mail*. The City of Angels rests on soft clay and the cost of pilings is usually estimated at about 15-20 per cent of the total cost of a building. Pilings for skyscrapers, such as the ninety-storey Baiyoke Towers II, go 200 feet deep to the sand level. The pressure of multi-storey buildings and the increasing demands for groundwater in a city located on a flood plain are most evident during the monsoon season when large parts of Bangkok are subject to regular flooding.

"Noise, pollution, all the dementia and detritus spawned by a modern metropolis have in Bangkok outstripped the infrastructure's ability to cope, like a pubescent boy constantly outgrowing new sets of clothes," writes Steve van Beek, long-time American expatriate, author and river-explorer. A current municipal plan to divide the city into twelve more manageable urban districts offers little hope of remedying the most serious problems of urban sprawl—dozens of slums caused by escalating land values, pollution of air, water and soil. Pathumwan slum, adjacent to the great gleaming post-modern shopping malls at Siam Square, has been walled off by the city to hide it from the tourists.

We are standing in front of a blank canvas but we let the artist paint anything," says prominent social critic Sulak Sivaraska, "because there is no control." He scorns the historic mismanagement and economic colonialism that has made Bangkok a "second-rate western city" with corporate palaces, American fast-food joints and socially fragmenting forces. Due to ineffective zoning and obsolete regulations, some residential areas abut toxic plants, slaughterhouses and petroleum tanks.

SEX IN THE CITY

Bangkok may seem like an "infernal city" with its three tropical seasons, aptly described as hot, hot and damn it's hot, but it is extraordinarily seductive. Paul Theroux was unsettled by the "hugely preposterous city of temples and brothels" but missed their mutual allure: release from the karmic chain of suffering and from consuming lust. Public and private merge in the busy marketplace of sex in the city that is devoid of the sense of pathos found in red light districts of western cities.

Poet Chitr Phoumisak in *Fishiness in the Night* (1964) blames Americans GIs for the sex industry:

There are the call girls—their creamy white, sweet complexions.

The widows of absent-minded husbands—spreading their legs wide open for trade.

The sex boats meandering on the river, places for careless orgies.

Saen Saeb Canal wincing from the madness of lust, suffocating from its fish smells.

(In the past) the Northeast was alive with the sound of the *khaen* [north-eastern mouth organ] echoing off the rain clouds.

Maidens were most, and in their manner turned away from the gaze of men.

(But now) they are delirious over their foreign soldiers, boasting of lovers who throw money at them.

They promenade, proposing their beautiful flesh for sale along the side of the road.

But sex for sale has always been readily available and pervasive in Bangkok, primarily because the local market sought it out. The Chinese had floating brothels on the river soon after the city was founded in 1782. During the Japanese occupation of Thailand, girls at the Venus and Mosquito Bar opposite the port at Klong Toey dressed to play up to the secret fantasies of sailors: Japanese kimono, schoolgirl uniform or Hollywood glamour girl.

An old Bangkok hand listed the top ten brothels in mid-twentieth century Bangkok with an addendum: the brothel boats that paddled around the Chaloemlok Bridge in Pratunam near the end of the Klong Saen Sap (one the most popular with the local rather than the foreign clientele). William Warren, an American writer who lived on the canal after he came to Bangkok in the 1960s, recalls that each *sampan* had a "curtained area behind which a prostitute lolled on cushions, soliciting customers who waited beneath bridges."

The King and I (1956) fixed Bangkok in the popular imagination as an exotic destination for highly sexualized western men. Yul Brenner acted out a western male fantasy of an uncouth Oriental king and lord of a harem. The White Leopard, the famous bar-girl in Jack Reynold's *A Woman of Bangkok* (1956) sizes up her foreign customers.

By and large she preferred Americans to all the rest. The English were too sentimental: they always fell a little bit in love with even a dancing-girl, even though they were going to be in town only one night and never see her again... As for the Dutch, they were always fat and quarrelsome about money. The French paid too little and never gave a girl any peace all night, and also they wanted to do things that the Buddha doesn't approve of. But the Americans knew how to treat a girl like her. They had plenty of money and were free with it when out to enjoy themselves.

The first soft-porn movie *Emmanuelle* was filmed in Bangkok in the 1960s and the arrival of American soldiers on leave during the Vietnam War further distorted the image of the city. Notorious night-life places sprouted up during the war, among the most famous being The Holly-wood Hotel, The Grace Hotel, Golden Gate Massage Parlor, Lucky Strike Bowling Alley.

Mass international tourism turned the flesh trade into a major service industry and billion dollar foreign-currency earner. One out of two visitors arriving by air today is an unaccompanied male. Prostitution is an integral part of the overall economy but the Thai sex trade has a unique feature—massage parlours—that market "clean sex". They also predated international sex tourism and are popular all over the country.

One Night in Bangkok, a pop tune from the Vietnam era, is a favourite siren song for pasty, beer-bellied western sex tourists. Its message is enacted every night in the maze of bars in Patpong, Soi Cowboy, Nana Entertainment Center, in the up-scale sprawling entertainment centres of Ratchchadapisek, in Turkish baths and tourist hotels, and here and there and almost everywhere.

> One night in Bangkok and the world's your oyster.
> The bars are temples but the pearls ain't free
> You'll find a god in every golden cloister
> And if you're lucky then the god's a she
> I can feel an angel sliding up to me.

Sex workers in bars are not obliged to sell their services and don't have to go with any man who pays the fee. Yet there is no denying "the overall ambience of complicity, a knowingness that has seeped into the very fabric of this Asian Babylon and its economy, a sybaritic scent so pervasive that it cannot but affect the general atmosphere and social life," as an American writer has so well-observed. In what other city could a place called the *No Hands Restaurant* provide a full dinner menu with *à la carte* post-prandial services?

For a glimpse of those who have been expelled from the garden, go to the Nana Hotel (soi 4 Nana Tai, off Sukhumvit Road). A guard sits opposite the elevator to take the identity cards of the Thai women who are going up to bedrooms with customers. Adjacent to his desk is a "portrait" gallery of more than a hundred photocopied identity cards. Some of the previous owners were killed by their lovers or had murdered them. Most were victims of theft by wily women who resorted to criminal steps to attain their end: "First we win your hearts; then we win your wallets."

POST-MODERN CITY

The Buddhist conception of time is cyclical; change is inherent, inexorable and unbending. In the eyes of the great nineteenth-century Thai poet Sunthorn Phu, the destruction of past capitals was congruent with the Buddhist doctrine of impermanence. Reading Bangkok in his way, the more the city changes, the more it becomes what it truly is. For many preservationists, however, the Buddhist philosophy of impermanence has too readily allowed demolition of the old. Fortunately some local activists have been successful in their opposition to the westernized fashion of recasting *bijoux* in a sparkling new brooch, usually at the expense of old neighbourhoods.

It is rather ironic that some contemporary urban planners and cultural theorists now admire the unplanned character of Bangkok and the fact that it has no downtown areas or a city centre. Singaporean architect William S. W. Lim articulates their view:

The idea of cleaning up [an existing city] and re-creating a modern, orderly city [like Singapore] is out of fashion. In an age of mobile phone and e-mail communication, cities don't need centres… Bangkok has tall buildings all over the place; there's no typical concentric structure where you have a downtown with a high land value and the outer parts with a low land value. The even distribution is exactly what contemporary thinking is all about.

But progress has exacted a heavy price on Bangkok. Huge issues face the city: gridlock traffic, swelling population, the flooding and pollution of the Chao Phraya river and remaining canals. "We have too many solutions; that's the problem," says architect-historian Sumet Jumsai. Many are advanced by people with no sense of history who "should not be allowed to plan anything in this world," he complains. His hero is Buckminster Fuller, the American inventor, futurologist and global-philosopher who championed floating cities.

Dr. Sumet has ardently proposed floating cities on the Gulf of Siam that would provide energy-efficient, inexpensive housing for the capital to which they would be connected by a modern mass transit system. He also envisages floating parks extending from the banks of the Chao Phraya. Perhaps the unique "city in a garden" and the amphibious life of Old Bangkok might one day be recalled down by the riverside.

Part One

CITY OF KINGS

One

SUKHOTHAI AND AYUDHYA

According to the "great trek" theory that once claimed wide support among scholars, the Thai people emigrated from southern China, conquered and absorbed the civilizations of indigenous people—the Mon and the Khmers—and began to call themselves Thai, the Free. Historians are now of one mind that that the Thai or Tai (an ethnic identification) were more or less *in situ* in South Yunnan, the Shan States, Laos, North Vietnam and the Chao Phraya basin. One of their leaders, known as King Ramkhamhaeng the Great (reg. 1277-98), founded a city on a Khmer site. By consolidating and uniting the disparate Thai communities, mainly through political alliances and dynastic marriages, he formed the first Siamese kingdom of Sukhothai in central Thailand. He seems to have deliberately rejected the Khmer idea of divine kingship and, absorbing the teachings of the Buddhist monks who by then had come from Ceylon to the kingdom, he fashioned himself as a wise and compassionate monarch. He was said to have heard the petition of any subject who rang the bell of the drum tower at the palace gate to summon him. The citizen's right to appeal directly to the king, as inscribed in King Ramkhamhaeng's stele of 1292 (Bangkok, National Museum), is still practised today.

Sukhothai was the cradle of Thai civilization as the stele boasts: "This city of Sukhothai is prosperous. In the water there are fish, in the fields there is rice." The Chinese were attracted by these bumper rice crops, so much so that the Mongol Kublai Khan sent an ambassador to establish friendly relations with the Sukhothai king. Trade was promoted, eventually developing into a full-blown commercial relationship. Legend has it that five hundred Chinese potters were sent as a diplomatic gift to the king of Sukhothai.

Art and literature were nourished during the heyday of Sukhothai. The elegant, sensuous, three-dimensional walking Buddha was an important artistic innovation, as were the lotus-bud shaped temple finials. King Ramkhamhaeng's grandson wrote the first complete Thai book, later known as the *Tri-Bhumi P'ra Ruang* (The Three Realms by P'ra Ruang). It was principally a formulation of Buddhist cosmology but provided a pivotal role for the king as the absolute power to ensure social order. This new conception of kingship would be consolidated by the dynasty of kings who governed the next Siamese capital for more than four centuries.

In the mid-fourteenth century a new capital was built on an island at the confluence of three rivers. Its legendary foundation by King Ramathibodi I (U Thong) is recorded by a Brahman scribe in the minute detail of court ritual: "In the Chula Era 713, the year of the Tiger, on Friday, the sixth of the waning month at 9:54 in the morning the foundation of Ayudhia was laid." This was, in the words of the poets, the Divine Blessed City of Ayudhya.

Later, a Dutch trader living in Ayudhya related a more colourful account of the city's foundation. He claims to have consulted Siamese histories and wise old men who confirmed the tale of Prince U Thong, the son of a Chinese trader. The prince had to flee the country after he was found to have violated a number of the wives of top mandarins. His wanderings finally led him to Siam, where he was told of a beautiful island that was strangely uninhabited. A hermit explained that the site had been abandoned because of a dragon that lived in a swamp in the middle of the city. When provoked it spurted poisonous saliva from its mouth that caused epidemics and a horrid stench. The prince heroically slew the dragon, filled in the swamp and founded the city of Ayudhya.

Ayudhya derives from the Indian Sanskrit Ayodhya, home of the Lord Rama, avatar of Vishnu and hero of the Indian epic the *Ramayana*. The kings of Ayudhya were fascinated by the Indian-derived traditions of Khmer culture and fully embraced the idea of divine kingship based on the cult of the *devaraja* (Sanskrit for "divine king"), who was revered as the earthly incarnation of the god Shiva; this marked a distinct departure from the benevolent monarchy of King Ramkhamhaeng at Sukhothai. Brahman priests provided the pomp and ceremony for court etiquette. Theravada Buddhism remained the official religion of the kingdom, however, and the role of the king encompassed a defence of the faith and the proclamation of only such laws as were appropriate to the preservation of the Buddha's teachings.

Ayudhya rose to become the strongest and most prosperous and powerful city in Southeast Asia. Natural water barriers buffered it and for much of the year it was an essentially nautical city as the area surrounding it was inundated during the long monsoon season. From the mid-fourteenth century all the major trading nations dispatched their ships to Ayudhya.

North-east monsoon winds brought traders from China, Japan, Korea, Annam and Champa (Vietnam) as well as from seaports along the Indian and Persian coasts. Ships embarked with goods from afar and departed with holds full of Siamese export: rice, metals, teak, dyes, perfumes, sealing wax, ivory, elephants and peacock tails. By the beginning of the sixteenth century the links with Europe were firmly established: the Portuguese had been the first foreigners to sign a treaty of trade (1516) with the king of Ayudhya. Then came the Dutch, followed by the English, the French and others.

Traders were warmly welcomed by the king since they competed against each other and courted his favour. The kings had a lucrative monopoly on international trade. Each group of foreigners was granted a piece of land for settlement located outside the city. They were under the jurisdiction of the minister of trade (*kosathibodi*) but were free to select their own head (*kapiton*) who was empowered to look after everyday affairs and handle judicial matters. All foreigners were allowed to observe their own laws, customs and religious practices. Since the Chinese were exempted from *corvée* duty and could move freely throughout the kingdom, they controlled internal trade and rose to important places in the military and administration. Only the Chinese were allowed to live inside the walls since they were not perceived as foreigners. By the seventeenth century they had become the economic backbone of Siam and numbered about three thousand.

DIPLOMATIC EXCHANGES

Major disputes with the Dutch and the English East India Company prompted King Narai the Great (reg. 1656-88) to send four embassies to the court of France with the aim of encouraging new trade. (The first vessel left Ayudhya in December 1680 and sank off Madagascar taking everybody and everything down with it.) The second embassy left in January 1684, went to England first and had two audiences with King Charles II. Then it proceeded on to France where the Siamese emissaries were graciously received at a splendid reception by the Sun King. But after they left Paris the French grumbled aloud at their *gaucherie*. They had yawned openly, nodded off at the opera and refused to kneel during Mass at Nôtre Dame. But His Most Catholic Majesty King Louis XIV was not dissuaded by a few *faux pas*. He had just acquired a new mistress whose pious influence induced in him even greater devotion to the Catholic cause. He was stirred by the "glowing vision of bringing a non-Christian monarch into the true doctrine," as Prince Chula Chakrabongse later put it. The king sent two official embassies to King Narai and the court of Ayudhya: "pour la gloire de Dieu et de la France", he proclaimed.

The first French delegation was received in the Royal Palace at Lopburi in 1685. The diplomatic letter from the French king was first placed on a gold salver; this was transported in a gilded royal barge propelled by sixty oarsmen in scarlet robes, then ceremonially carried on a tiered gold palanquin by ten men, also in red raiment. The French envoy led his small cortege into the glittering reception chamber that was dominated by the presence of the Siamese sovereign. He sat completely motionless on a throne nearly nine feet above ground, as was his courtly protocol. But the Sun King had given strict orders that the letter be delivered directly into King Narai's hands. The French cleverly avoided a diplomatic fiasco by fashioning a stick so that the ambassador Chevalier de Chaumont could raise it up accordingly. "He moved proudly towards the throne, holding the golden cup in which was the letter, and presented the letter to the King without raising his elbow, as if the King were at the same level as he," wrote the Abbé de Choisy. Thus "the good King was obliged to lean half out the window to take the letter, which he did laughing... [then] he lifted it up to be level with his head, which is the greatest honour he could ever show it." The king, who had a keen interest in astronomy, was later introduced to six Jesuit astronomers who had brought telescopes as gifts.

The embassy to France led by Kosa Pan (1686-87) was a sensational success; the "exotic" dress and demeanor of the group caused much comment in patrician French society. A fragmentary account written by Kosa Pan describes the reception by King Louis XIV. As the three Siamese approached the Bourbon monarch they performed the *wai* at intervals. They then prostrated themselves at the foot of the throne, offering him a form of honour "that extended almost to adoration."

The second—more lavish—French diplomatic delegation, intended to seal the conversion of King Narai and to establish garrisons in the ports of Bangkok and Mergui, departed from Brest two years later. Five warships carried the official party, including about a dozen Jesuits and an expeditionary force of thirteen hundred soldiers. But this time they were not as warmly received and were kept waiting a month for a royal reception.

FALL OF AYUDHYA

Travellers' accounts (including a few Persian and Japanese) from the sixteenth to the eighteenth centuries describe a breathtaking cosmopolitan city of about a million people that included over 500 temples and monasteries, 24 fortresses and about a hundred gates and 35 miles of boat-filled canals. Highly skilled artisans embellished the city. Beautiful "forbidden" women who spent their entire lives in the inner sanctums of the palace produced numerous progeny for the kings.

The ecology of the widely scattered city was noted less glowingly by the intrepid German naturalist Engelbert Kaempfer in his *Description of the Kingdom of Siam*, compiled in 1690.

> ...the streets run in straight lines along the canals; some of them are tolerably large, but the greater part very narrow and all, generally speaking, foul and dirty. Some also overflow'd at high water. Considering the bigness of the city, it is not very populous and in some parts but thinly inhabited, particularly on the West side on account of its remoteness, and toward the south by reason of the morassy ground, over which people make shift to get upon planks or paltry bridges. There are abundance of empty spaces and large gardens behind the streets wherein they let Nature work, so that they are full of grass, Herbs, Shrubs and Trees that grow Wild.

Kaempfer also had a connoisseur's eye. After describing the three most impressive royal palaces, he turns to Buddhist temples which he considers more exceptional than the Gothic cathedrals of Europe. "They do not equal our churches in bigness, but far exceed them in outward beauty, by reason of the many bended roofs, gilt frontispieces, advanced styles, columns, pillars and other ornaments. Within they are adorned with many images as big as the life and bigger, skilfully formed of a mixture of plaster, resin, oil and hair, the outside of which is first varnished over black then gilt." Less than a century later, all the precious images of Lord Buddha were melted down for their gold value by the Burmese who utterly and completely vanquished the capital in 1767.

A number of Ayudhya's nobles had tried to constrain the ambitions of the Burmese dynasty. They enjoined Buddhist fellowship. "It will be like when elephants fight," they pleaded. "The plants and grass on the ground get crushed... So ask your lord to ally the two countries as a single golden land. Both kings will gain fame for their kindness in freeing their people from worry." But the Burmese had grandiose ambitions: to obliterate the rival capital of Ayudhya. In order to ensure success they sent a huge contingent of three armies that camped near temples on the higher ground outside the capital and laid siege for two years. They had first captured the cities and towns up river to control the food supplies to their troops as well as to cut off provisions to the capital. During most of April 1767, with temperatures soaring to nearly 40 degrees, the Burmese volleyed their cannons from the base of the Wat Na Pramen directly across the Lopburi river from the palace. The *Chronicles of Ayudhya* tersely recorded the final downfall.

> On Tuesday, the 5th month, the 9th day of the waxing moon, the year of the Pig, around 4 p.m. The Burmese fired at the capital from the highpoint of Wat Ka Pong, Wat Mae Nang Plaem. Then they set fire to the wall; as the wall crumbled, they marched into the capital. They set fire to the palace and the Wat Phra Si Sanphet. The Royal Family and high officials fled with their families.

The Kingdom of Ayudhya had endured for 417 years through five dynasties and 34 kings. Surviving members of the royal family (reportedly about 2,000) were led away to Burma as war captives. With them went the highly-skilled artisans and poets who would spend the rest of their lives in slavery. A cosmopolitan city with a million inhabitants, more populous than Paris or London at the same time, was reduced to barely ten thousand. Temples were set afire. Manuscripts containing much of the written history of the Siamese people and their religious records were destroyed. Precious objects were looted. Mosques, Hindu shrines and Catholic churches were plundered. A Dutch trader lamented the wanton destruction: "On the 28th of April 1767 the city was taken by assault. The riches of the palace and pagodas became a heap of ashes and ruins; the golden images of the false gods were melted, and the blind rage of these barbarians deprived them of the rewards which had awakened their cupidity."

Ayudhya smouldered for months and the entire countryside was laid waste and looted. A Buddhist monk vividly describes the ensuing chaos.

> When Ayudhya fell… the king fled from the city into the forest. Starving when the enemy captured him, his strength failed and he died a natural death. The populace was afflicted with a variety of ills by the enemy. Some wandered about, starving, searching for food. They were bereft of their families, their children and wives, and stripped of their possessions and tools… They had no rice, no fish, no clothing. They were thin, their bodies wasting away. They found only the leaves of trees

and grass to eat… In desperation many turned to dacoits… They gathered in bands, and plundered for rice and paddy and salt. Some found food and others could not. They grew thinner, and their flesh and blood wasted away. Afflicted with a thousand evils, some died and some lived on.

The fall of Ayudhya was a devastating blow for the Siamese, made more poignant because it was brought about by fellow Buddhists. Ankham Kalayanapongs, one of Thailand's National Artists, evokes the wasteland.

> One hundred thousand beasts have played a trick
> and ground the Royal City into dust.
> Shut out, the holy palanquin rolls on the ground.
> Dogs, pigs, and crows devour our heaven,
> Tears from the eyes of the guardian spirits turn
> to blood that floods and flows around the lost,
> defeated town.

Ayudhya's collapse was due to many factors, foremost of which was constant warfare during three centuries after a Burmese king was spurned in his request for one of the seven white elephants in the royal stables of Ayudhya. Historians Chris Baker and Pasuk Phongpaichit underscore the role played by the great expansion of commerce, undermining royal power. Intense rivalry among nobles for revenue from the lucrative rice trade and unveiled competition for wealth internally weakened the kingdom.

Refugees who returned after the fall to live on their raft houses or on boats found food supplies at a bare minimum. Many resorted to stealing from the ruined temples and pagodas. The enterprising Chinese in Ayudhya had a real gift for finding booty in the rubble. In an excerpt from a letter a court functionary describes a successful treasure hunt:

> It is only because of the industrious nature and perseverance of the Chinese that Siam has recovered as quickly as it has. Without the Chinese there would be no gold or silver in Siam as the Burmese took it all… The Chinese seem to have a knack of discovering hidden caches. When a group of Chinese descended on the ruins of Wat Pha Thai, they uncovered a huge amount of gold. It took three hours to take it away.

At another temple called by the royalty Wat Pradu, they discovered 5 hai [earthen] jars of silver. The Chinese have waged war on bronze cast Buddha images, weapons, tools, window shutters, doors, posts. Some of the temples are now just like old ovens. The walls are black and they are filled with burned rubble and coal. The Buddha images have been broken and shattered.

Even though the capital had been transferred to Bangkok after the destruction of Ayudhya, the old city slowly recovered and experienced a significant economic boom during the reign of King Rama IV (1851-68). An abundance of food was by that time available at the international market as well as a great variety of local-grown produce sold in the floating markets on the rivers. Ayudhya became a province in 1894 and was connected by rail to the capital at Bangkok. Old bricks were used as landfill for the railroad tracks. During an inaugural run in 1900 a Belgian traveller climbed an old guard tower for the wider view of a city that could still only be visited by water as the interior was still completely overgrown. Surrounding the island was a floating city of about 40,000. Double rows of water-born native shops plied their wares to the local markets and downstream to the new capital at Bangkok.

By the mid-twentieth century government-sponsored infrastructure projects—bridges, highways and commercial shop houses—began to deal a death sentence to the river as the main artery of the life of Ayudhya. Land titles, which covered ancient monuments, were sold to the private sector. The sale of once restricted island property led to legalized historical destruction and industrial activity began to boom in the late 1960s. Thanks largely to the advocacy of Sumet Jumsai, the concept of National Historical Parks was instituted. In 1976 the Fine Arts Department designated twenty per cent of the island as a protected historical park and in 1991 Ayudhya was named a World Heritage Site by UNESCO.

Two

THE GRAND PALACE

It is an old tradition that the Grand Palace should always be viewed for the first time from the Chao Phraya river either early in the morning when it glitters or after sunset when it glows. As the ferry boat rounds the wide curve of the river, the gilded roofs and spires appear soaring high above luminous chalk white walls. Like the golden birds of Byzantium that once wakened a drowsy emperor, it is a startling sight. "No painting could give any idea of it," exclaimed a young Napoleonic exile, the Marquis de Beauvoir, who spent a week in Bangkok in 1867. "The tropical sun alternately casts rays of gold, crimson, pale pink and misty blue, which play like a thousand electric lights on the marble minarets, the porcelain domes, the crystal spires, the glistening gables, and the brilliant dresses of a strange people.

The moonlit view from outside the palace was no less magical for a Danish writer Ebbe Kornerup, who found its turrets and temples "fantastically lovely, with concave glazed roofs, pointed gables, and three spires. Do we dream or wake? Siam reveals herself [as] enchanting, unique. There are not so many places in the world where one may find so amazing and excellent a pile as the King's palace in Bangkok.

The Grand Palace complex, official residence of the Lords of Life (as Thai kings are reverentially known), is like a city within a city. It is a stunning architectural ensemble, oriented to the East, which occupies a rectangular piece of land of nearly a square mile. It has been greatly embellished over the years by successive Chakri monarchs but the original plan and Khmer cosmology underpin it. The ruler's function was to harmonize activities on earth with the cosmic forces of the universe. To this end, the Grand Palace was organized as a universe in miniature. The king's royal residence was the symbolic Mount Meru, sacred city of the gods; his four chief ministers were counterparts of the guardian deities of the four cardinal points of the universe. It is imbued with history, tradition and sanctity as the names of palace gates suggest: Gate of Knowledge, Gate of Merit, Gate of Earth and Gate of Heaven.

The first Chakri monarch wisely selected a ready-made fortified site, the ruins of a brick fort, for his palace in splendid isolation on Rattanakosin Island. Its layout and situation were intended to mirror as closely as possible the old palace of the vanquished capital at Ayudhya. The three pillars of the kingdom—monarchy, Buddhism and national administration—were concentrated within the crenellated walls. This required the construction of numerous buildings, the most prestigious of which was the Royal Chapel or Temple of the Emerald Buddha (Wat Phra Kaeo), as well as a royal residence, throne halls, administrative offices, the regiment of the guards, the regiment of the artillery, the stables for horses and elephants, the forbidden city of the harem containing the king's private residence, homes of the queens, consorts, children and attendants, shops and a flower garden.

The Grand Palace complex is divided into four distinct areas: Outer Court, Central Court, Inner Court and the Temple of the Emerald Buddha. The first part once encompassed ministerial offices, barracks, palace guards (and a mint and arsenal during the reign of King Mongkut). The central part contained the royal residences where all important state receptions and ceremonies took place. The Inner Court, also known as the Inside, was directly behind the Phra Maha Monthien (Great Residence) Group. It was a forbidden city enclosed by a massive, high wall; inner doors of great weight and size were guarded by policewomen. Female members of the royal family lived in brick mansions with their attendants while the king's concubines as well as officials and guards inhabited more traditional Siamese-style wooden houses. The Inside remains off limits, except through special permission of the Minister of the Royal Household.

Visitors today are given access to enter the Royal Chapel, three-throne halls, a museum and the Royal Chapel Museum. For a comprehensive armchair visit, M. R. Naengnoi Suksri's beautifully illustrated guide, *The Grand Palace Bangkok* (2001), takes you to inaccessible places and includes useful plans and supplementary material.

The Grand Palace is charged with religious and royal symbolism meant to convey the king's sacred and absolute power. Every aspect of the architecture reflects his lofty status, especially the multi-tiered parasols and roofs, the carved and gilded pediments and *nagas* (mythic serpents, symbol of water and auspiciousness) and the long-petalled lotus-shaped capitals.

Thai architectural and decorative styles predominate but they are blended, sometimes fused, with Khmer and Chinese forms and fashioned to extraordinary visual effect.

Following the obligatory tourist circuit from the entrance on Thanon Na Phra Lan, one is greeted by a statue installed by King Rama III of a hermit monk, physician to Buddha, and father of Thai herbal medicine. His yogic position and attitude of calm seem to have little effect on the swarms of tourists who ignore him, en route to the legendary Emerald Buddha.

The temple grounds are guarded against evil spirits by fifteen-foot tall giants from the *Ramakien* and bronze Khmer lions. Their ferocity is tempered by the sculptures of Kinnon and Kinnaree on the elevated terrace. These lovely hybrids (half-human and half-bird) of the legendary Himaphan Forest in the Himalayas seem like charming hosts for the visit to three sacred monuments. From left to right: Phra Si Rattana Chedi, a stupendous golden Sri Lankan-style reliquary. Next is Phra Mondop, a square Khmer-style pavilion that enshrines the *Tripitika* (the sacred Buddhist scriptures recorded on palm-leaf paper and stored in a precious mother-of-pearl box). The last monument, Phra Thep Bidorn (the Royal Pantheon), houses life-size effigies of the first eight kings of the Chakri dynasty. (It is open only on Chakri day on 6 April when the public come to pay their respects.) King Mongkut wanted to transport a complete Vishnu temple from Angkor to the Royal Palace but wisely settled for a miniature replica of Angkor Wat, adjacent to Phra Mondop.

Royal temples are a riot of colour, "a polychrome aesthetic that clothes the sacred in layer upon layer upon glittering layer and expresses adoration through a process of unrestrained accumulation," in Alistair Shearer's theophanic prose. Spires and *chedi* (bell-shaped reliquaries) are coated by millions of paper-thin gold leaf flakes; golden pediments, translucent glass mosaic, rainbow-hued mother-of-pearl, and Chinese porcelain tiles and pastel ceramic bits are combined to create a resplendent effect. Brilliant exteriors contrast with the inner darkness that intensifies the iconic impact of the principal Buddha image.

Thai Buddhist temples are constructed as objects of veneration; the symbolism of each architectural feature is of spiritual importance. This was of little interest to Somerset Maugham when he visited Bangkok in 1923. He may even have had a touch of the Stendhal syndrome—a sense of disorientation and feeling of giddiness brought on by an extraordinarily beautiful masterpiece or a large concentration of art in a single place. He writes of Bangkok's temples:

> They are unlike anything in the world, so that you are taken aback, and you cannot fit them into the scheme of things you know. It makes you laugh with delight to think that anything so fantastic could exist on this sombre earth. They are gorgeous; they glitter with gold and whitewash, yet are not garish; against that vivid sky, in that dazzling sunlight, they hold their own, defying the brilliancy of nature and supplementing it with the ingenuity and playful boldness of man.

TEMPLE OF THE EMERALD BUDDHA

The most sacred place in Thailand and the centrepiece of the Grand Palace is the Royal Chapel or Temple of the Emerald Buddha (Wat Phra Kaeo) at the north-east corner of the palace grounds. The complex surrounding the royal chapel contains diverse buildings, monuments and courtyards that serve various functional, symbolic and spiritual purposes. Since burning incense and joss sticks is not permitted in the temple, two small Buddha statues within its enclosure are visited by Thais who wish to make offerings of eggs, pig snouts, fruits, soft drinks and other edible items.

The visitor passes through two outer walls separating the temple from the compound which emphasize its sacred nature. Four boundary stones covered with gold leaf designate the temple as a sacred place where monks may be ordained. It is the private chapel of the king as well as the site of grand royal ceremonies.

The gilded exterior of the temple is lavishly decorated: the three pairs of doors are inlaid with mother-of-pearl that shines like fire opals, the surrounding walls are imbedded with reflective glass mosaic and colourful vegetation made of Chinese porcelain. Southeast Asian caryatids—hundreds of gilded *garudas* (half bird/half man) at the base of the temple walls—seem to lift the rectangular hall from the marble base. On the pediments is Vishnu on his private *garuda*, a traditional Brahmanic symbol of kingship, which extends his protective wings as guardian of the universe.

Inside the temple, which is also highly ornamented and continually embellished to enhance the aura of the most venerated icon in the country, sits the surprisingly small Emerald Buddha. It is only twenty-six inches,

but is positioned on a gold-leafed wooden throne about forty feet in height, designed to resemble the aerial chariot of celestial beings in Hindu mythology. Carved out of jade, or jasper, the figure glows in the relative darkness of the temple. An icon believed to possess great potency, it was paraded through the city in 1820 in the hope of purification from a terrible cholera epidemic. Twice a year ministers drank the water of allegiance before it, prostrating themselves in front of their sovereign on a carpet of woven silver. It was believed that a grisly fate would befall anyone who swore falsely before the image.

The origin of the Emerald Buddha remains shrouded in mystery. It is surely one of the best-travelled statues in existence, having journeyed for a thousand years from Ceylon via Burma to the Kingdom of Lanna. Legend has it that the statue was rediscovered by accident in the fifteenth century when lightning cracked open an ancient *stupa* in Chiang Rai. The king of Chiang Mai tried to transport it to that city but the elephant refused to budge further than Lampang, where the king recognized the omen and had a temple built to house it. A Laotian king took possession of it in 1555 but King Taksin was determined to win it back. After Chao Phraya Chakri vanquished Vientiane in 1779, the prized Buddha was installed in Wat Arun in Thonburi. There it remained until the first Chakri monarch King Rama I translated it with great ceremony in the splendid new royal chapel. Two large gilded images of the Buddha dressed in the regalia of Siamese kings were placed before it by King Rama III.

King Mongkut had a beautiful new temple built for the sacred icon but it burned down in 1863. Tradition has it that after the temple was completed, the king had a dream in which the statue appeared to him and told him that it did not want to be moved. It must then have seemed less like a dream and more like a nightmare when he was approached by the British consul in Bangkok who had been authorized to negotiate the purchase of the statue for £40,000. Some years later, a French diplomat was more forcefully rebuked when he demanded that the Emerald Buddha be handed over to France as partial reparation for Siam's rather insignificant intervention in the Indo-China War.

Within the royal arcade framing the royal temple are more than three thousand feet of continuous painting contained within 178 panels. This is a lavish illustration of *Ramakien*, the longest prose work in Southeast Asia with 52,086 verses. Based on the Indian *Ramayana*, a Thai-language version of the epic was commissioned by King Rama I in 1798, more profane than the original and more entertaining. In a nutshell, the story is an allegory of the triumph of good over evil. Beautiful Sita, bride of the virtuous Rama, who is the earthly reincarnation of the Hindu God Vishnu, is kidnapped by the demon king Thotsakan who has numerous heads and arms. He imprisons her in his fortress on the island of Lanka in Ceylon. Various scenes (often set against magnificent architectural settings and evocative landscapes) depict Rama's many fierce battles with the giant to win back his wife and demonstrate his close alliance with Hanuman, the canny general of a monkey army. Through their skill, cunning and savvy, they finally kill Thotsakan and rescue Sita.

AMARIN WINICHAI AUDIENCE HALL

This hall, a Lego-like fusion of rectangle and square, is the most important audience hall for state ceremonies. Officials of state, dignitaries and ambassadors were formerly received here, and still are by King Bhumibol Adulyadej, the ninth king of the Chakri Dynasty and the reincarnation of Vishnu.

The richly decorated room is dominated by an intricately carved and gilded throne shaped like a boat with a pagoda-like seat in the middle for the king and a nine-tiered white parasol that signifies the seat of a king. A marble staircase that once flanked it led to an upper level where a curtained window gave onto the hall some ten feet beneath. From this height the king gave audience and the ceremony was carefully crafted to impress the visitor.

In 1822 the Scotsman and Malay scholar John Crawfurd was given an icy reception in the hall by King Rama II. Crawfurd had been sent as emissary of the Governor General of India to try to reduce import duties and to change the system of royal monopoly. His vivid account merits a complete transcription.

Facing them in the hall of audience the visitors saw a large Chinese mirror intended apparently as a screen to conceal the interior of the court. Advancing to this they were received with a great flourish of wind instruments and a discordant yell, which they subsequently discovered hailed the advent of the king. Mr. Crawfurd and the other members of the missions took off their hats, and bowed in the European manner. Meanwhile, the courtiers prostrated themselves in Siamese fashion, and in a twinkling the floor was so thickly covered with the forms of mandarins and attendants that it was difficult to move without stepping on someone. The view which was presented at the moment was more singular than impressive. The hall of audience was a well-proportioned and spacious apartment about thirty feet high. The walls and ceiling were painted a bright vermilion; the cornices of the walls were gilded and the ceiling was thickly spangled with stars in very rich gilding. A number of English lustres of good quality were suspended from the ceiling, but the effect they produced was marred by the presence of pillars supporting the roof by some miserable oil lamps. The throne was situated at the upper end of the hall. It was richly gilded all over, was about fifteen feet high, and in shape and look very much like a handsome pulpit. In front of the throne, and rising from the floor in sizes decreasing as they ascended, were numbers of gilded umbrellas. The king as he appeared seated on the throne struck the mission as looking more like a statue in a niche than a sentient being. He was short and rather fat, and wore a loose gown of gold tissue with very wide sleeves. His head was devoid of a crown or any other covering, but near him was a sceptre or baton of gold. On the left of the throne were exhibited the presents, which the envoy firmly believed were represented as tribute from the English Government. There were a few minutes of profound silence, broken at length by the king addressing Mr. Crawfurd. He put a few insignificant questions and concluded with these few words: "I am glad to see here an envoy from the Governor-General of India. Whatever you have to say communicate to my chief minister. What we want from you is a good supply of firearms—firearms and good gunpowder." As soon as the last words were uttered a loud stroke was heard, as if given by a wand against a piece of wainscoting. It was a signal apparently for the closing of the ceremony; for immediately curtains were lowered and completely concealed the king and his throne from view. A great flourish of wind instruments heralded the disappearance of Majesty, and the courtiers, to further emphasize the action, stretched their faces along the ground several times. The members of the mission, in accordance with their preconceived arrangement, contented themselves with bowing. While the audience was in progress a heavy shower of rain fell, and the king graciously sent to each of the strangers a small common umbrella as a protection from the elements. But as a counterpoise to this thoughtfulness they were prohibited from putting on their boots, so that they had to march through the miry courtyards in their stockinged feet.

The new audience hall of Ananda Samakhom (later destroyed) was the setting for the most important diplomatic event of nineteenth-century Siamese history: the historic trade treaty signed by King Rama IV and Sir John Bowring on behalf of the Queen of England in 1855. This was the second state reception of a foreign embassy in Siamese history and it had been decided to follow the mode of reception given to the ambassadors of Louis XIV when they were received in Ayudhya in 1685. Gilded barges and six accompanying boats brought the embassy. Five hundred men clad in scarlet faced with green and white chanted as they rowed, turning their oars with great gusto at they sang, "Row, row, we smell rice" (*Pai pai rao hom kao*).

In *The Kingdom and the People of Siam* (1857) Bowring recounts his initial reception in the throne hall of the Grand Palace on the clear moonlit night of 4 April 1855. The king sat on a richly ornamented throne, wearing a crimson gown, gold girdle, a short dagger and a glittering headdress of diamond and precious stones. Following introductions, the king offered Bowring a cigar. Then after tea and sweetmeats, he gave the English diplomat a tour of his private apartments that were "filled with various instruments, philosophical and mathematical, a great variety of Parisian clocks and pendules, thermometers, barometers, in a word all the instruments and appliances which might be found in the study or library of any opulent philosopher in Europe." After the grand reception in honour of the treaty, Bowring returned to his quarters in what was known as the English Factory. The self-proclaimed hyperpolyglot (he claimed to know 200 languages and to speak 100) struggled to compose his thoughts: "How can I describe the barbaric grandeur, the parade, the show, the glitter, the real magnificence; the profuse decorations of today's royal audience?"

In 1873 western diplomats, British and French gunboat captains, Siamese nobility and distinguished officials gathered for the re-coronation of King Mongkut's son, King Chulalongkorn. The curtains before the throne were drawn back. The heads of the foreigners were bowed; the Siamese prostrated on the floor, their palms joined. They raised themselves on their knees and leaning on their elbows, touched the richly carpeted floor three times with their heads. To their utter and complete astonishment, the king rose from his throne. Then he read a decree that reversed an age-old practice. "The custom of prostration and human worship in Siam is manifestly an oppressive exaction which an inferior must perform to a superior… His Majesty proposed to substitute in place of crouching and crawling, standing and walking; and instead of prostration on all-fours and bowing with palm-joined hands to the ground, a graceful bow to the head." After the king had concluded his historic speech the entire assembly stood upright and bowed as he had requested. "I can assure you," wrote Prince Damrong, one of his most accomplished brothers who was present at the event, "that it was a most impressive and memorable sight."

Westerners were bowled over by raiment at royal receptions and the unsuitability of their formal dress in a tropical climate. A Belgian government advisor recounts King Chulalongkorn's birthday celebration.

How unforgettably splendid it was! What a wealth of costumes in this whole presence of the ranking princes, the ministers, the noblemen, the Malay rajahs and the officers! Among them an Arab sheik majestically draped himself in a large, golden-yellow coat. In this environment, with our black tailcoats, we resemble to some extent the crows on the gilded roofs of the wats and we suffer terribly from the mid-day heat which is suffocating in this crowd.

CHAKRI MAHAPRASAT THRONE HALL

In 1875 King Chulalongkorn undertook the customary royal building project in the Grand Palace to commemorate his reign. A British architect was engaged to build the Chakri Mahaprasat Building. It was inaugurated in 1882 and has been used ever since for ceremonial functions. Although the overall design is neoclassical the heavily rusticated ground floor mimics the traditional Siamese-style podium and signifies the foothills of Mount Meru. The ornamental *piano nobile* represents the celestial abode. This concept is further reinforced by the Siamese roof rising from three to seven spires. Ashes of eight Chakri kings rest under the central spire; the two that flank it contain ashes of other prominent members of the royal family.

Thais humorously refer to the building as the *farang gap chada*—the foreigner with the Thai dancer's headdress. This was not lost on the Thailand Tobacco Monopoly. An advertisement for Gold City cigarettes from the 1950s features the building set right in the heart of Marlboro country.

The mid-section of the Chakri Mahaprasat contains an immense throne hall adjoined by long reception rooms. The golden throne with its nine-tiered umbrella dominates the largest hall. Its East meets West interior decoration includes English antiques, portraits and busts of Chakri kings and queens, European royalty, and depictions of famous diplomatic missions: the receptions by Louis XIV of the mission sent by King Narai of Ayudhya, by Queen Victoria of King Rama IV's ambassador, by the Emperor Napoleon III of a Siamese mission at Fontainebleau.

General Ulysses S. Grant was surprised to find there his likeness—a bronze bust in a portrait gallery of contemporary sovereigns and heads of state. While pleased at the place of honour he was accorded, he stated for the record that the sculpture "did not much look like the General, and seems to have been made by a French or English artist from photographs."

The Chakri Mahaprasat Building also served as the royal residence for nearly a decade until the new palace in Suan Dusit was completed at the end of the nineteenth century. The apartments of the First Queen of King Chulalongkorn were connected by a passageway behind the throne hall. The king had 36 consorts who bore him 78 children. One child died *in utero* when Queen Sunanta, a daughter of King Mongkut, drowned in the lake of the summer palace at Bang Pa-In after her motorboat was overturned. Since Sunanta was a royal and the penalty for touching her was death, no one intervened to save her and the unborn child.

Soon after Queen Sunanta's premature death her older sister Queen Saowapa, who had married the king at the age of sixteen, was elevated to the rank of First Queen, a position she held for fifteen years. Described by a contemporary as "hardly pretty, but well formed and of versatile tact", she was a light-hearted woman who also possessed an unusual and assertive character.

Queen Saowapa was exceptionally well-spoken on a variety of subjects and highly intuitive. She exercised considerable influence over King Chulalongkorn who named her regent when he visited Europe in 1897. The English physician Dr. Malcolm Smith, who became her medical attendant and chief source of information about current affairs in Europe after the king's death in 1910, was impressed by her intellect and vitality. He described her as slim and unusually well-preserved for her age. "The years dealt lightly with her. Until her long illness after the death of the King, her face was almost unlined and her hair always thick and black." She took great care with her toilette. Maids ladled water upon her that had been specially scented by freshly cut flowers and aromatic herbs. Then her body was daubed with powder. Her clothes were kept in a large, sealed earthenware jar perfumed by scented candle smoke. She often ate unusual dishes—blackbirds and comb of the wild bee. Following ancient custom derived from the Celestial Kingdom, an hourly chronicle was prepared for the king that included her food and drink and her state of health (with remarks upon the contents of the chamber pot).

The monarch's far grander apartment was adjacent. His bedroom was richly decorated with gold. A huge bed in the centre was actually composed of three beds. The middle one, higher and larger than the others, was reserved for the royal couple and the lower beds were reserved for attending servants.

The king was a night-owl who liked to work when it was cool and rarely rose before noon. The official opening of his window was a sign that he was awake; then the news was quickly carried to the apartments of the queens, princesses and minor wives. After a full day of royal duties, public functions, a late afternoon excursion in his English Victoria and ministerial meetings, he retired to bed between 3 and 4 a.m.

After her husband died in 1910 Queen Saowapa moved to Phayathai palace where she "shunned the light of day like some nocturnal creature," retiring at 6 a.m. and awakening at 6 p.m. Nothing was permitted to destroy her tranquility. Traffic was rerouted; every garden noise was curtailed. A patrol consisting of an old woman and two men with noiseless weapons—blow-pipes and clay bullets—ensured that even the birds stayed away.

While the king abolished prostration before him, the queen obliged everyone, no matter what their rank or relationship, to come into her presence on their hands and knees. When departing, they crawled out backwards. "When hampered by top-boots and a sword, for men were in uniform, it was not a dignified proceeding," reported Dr. Smith. "Those serving her in the room moved about in the same way. No one, myself excepted, ever stood up."

King Rama VI was the last sovereign in residence until the 1920s when he moved to the posh European suburb called Dusit developed by his father King Chulalongkorn following his first European tour in 1897. He built Chitralada Palace where the reigning monarch has lived since his coronation in 1946.

Dusit Mahaprasat

The earliest Dusit Maha Prasat was built by King Rama I for the great court ceremonies, such as the coronation of kings and the lying-in-state of royal remains. Three days before his coronation in 1782 Brahman priests lit fires at altars before images of Hindu deities and offered gifts. Nine basins of water placed before the altars were purified by these rites. Then leaves steeped in the hallowed water were sent to the king, who brushed his body with some and burned others, reciting chants that were to absolve him from all sin.

Royal astrologers had warned the king of fire in the palace. A few years after his coronation the first throne hall, a wooden structure built at his behest, was struck by lightning and burned to the ground but he carried the throne to safety with his own hands. Just after this disaster the king predicted that "the City and the dynasty will be glorious from now on, and my descendants will rule over the country for 150 years." In uncanny fulfillment of his prediction, the absolute rule of the Chakri dynasty ended with the coup of 1932, exactly one hundred and fifty years after his coronation.

The new throne hall is an exquisitely proportioned building of brick, mortar and stone. It is regarded as one of the finest examples of Siamese architecture and the most beautiful building within the Grand Palace complex. It is cruciform shape, with a gilded nine-tiered roof supported by mythical birds. Its four façades are covered with magnificent sculpture and topped by a gilded spire. Its centrepiece is a mother-of-pearl throne surmounted by the nine-tiered white canopy, symbol of a duly crowned king. A pavilion in front of it was used by the king to dismount from his elephant and to change robes before proceeding inside.

The death of a king entailed equally elaborate rituals. The Marquis de Beauvoir paid his respects to the deputy King, Phra Pinklao, who had died in 1866, leaving a vivid account of the event.

> The said king [the second king] has been dead nine months; after endless extraordinary ceremonies, it seems that, according to an old and solemn custom, they place the corpse on an iron-wood throne with a hole in the seat, and by means of a funnel introduced into his throat made him swallow thirty-eight quarts of mercury. This operation fried him very quickly; the quicksilver more or less mixed was gradually collected in a sculptured bronze vase placed beneath the throne. Every morning all the chief officers of state came with great pomp to fetch the vase and then emptied it with reverence into the river. When his majesty No. 2 was reduced to the dryness of an old chip, they doubled him in half, drawing his legs up to the forehead, and tying him up like a sausage, they deposited him in a golden urn, at the top of a magnificent catafalque.
>
> The dead king squeezed into his jar on the summit of the altar holds his court exactly as if he lived. They told us how to bow before him; which we did to the great satisfaction of the mandarins who lined the walls to right and left, smoking their cigarettes while prostrated with

their foreheads to the ground; they wore white in sign of mourning. One of the pages fetched some large cigars from the catafalque, which they brought us in a basket of red filigree work. They mumbled a few words, which were translated to the effect that, "It is the second king who offer them to us, and that he lights them with one of his mortuary torches."

Long ropes of white and gold extended from the pedestals of the vase, like the threads of a spider's web: at the end of each is a mandarin in adoration. According to their belief these ropes carry their words and prayers to the king, and they press them to their lips with the most intense feeling and belief. A large gold basket is on the first step of the mausoleum, filled with letters and petitions addressed to the deceased within the last week.

His harem has also been kept for the last nine months for his sole use. At sunrise and sunset his hundreds of wives come and speak through the white cords to this peaceful and most inoffensive husband. In the eyes of the Siamese this is not widowhood; it is conjugal life, only drawn out. They only cease to be his on the day he is placed over the fire.

WAT PHRA KAEO MUSEUM

Among the precious objects that make a visit to the museum so enjoyable are various offerings to the sacred image and the seasonal costumes of the Emerald Buddha. At the start of each of the three Thai seasons the sovereign reverently dresses the image: a gold and blue tunic for summer, a gilded robe flecked with blue drops for the monsoon season and a heavy gold chain encased in enamel to be worn during the cooler months.

Adjacent to a model of the earliest palace is another model of the complex as it appears today. If you are in the mood, take a trip to visit to Rama II's Garden of Night, once located in the Inside, which can now only be visited imaginatively.

THE INSIDE (THE HAREM)

The French prelate Bishop Pallegoix, who was resident in Bangkok for a large portion of the reign of King Mongkut, heard tale of a marvellous garden.

It is said that in the third enclosure, there is a delightful and quite curious garden. It is a vast enclosure containing everything great one can find in the world in miniature size. There are artificial mountains, forests, rivers, a lake with isles and rocks, small vessels, boats, a bazaar or market held by women of the palace, temples, pavilions, belvederes, statues and trees with flowers and fruits brought from foreign countries. During the night, this garden is illuminated by lanterns and center lights. It is there that the ladies of the seraglio take their baths and engage in all kinds of entertainment to console themselves for being sequestered from the world.

The Garden of Night had been the brainchild of King Rama II (1809-24) who indulged his love for poetry, art and music there. Descriptions evoke an idyllic place of pleasure like the island of Cythera in Watteau's famous painting. The Inside belonged to the king alone and for most of the "forbidden" women of the cloistered city, it was a butterfly existence. They were enclosed by three guarded walls; inside the third enclosure were the king's private apartments and the living quarters for the harem. Once the king's sons reached puberty they were sent to live with relatives or with officials outside the palace. The monarch reigned supreme.

The population of the harem town consisted of about 3,000 women who ran the inner sanctum's government, institutions, law courts, police force and jail. Men were only admitted for construction or repair work or for medical visits. It was a complex, congested warren of narrow streets, houses, markets and small shops. Each queen had her own household of two or three hundred women; ladies in waiting had, in turn, servants of their own. Every minor wife had a separate living area and retinue as well, the size depending on the number of children she had.

But the Inside was not a place of great comfort, especially in the torrid heat of Bangkok. Sanitation was in the hands of the pail brigade and ventilation was poor, especially when the intense sun beat down upon the granite pavements. Royal and religious festivals were the principal diversions in a rather monotonous routine. Palace laws, the promulgation of which dated from Ayudhya, were strict. They regulated the conduct of the lives of the harem women and their children, depending on their degree of rank. Only the children of the king could be born in the palace and no one except the wives and offspring could die there. If they could not get out fast enough, special exorcism rites were performed by Brahman priests.

King Mongkut broke with precedent and occasionally allowed some of his wives to leave the palace precincts. If a royal lady was granted permission to leave she had to be accompanied by chaperones from her household. Upon their return, they had to give full and detailed account of the excursion for a report that was sent to the king.

Control of the city was in the hands of the fearsome Directress of the Inside and her various officials who were charged with the minor wives, serving maids and the king's kitchen. The female police force consisted of more than two hundred officers (with their own station house and cells). They wore a uniform of a blue *panung* (a loin cloth worn like an Indian *dhoti*, from which garment it surely originated) and a white jacket with a cream-coloured scarf across the breast. Their duties were to guard the gates, to accompany any men who entered, to control traffic, and to act like town criers, clearing the path when a person of importance walked the streets. At night they patrolled the streets with torches and lamps. They were forbidden to marry but allowed to move freely in and out of the walls. This made them highly sought after as couriers, especially of *billets doux* that nurtured fantasy and little else. Clandestine affairs were scarcely possible and very dangerous.

The young Marquis de Beauvoir and his companion the Duke de Penthièvre enjoyed a rare hour-long visit inside the harem in 1867 in the company of King Mongkut who was the last monarch to live full-time in the palace.

> By some signal favour, indeed one almost unknown to strangers, as we were told by the general and Père Larnaudie, we were permitted to cross the threshold of the harem! Groups of fifteen or twenty women taken by surprise by this unexpected visit instantly threw themselves down on the coloured mats which covered the floor, supporting themselves on their elbows and knees, and looking terribly frightened. There must have been 160 of them, some taking refuge on the steps of the winding staircases, on the projecting balconies, or in the kiosques joined to the rooms by marble bridges; others again fled to the shady avenues in the garden. Through the chinks of half-open doors sparkled bright eyes, animated with the liveliest curiosity. Some of them were ancient matrons, with baggy, dried-up skins, who squatted down on one side in their short

yellow skirts; then there were gentle nymphs of chocolate colour, languid young Sultanas, with a ribbon, narrower than the width of a hand, worn across the shoulder instead of a bodice, a little blue scarf, and diamonds on their necks, hands, and feet, who crowd together like bees in a hive.

The harshest view of the Inside is contained in the *English Governess at the Siamese Court* (1870) by the English school teacher Anna Leonowens—the first English teacher for the king's numerous children, made more famous by the film *The King and I*. She arrived in Bangkok from Singapore on 15 March 1862 with her young son Louis aboard the *Chao Phraya* steamer. It was the worst time of year, the hot, dry season when cholera often struck. As the steamer approached the gleaming Grand Palace, the royal enclave surrounded by thick whitewashed walls must have offered promise of clean water and spacious quarters. Finally, she and little Louis would rest in comfort, perhaps cooled by *punkahs*—suspended sheets pulled back and forth by Indian boys—as in Singapore.

When the 27-year-old schoolmarm descended the gangplank to meet the prime minister at the Tha Tien landing, her demeanour was surely as sober as her Victorian attire. Freudians may sense a barely repressed erotic charge in Anna's feigned protest at his appearance. Although the nobleman wore bright red Siamese pantaloons that ended at his calves, "to cover his audacious chest and shoulders he had only his own brown polished skin." But any subconscious attraction vanished in a flash after her shining prince quite bluntly informed her that there was no place in the palace. A foreign woman was unwelcome inside the Royal City of Women.

Poor Anna. She was completely on her own, and in a very foreign city. She was so forlorn that she could not even muster up the courage to ask him for a hotel recommendation. Once the gilded barge had glided away, the floodgate of emotion broke open: "The situation was as Oriental as the scene, heartless arbitrary insolence on the part of my employers; home-lessness, forlornness, helplessness, mortification, indignation on mine... My tears fell thick and fast and, weary and despairing, I closed my eyes, and tried to shut out heaven and earth; but the reflection would return to mock and goad me that, by my own act, I had placed myself in this posi-tion." They spent a lonely night on deck; then she found herself in two squalid rooms at the end of a Bangkok fish-market until a proper house could be readied.

When Phra Mongkut left the monkhood in 1851 to take up his duties as King Rama IV, he had to resume a life that he had once forsaken. It was simply a tradition handed down over the centuries for the sovereign to have as many wives and children as possible. The celibate priest (he had fathered a child before putting on the robes) went straight from his monastic cell into the harem. During seventeen years on the throne, he had 35 wives and sired 84 children.

Anna acquired unique and almost unlimited access to the royal harem and wrote the only account in existence by a westerner of life within its walls. Like everyone else, she was constantly watched while at the court. On occasion she acted as the king's secretary and undertook other tasks. As her workload expanded, and her salary remained the same, her position became less attractive. She also worried about her personal safety since her interaction with the king caused much jealousy among ministers. After five years at court, she requested leave of absence to "rest" in Singapore. She left Siam with the hope that King Mongkut would summon her back under more favourable economic and personal conditions. But the king died and his son, her pupil, made a point of not inviting her to return.

Anna's books have had a complex critical fortune. Critics have found fault in her reinvention of her personal history as well as her penchant for melodrama at the expense of truth. "Anna is a terrible liar, but she is a fine writer," writes Susan Morgan in the preface to a recent edition (1991) of her second novel *The Romance of the Harem* (1874). One is never sure if she is writing fictionalized history or historical fiction but her accounts are enthralling.

She was fanatically anti-polygamous and paints a very dark picture of life in the harem.

> Within the close and gloomy lanes of this city within a city, through which many lovely women are wont to come and go, many little feet to patter, and many baby citizens to be borne in the arms of their dodging slaves, there is but cloud and chill, and famishing and stinting and beating of wings against golden bars. In the order of nature, evening melts softly into night, and darkness retreats with dignity and grace before the advancing triumphs of the morning; but here light and darkness are monstrously mixed and the result is a glaring gloom that is

neither of the day nor of the night, nor of life nor of death, nor of earth nor of—yes, hell!

Anna sympathetically recounts tragic tales of Siamese women who were victims of the palatine prison. Khun Choy's tale of woe is particularly compelling. She was a dancer who became a favourite of King Mongkut. But she was secretly in love with a prince, whose own wife loved him so desperately that she became a go-between. A message was intercepted, they were brought to trial, and all were sentenced to a most gruesome death. Anna claims that Choy's life was spared through the good offices of Sir Robert H. Schomburgk (she misspells his name). There is a distinct air of plausibility to this story as Shomburgk did indeed serve as British Consul in Bangkok from 1857 to 1862, departing the year she arrived. As a British subject it is highly unlikely that she would have dared invent a diplomatic intervention that could have brought her before the Foreign Office for perjury.

The confinement of the harem was relieved for a few privileged royal women during the Fifth Reign. King Chulalongkorn's pleasure in travel meant that the most fortunate were given the chance to visit places that before had existed only in travellers' tales. They accompanied the king on river picnics, on excursions on the royal yacht in the Gulf of Siam. Some had the opportunity to live in a more Europeanized life in the newly completed royal residence of Chitralada Palace at Dusit Park.

One brave princess rebelled against the harem and all that it represented as she later recounted in her autobiography *The Treasured One: the Story of Rudivoravan, Princess of Siam* (1958). The princess, who was born in 1911, the youngest daughter and twenty-second child of Prince Narathip Prabhanbongse, was brought as a girl to the harem by her mother (who as a commoner was allowed only one night to settle her in). After a terrible inspection by the "Amazon-like" women, the young girl was led to the house of her aunt and cousins. "It was the hour for dinner and we children had it together. We ate in a kind of Roman style, reclining on the floor and resting on one elbow. I had a woman attendant, whose name was Term, to feed me. It seems ridiculous now, but it was then still the custom to feed children until they were quite big and to carry them about." After dinner they went to bed, "as soon as the rice is laid down neatly in your stomach," according to the old Siamese saying. Then she was bathed:

A large china barrel covered with beautiful designs stood in a corner, on a zinc floor. My aunt undressed me but wrapped a band of red material below my waist. A Siamese girl never bathes unclothed, and for royalty the covering must be red. My aunt put water from the barrel into a silver bowl, and poured it over me… When, finally, I was ready and placed in the four-poster bed in the room which was to be mine, my mother came and lay beside me. She sang me a little song. Her voice was sweet—*A small bird lies in the nest.* For the last time I went to sleep wholly her child.

The princess stayed on in the Grand Palace for five years, playing in the secluded pavilions within the walled city. Later in life the bird finally flew the nest. Princess Rudivoravan divorced a prince, breaking conventions of status and risking her security, to marry a commoner and moved to the United States. After a long and eventful life there she ended up as a broadcaster for the Voice of America and royally charmed audiences around the world.

Three

THE RIVER OF KINGS

The Maenam Chao Phraya flows from the mountains of northern Thailand. After it irrigates the country's heartland, it suddenly turns east; then spills out into the Gulf of Thailand. For almost half the year monsoon rains fall on a fertile basin, once a vast sea of mud that was transformed into one of the world's greatest rice baskets. The Chao Phraya valley was a kind of pre-lapsarian paradise of flora and fauna. The Abbé de Choisy made an evocative entry in the journal of his *Voyage au Siam* (1685): "Both banks of the river are edged with betel-nut palms and coconut trees, which are green and laden with fruit, monkeys and birds. Some birds are all blue, others all red, and still others entirely yellow. The prettiest are the egrets, which are completely snow-white and have on their heads a true aigrette spray."

The river imposed itself on King Rama I in a more intimate way. While en route to battle with the Burmese in 1786, he wrote a *nirat* poem in which the riverine scenery personified his nostalgia for home.

> Next we came to a spirit shrine
> Guardian spirit of the riverine estuary and wharfs.
> It stood forlorn amidst the solitude.
> It indeed resembled me, far away and lonely.

Like his predecessors in Ayudhya, King Rama I sought to legitimize his power through royal pageantry, especially spectacular barge proces-

sions. He commissioned the magnificent gold and scarlet royal barges displayed in the popular film, *Around the World in 80 Days*, now preserved in the Royal Barge Museum in Thonburi. The stunning barge processions were halted after the coup of 1932 toppled the absolute monarchy. Today barges are brought out on very special occasions, such as the sixtieth anniversary of King Rama IX's accession to the throne celebrated in December 2006.

CITY OF WATER

Bangkok was shaped by water. The river was the principal metaphor for life itself; its rippling currents confirmed Buddhist belief in impermanence; it brought forth fish and watered the rice paddies. The river served as the great commercial highway for Asian and intercity trade and for swarming mobile markets. It was a theatrical stage for royal ritual, the vital artery for communication, the great liquid ribbon of daily life and the main water source for the capital.

By the mid-nineteenth century the river and canal network was estimated to have 7,000 houses that "float, rising and falling, as if breathing with the tide and the flow" and a floating populace of 350,000 people. The land-dwellers were royalty, nobility, monks. Peasants rowed foodstuffs via canals to the city markets and fished the river and gulf. A Scotsman

John Crawfurd in1822 was one of the earliest to note the great disparity between glittering temple roofs and "mean huts and hovels".

King Rama III (1824-51) actively encouraged Chinese trading. Broad, bat-like sails of numerous Chinese junks cast dark shadows in mid-afternoon cooling the verandahs of the floating row houses. The Siamese aristocracy built mansions on the east bank of Thonburi, hidden from sight by moss-covered walls. Waterways and drawbridges spanned "tranquil canals of greenish water between brick quays covered by parasite grasses," a foreign visitor noted. A community of Indian traders had already established itself on the west bank but they were a discreet presence.

Some years later King Mongkut, an authority on Siamese history, decided to set foreigners straight regarding the correct name of the river in a letter to the missionary press. "It is wrong for the Americans and some other nations to call the Bangkok river simply 'Maenam', for it has a specific name. It is the custom of the Siamese to call the stream nearest to them the Maenam and add the names of one of the principal towns or villages on its bank to it, such as the Maenam Bangkok, Maenam Krung, Maenam Ta Chin etc. The true name of the Bangkok river is the Chao Phraya but it has become obsolete."

Tropical beauty and realms of the spirit along the waterway spawned a rich native genre of traditional sung poems about boat processions, describing the luscious scenery, singing birds and the object of a poet's affection. This nineteenth-century boat song (in translation) has a rhythmic beat in time with the rowing of oars.

Boatman's Song

A happy and reckless youth I am,
As I ply my boat on the deep Maenam;
My song shall end, and my song begin,
In praise of you, my darling Chin.

As for thy nose, I'm certain that
None other has one so wide and flat:
And the ebony's bark, in its core beneath,
Was never so black as your shiny teeth.

Begin with the head and end with the toes:
My praise is as strong as the tide that flows.

The River of Kings, as it is now described in glossy tourist brochures, made an extraordinary impression on nineteenth-century travellers who entered the city by river from the Gulf of Siam. Low banks fringed with coconut trees and palms gracefully swayed over wooden houses nestling in their shade, glittering temples and pagodas broke through a frame of leaves like a daylight illumination and endless rice-fields stretch far into the horizon.

About an hour before dawn in 1835 a steamer carrying an American writer passed the lower end of the city. The night resounded with clanging noises made by vast numbers of Chinese blacksmiths and glowing red forges were the only light.

> We now threaded our way among junks, boats, and floating houses, jumbled together in glorious confusion, and totally concealing the banks from view. Hundreds of small canoes, some not larger than clothes-baskets, were passing to an fro, many of them containing talapoins or priests, paddling lazily from house to house, collecting presents of provisions. The occupants of the floating houses were taking down the shutters which formed the fronts, exposing their wares for sale; printed calicoes, paper-umbrella, sweetmeats, fruits, pots, pans & c., being placed in situations the best calculated to attract the notice of the passers-by. This occupation was carried on entirely by women, the men being either seated on the platforms smoking their segars, or making preparations to take a cruise in their canoes.

An Englishman named Frederick A. Neale, who was a British naval officer, first came upon Bangkok in 1852.

> The glories of the floating city burst upon our admiring gaze, like some resplendent ray of sunlight through an envious cloud. It was night—dark night; neither moon nor stars were in the heavens. But what cared Bangkok, with its million globes that lighted the river's broad surface from side to side, for night or darkness! It was like a fairy-land where houris dwell, whose eyes shed luster... As far as the

eyes could reach, on either side of the river, there was one endless succession of lights—lights variegated, and of every imaginable colour
and shape, and such only as Chinese ingenuity could ever invent; every
little floating house has two or more of these lights, the yards and
masts of the vessels and junks (and these were by no mean few) were
decorated in a like manner, the lofty pagodas or minarets of the wats
were one blaze of light. It was the most striking, the most beautiful
panorama I had ever witnessed...

Some thirty years later Joseph Conrad, an obscure, thirty-year-old
Polish seaman—who would later anchor his talents in literature—must
have climbed the central *prang* of the Temple of the Dawn in Thonburi
(Wat Arun) or ascended to the summit of the Golden Mount to have had
this view of the city, later penned in *The Shadow Line* (1917).

There it was, spread out largely on both banks, the Oriental capital
which had yet suffered no white conqueror; an expanse of brown houses
of bamboo, of mats, of leaves, of a vegetable-matter style of architecture, sprung out of the brown soil on the banks of the muddy river. It
was amazing to think that in those miles of human habitations there
was not probably half a dozen pounds of nails.

Some of those houses of sticks and grass, like the nests of an aquatic
race, clung to the shores, others seemed to grow out of the water; others
again floated in long anchored rows in the very middle of the stream.
Here and there in the distance, above the crowded mob of low, brown
roof ridges, towered great piles of masonry, king's palaces, temples, gorgeous and dilapidated, crumbling under the vertical sunlight, tremendous, overpowering, almost palpable, which seemed to enter one's breast
with the breath of one's nostrils and soak into one's limbs through every
pore of the skin.

But the river and canal water was always unhealthy; a foreigner likened
it in 1904 to "yellow ooze that carries all the capital's filth to the sea." A
familiar Siamese adage *Nam khuen hai rip tak* ("When the water rises,
hurry to collect some") gives a native solution. The locals collected rainwater during the monsoon season and stored it in the large glazed earthenware jars that are still are a fixture on canal side homes. The river is still

used for swimming and bathing though obviously not as much as in earlier times.

Each floating house generally consisted of three teak units with palm leaf roofs hitched together like train carriages. A shop house facing the river, sleeping cabin and cooking hut floated on thick bamboo pontoons. Their rustic simplicity and harmony with nature lent great appeal, as did the open style of living that invited voyeurism, though the floating brothels plied their trade "on rafts next to the river banks, so as to be hidden from the public gaze," as a foreign visitor noted.

The floating streets had real advantages wrote George Windsor Earl in *The Eastern Seas of Voyages and Adventures in the Indian Archipelago in 1823, 1833 and 1834.*

> The best shops are built on wooden floats on the river; indeed when the waters are out, they flood the whole town, the only communication between the different dwellings being by means of boats. At this period of the year, when the river becomes swelled by the rains, whole streets of floating houses, together with their inhabitants, sometimes break adrift from their moorings, and are carried down the river, to the utter confusion of the shipping. These floating streets, nevertheless, possess their advantages. A troublesome neighbour may be ejected, house, family, pots and pans, and all, all sent floating away to find another site for his habitation. A tradesman, too, if he finds an opposition shop taking away his custom, can remove to another spot with very little difficulty.

Floating houses were fastened by chains to huge poles driven deep in the river bed. Sometimes they took off rather quickly for another mooring, either at the owner's whim, perhaps to escape creditors, or when the water level altered too rapidly. Sir John Bowring, who came to Bangkok in 1855, was bemused by the sight of houses "moving up and down the river, conveying all the belongings of a family to some newly selected locality." But an American missionary of the time expressed considerable alarm at finding himself in a houseboat suddenly "adrift at the mercy of the tide [that] floated down river many miles before it could be made to submit to the power of the ropes and cables, with which we endeavored many times in vain to stop her."

The sampan and small, moveable gangplank to the river bank accommodated the amphibious way of life. Fournereau observed that for the Siamese, aquatic life was also preferable to land-dwelling. Refuse flowed rapidly away on the mid-river current, adjustable partitions allowed air circulation, and bathing was a real cinch. The verandah was multi-functional, serving as a shop during the day for "teas, silks, porcelains, cigars, spices, vegetable, tinware. One finds everything there and it is with real pleasure that one's boat glides with the water while watching buyers enter the shops, and make their choices [as they] squat on the verandah, load their frail vessels and leave for the next house."

Wealthier merchants had more spacious verandahs, protective railings, rattan chairs and ornamental flowers and shrubs. At night it seemed as if there was only one form of entertainment for families:

> …squatting on mats or on chairs and inhaling the night breeze that licks the river; then the time passes quietly because to the charms of conversation is added the delicate aroma of quite a number of cups of tea, a few betel chews and the smoke of tobacco laced with opium; so much and so good that sometimes the entire family lets itself slip gently into sleep until the freshness of the night comes to call it back to order.
>
> Then the family enters its floating home which almost all are adorned with a more or less sculpted and gilded altar according to the wealth of the owner and on which a Buddha of some kind of lares stand. The whole with the obligatory accompaniments of gilded paper or tinsel is essentially Chinese in appearance: embroidered silk cloths, statues, and copper vases serve as ornaments. Sticks of odoriferous wood burn in incense burners and, coconut oil slowly burns in urns.

Bowring's impressionistic portrait of the river's natural beauty (1855) is one of the final pictures we have before the treaty he negotiated brought the trade and rapid development which eventually dislodged the river dwellers from their ecological home and dislocated them from the traditional aquatic culture.

> Now and then a bamboo hut is seen amidst the foliage, whose varieties of bright and beautiful green no art could copy. Fruits and flowers hang by the thousands in branches. We observed that even the wild animals

were scarcely scared by our approach. Fishes glided over the mud-banks, and birds either sat looking at us as we passed, or winged their way around and above us. The almost naked people sat and looked at us as we glided by; and their habitations were generally marked out by a small creek, with a rude boat and one or more pariah dogs.

RIVER UNDER THREAT

Almost as soon as the ink was dry on the trade treaties signed in the mid-nineteenth century, foreign vessels made haste to the port of Bangkok. Chinese middlemen erected rice mills and foreign merchants had large warehouses built at the river's edge. The Portuguese consulate was soon joined by new consulates and the stretch of river before them was called Legation Row. They looked incongruous, like cardboard huts in an exotic theme park.

After this date, roads and land-based transport began the relentless transformation of the city away from the river and up to the sky. Soon to disappear were such unique features as the Chinese floating theatre that the American writer Frank Vincent Jr. saw in 1871.

By 1898, when Ernest Young published *The Kingdom of the Yellow Robe*, the harbour had become a regular port of call for coastal steamers and tall ships transporting rice from Siam to Singapore or Hong Kong, cattle to Malaysia, "cheap tin and trumpery from Birmingham, Manchester or Germany; silks from China and Bombay." The floating city of houseboats "moored in every available inch of space" was supplemented by rice barges from up-country that consigned their harvest to merchants in Bangkok and headed back home after a few days in the capital. A huge floating market moved at its own gently gliding rhythm from Tha Tien pier to Pak Klong Talaat (site of the fruit and vegetable market today).

By the turn of the century trade was "in the hands of the foreigners," as Young reports. Each ethnic group in the city had a specific activity in a diversified economic system, according to H. Warington Smyth in 1898.

The coolies, boat-builders, carpenters, and sawyers are all Chinese, and Chinamen form the majority of the market-gardeners, smiths and tradesmen. The Malays work the machinery of the mills and are padi cultivators, and they share the fishing with the Anamites [Vietnamese] and Siamese. The latter are the boat and raft men, and cultivate the fruit and padi of the suburbs. The Javanese are gardeners, the Bombay men are merchants, the Tamils cattlemen and shopkeepers, the Burmese gem dealers and country pedlars, the Singhalese goldsmiths and jewelers, and the Bengalis are the tailors.

But pollution had arrived with the Europeans and Americans. By 1892 "European rice mills thrust up their high factory chimneys and dirty this beautiful sky with thick and nauseating smoke," a foreigner observed somewhat ruefully. They were manned by great waves of Chinese immigrant coolies. "Under the burning sky, their skin shiny with sweat, Chinese, almost naked, drop bags for rice, break up rafts of heavy teakwood logs, so that elephants can pick them up with their trunks and bring them to the roaring saws," he further noted.

Due to the increasing value of international commerce and rowdy seamen from foreign ships, river police were newly introduced to maintain order. In *Lord Jim*, Conrad describes a bar-room scuffle involving a "crosseyed Dane of sorts whose visiting card recited under his misbegotten name: first lieutenant of the Royal Siamese Navy" and Jim, the brittle ex-mate of the *Patna* who snapped at a "scornful remark" made at his expense. "It was very lucky for the Dane that he could swim, because the room opened on a veranda and the Maenam flowed very wide and black. A boat-load of Chinamen, bound, as likely as not, on some thieving expedition, fished out the officer of the King of Siam, and Jim turned up at about midnight on board my ship without a hat."

On a steam boat ferry along "the great nautical boulevard" from Sathorn pier to Tha Tien pier, the Belgian Charles Buls pointed out in 1900 the major landmarks on the left bank. Apart from the temples, most buildings had gone up in the second half of the nineteenth century: rice mills, warehouses, Assumption College, the Oriental Hotel, the Customs House, the Postal and Telegraphic Services, the various consulates, the Hongkong-Shanghai Bank, Holy Rosary Church (then under construction) and private secondary schools. Buls admired Italianate princely palaces and the rebuilt Santa Cruz Church near Wat Arun, one of the most ancient temples in Bangkok

Prince Wilhelm II of Sweden, who came to Bangkok for the coronation of King Rama VI in December 1911, was transported by the river scene:

Along the banks glittered long rows of coloured paper lanterns, broken here and there by more prosaic electric-arc lamps, whose dazzling rays were reflected a thousandfold in the pitch-black water. Behind them, against the velvety tropical sky, rose the black masses of the pagodas, some off them outlines with flickering temple-lamps, which made them look like gigantic isosceles triangles. The river swarmed with illuminated boats, from which one cracker after another was thrown into the water, sputtered, shone, and disappeared. But the finest sight of all was a winding procession of all the old historic boats gliding down the steam. Their slender forms were outlined with lights, and on the larger ones seven gleaming paraphernalia were erected in a long row, reflecting their umbrella-like outlines in the glittering waters of the Maenam. As these dream-like craft came nearer, their scarlet-clad rowers sang one old war-song after another, which rang out clear and brisk, though sometimes with an undertone of melancholy, in the listening night.

Already by the 1920s, municipal authorities aimed to clear the river of houseboat communities from the market areas near Pak Klong Talaat and the old Klong Toey market where they had naturally congregated. Prime Minister Phibul thought some of the floating houses were a blot on the modern city he envisaged and evicted most of them in the 1950s. Within ten years a new flood prevention system was necessitated by the filling in of canals and pressure on the water table due to multi-storey buildings that mushroomed during an era of rapid economic expansion.

The environmental impact of explosive growth since the Second World War had a nearly disastrous effect on the river. Kukrit Pramoj, one of the first writers to express concern about its viability, warned in *The Chao Phraya Is on the Verge of Dying* (1970) that the river would soon become a "stream of poison" unless people cared for their neglected Maenam. Environmental groups have made some headway but the river is choked by water hyacinth brought from Indonesia in 1872 by one of the consorts of Rama V and littered with non-biodegradable objects. Garbage boats make regular collections along the river but the refuse is unsightly.

To Sumet Jumsai Bangkok is now an outlandish place—an "alien organism"—as he calls it. The city is sinking at the rate of four inches per year and during the rainy season about forty per cent of the surface area is inundated. Its skyline could pass for that of Miami or Beirut but for the

hundreds of Buddhist temples. When viewed at sunset from the river their majestic roofs seem to glow like huge floating candles above it. It is at that moment that the traveller becomes most wistful for the garden city that has been largely covered in asphalt and cement.

Although the Chao Phraya river has long ceded its primacy to roads, expressways, the elevated mass transit system and the underground, living memories are carried on its muddied waters. People still bathe in the river, kids dive off rusty barges, and tourists feed soft white bread to huge carp near Buddhist temples.

The forty-minute boat trip from the Sathorn Pier to the Nonthaburi stop spills over with life. It is worth enduring the blood-curdling whistles of the wiry men who guide the ferries to the pier and untie them after loading. In late afternoon the ferry fills with giggling schoolchildren in old-fashioned uniforms that are neatly pressed. Wisps of women carry huge plastic bags of vegetables. Buddhist monks and their novices (in a special section to protect them from being jostled by women) return to their temples. Small-boned hotel workers on the second shift in trim suits stand under bronzed Germans just back from the southern islands. Bleary-eyed medical students are lulled to sleep by the rocking motion.

There are now almost ten five-star luxury hotels on the river and exclusive deluxe condominium towers are going up fast on the Thonburi side but the riverscape still retains a lower hierarchy of historical memory and lived experience. Clapboard houses with corrugated tin roofs. Minarets. Chinese pagodas. Palladian-style villas. Modern hospitals. Exclusive private schools. Neo-traditional wooden houses. Royal temples. Boat homes for authorized river workers. Gilded *chedi*. University dorms. Family restaurants. Glass box apartments. Spirit houses. The Oriental and Shangri-La riverfront hotels vie for the best firework display on New Year's Eve. Exploding rockets burst forth like newborn stars against a slate sky. Their sparkling fire cascades to the dark flowing water. Greetings from the sky ripple forth to the great womb of the mother of rivers at the sea.

The continuities and traditions of the aquatic Siamese lifestyle continue to flow in the daily and ceremonial life of Bangkok. Lustral water is poured over Thais at all of life's rites of passage—birth, marriage, death. Water (*nam*) is the ultimate metaphor in the Thai language. Tears are water from the eyes. Milk is water from the breasts. Ice is hard water. Honey is water from the bees. Sugar is water of the palm tree. Willingness is water from the heart. Many city streets are compounds named after water. Two major Buddhist holy days, Songkran and Loy Krathong, celebrate the symbolic importance of water.

Water is the agent of a stirring sensual awakening in Mishima's *Temple of the Dawn*. His anti-hero Honda is a cynical, middle-aged Japanese lawyer who has lost his passion. He is a guest at the famous Oriental Hotel; it is just after dawn.

> The unrelenting heat had already invaded the room. Having left his sweat-dampened bed and standing under the cold shower, Honda felt for the first time the morning on his skin. The experience was a strangely sensuous one. He who never contacted the external world without first filtering it through rational thought, here felt through his skin; only through his skin sensing the brilliant green of the tropical plants, the vermilion of the mimosa flowers, the golden décor adorning the temples, or the sudden blue lightning could he come into contact with the world about him. This was a totally exotic experience for him. The warm rains, the tepid showers. The external world was a richly colored liquid, and it was as if he were constantly bathing in it.

Four

KLONGS OF THONBURI

Scholars have traced the beginnings of Bangkok to a fishing settlement on a mud bank in an ox-bow of the Chao Phraya river at some stage around 1350. Rounding the ox-bow proved slow and cumbersome to travellers en route to Ayudhya, but it was another two centuries before a channel was cut across the mouth of the loop—thus reducing nearly a day's journey to the time it took to cook a pot of rice. It was then, about 1557, that a small walled town was built on the island to guard the canal; this soon developed into an important trading centre with a prosperous customs port. It was insignificant in size but bore the grandiloquent name of Thonburi Si Mahasamut, "the glorious and great oceanic city of wealth". Locals simply called it Thonburi or "money town". Foreigners called it Bangkok after a district of that name in the town.

"The City of *Bancock* is called *Fon* in Siamese, it not being known from where the name of *Bancock* is derived," wrote the Abbé de La Loubère, Envoy Extraordinary from the French king to the King of Siam in the years 1687-88, though Portuguese traders were the first to use it. "The Gardens which are in the Territory of *Bancock*... do supply this City with the Nourishment which the Natives of the Country love best, I mean a great quantity of Fruit," he observed. *Ban* signifies a village on a waterway and *kok* means wild plums which used to exist in some abundance.

The French emissary highlighted Thonburi's strategic importance as "the most important place in the Kingdom of Siam, for it is the only one along the coast which may offer any resistance to enemies." This is confirmed by Jeremias van Vliet in a letter to the directors of the East India Company:

> Bangkok is a small walled city about seven miles from the sea and amidst fertile fields. The rivers Menam and Taatsyn [Tachin river] meet at this point. Around the town there are many houses and rich farms. Bangkok is strong by nature and can be easily fortified, and kept by a prince, the supply of salt and fruits to the town of Judia [Ayudhya] would be prevented. Also all navigation on sea and passage of the Moors from Tessarim would be cut off.

A plan published by La Loubère shows the precise configuration of the fortified enclave. Two forts had been built by King Narai of Ayudhya, one of which still exists. The small brick fort of Vichaiprasit (near the entrance to Klong Bangkok Yai) was defended by Portuguese soldiers with the latest artillery as well as by about thirty French garrisons largely comprised of North African Muslims who had been conscripted by the French and had settled with local women. The fort also contained a royal guesthouse for foreign envoys and diplomatic missions en route to the populous capital of Ayudhya.

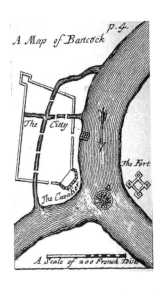

Following the destruction of the four-hundred-year-old Kingdom of Ayudhya by the Burmese in 1767 an ambitious Thai-Chinese soldier named Phraya Taksin rose from relatively low status as the ethnic Chinese governor of Tat to become a general and an extraordinary military tactician. The charismatic leader regrouped an army of Thai and Chinese warriors and recovered the honour of the nation. Luck was on his side for Burma suddenly found herself at war with China. Taksin routed the Burmese garrisons in Siam; then defeated various royal contenders and pretenders to the throne. He was regarded as a usurper who could claim no real blood ties to the Ayudhya kings; he was to be the only member of his dynasty. He crowned himself king (reg. 1767-82), taking the precaution of marrying several princesses of the old royal line; then he moved into the mansion of the former governor of Thonburi on the west bank of the Chao Phraya river. (This is across the river from Bangkok but is often referred to as *Bancock* in old maps.)

King Taksin fulfilled his vow to restore the temple in which he installed the precious Emerald Buddha—later transferred across the river by King Rama I. He built a royal palace adjacent to the temple complex. The king's page Nai Suan recounts the fine capital built by his beloved regent.

Thonburi was formerly thorny bush
Widespread weeds outgrew each other,
There remained only lifeless corpses.
After he settled down, all that was withered came to life again.
The location he chose was strategically correct.
It seemed its creation came from the experienced Vishnu.
It was to this source that all facets of the palace owed their beginning.
The completed palace appeared to be filled with pavilions of great width
on both left and right.

Piers driven into the water were parallel to the floating houses.
This was the arena where ladies could view the sky.
The audience hall was magnificently majestic,
The hall that housed his attire was indescribably gracious.

Fortresses, ditches, and barrages were built to give proper safeguard.
They yielded protection, both inside and outside the palace.
It was surrounded as well by a series of defence towers.
Each was well equipped with arsenals to show His Majesty's might.

The king's throne hall (largely rebuilt) is the only extant building of the old palace complex. It is located near the old city wall close to the Temple of the Dawn. For the past century it has been enclosed within the Royal Thai Navy complex and is therefore virtually inaccessible.

For most of his reign King Taksin was engaged in military campaigns. He fought an expensive war with the Burmese in 1779. Fines and import taxes enriched the war chest, but he began to suspect that his courtiers were engaged in illicit trade which deprived him of revenue. Merchants engaged in the flourishing illicit trade in salt, rice, valuable wood, rhinoceros and ivory suffered serious reprisals.

Gradually what remained of the old Ayudhya elite began to turn against Taksin, who was said to have become a paranoid tyrant. He had his family and a number of high officials tortured to extract confession for alleged crimes. Moreover, he claimed to have extraordinary spiritual merit; he made Lear-like demands for adulation and required monks to worship him as a reincarnation of Buddha. This outraged the elite and significantly weakened his political support. During the waning years of his reign Taksin apparently became a religious fanatic and believed that through concentrated private devotion he would be able to fly.

Some historians think that Taksin's bizarre behaviour may have been invented to justify the treachery that occurred when a palace coup finally erupted in early 1782 and Phraya Sen, a senior courtier, took charge of the capital. It was conveniently quelled by the war marshal Chao Phraya Chakri, from a prominent Ayudhya court family, who had expressly returned from Cambodia. (Four years earlier he had captured the powerful Emerald Buddha, which offered divine protection to any city that owned it.) General Chakri and King Taksin were old comrades both on and off the battlefield. The king requested a final interview with his old friend but his successor refused, though "with tears running down his face," a chronicler reported. Instead he was condemned to death by nobles he himself had appointed. On 7 March 1782 the king faced his executioners. He is reported to have said "since my *bun* [merit] is exhausted, I have arrived now at my death." He was executed according to royal etiquette—tied up in a velvet sack and bludgeoned on the back of the neck with a scented sandalwood club (to avoid spilling royal blood on earth.) He was forty-seven years old.

According to another version, a common criminal was executed in lieu of King Taksin who was smuggled to live out the rest of his life in peace at Nakorn Srithammaraj. His residence is still preserved there and the local people pay respect to this day.

A eucalyptus tree in the Wat Arun marks a shrine for miniature statues of Buddha which have lost their heads. Beneath the colourful gauze that marks it as a sacred tree is a statue of King Taksin. The base is surrounded by a bevy of decorated figurines—mainly dancers and good luck symbols—placed there for his entertainment in the hope that his spirit would act benevolently on behalf of the donors. Historical revisionism has given tragic Taksin a monumental comeback with an equestrian statue at Thonburi's major traffic circle of Wongwian Yai. (This was designed by Silpa Bhirasri, an Italian sculptor who brought modern art to Thailand during his four decades in the realm.)

Canals and Temples

It was regarded as one of the traditional duties of a Siamese king to make canals (*klongs*) and improve water navigation for his people. The *Royal*

Chronicles always mention the name of the canal dug on the orders of a king, saying who was in charge of the work, how much the labourers were paid and the length of the canal. Sometimes buffaloes and even the local people were required to trample up and down the bed of the canal to loosen the sediment that had accumulated and allow it to be washed away. The *Chronicles* also mention that it was the duty of the conscripts or *lek* to deepen the *klongs* and to clean them every summer.

A British travel writer at the end of the nineteenth century marvelled at the vibrancy of life on the canals: "The broad deep klongs with their double lines of house boats and their continual traffic of lumbering barges, cumbersome rafts, comfortable houseboats and tiny canoes are the great streets of the cities, and the highways of the plains... Moored in every available space are the houseboats in which thousands of the inhabitants spend the whole of their lives. They are born in the boat, are reared aboard, and are only taken permanently ashore when life is over." But it took the poetic licence of Somerset Maugham to see London's grey lanes reflected in the waterways when he visited Bangkok in 1925: "Little steamers, the omnibus of the thrifty, puff up and down quickly, crowded with passengers and as the rich in their great cars splash the passersby on a rainy day in London, so opulent Chinamen in motor launches speed a long with a wash that makes the tiny dugouts rock dangerously."

The *klongs* of Thonburi thread a rich vein through much Thai writing, proving malleable to the moods of the writers. Ussiri Thammachot mordantly confronts the contemporary canalscape in the short story *Nightfall on the Waterway* (2000).

> In a timeless moment of aloneness on the lightless klong with no passing boat to keep him company—a timeless moment in which the moving water made soft sounds like the breath of a dying man—he thought of death and suddenly realized that the quiet klong brought with it the smell of putrefaction. A rotting carcass of some animal, he thought. A dead puppy, or perhaps a piglet, that klong-side inhabitants never hesitated to throw in the waterway, relying on the current to bear it away while nature completed the process of decay and water finalized the disintegration of the once living flesh.

Yet Thonburi is still full of charm and I have often found escape in neighbourhoods that have a real village feel. After the canal boat tour, walking is the second best way to capture the vitality of the old life that is so often illustrated in Thai temple murals. There are a number of fascinating areas.

Kudi Farang, or the Foreigners' Quarter, near the Catholic Church of Santa Cruz was settled by descendants of the Portuguese who had built and fortified Thonburi during the reign of King Narai. King Taksin granted them land to build a church in 1769. When it fell into disrepair it was rebuilt by the energetic Bishop Pallegoix in 1834. Two architects from Turin designed the present church (1913) with its lovely Italian dome.

Kudi Yai, the Muslim quarter, was settled by a community of Sunni Muslims who migrated from Ayudhya. Thonburi is dotted with Shiite mosques and graveyards attesting to the long-thriving Muslim community. The earliest Muslims to settle were called Khaek Phae (Muslims of house boats) because they moored their craft along the banks of the Klong Bangkok Yai and earned their living as peddlers of perfumed powder, scented water, fragrant oil, spices and household goods.

Kudi Chin, the Chinese quarter south of the mouth of the Klong Bangkok Yai, was also settled by Chinese who had fled Ayudhya. Sanchao Kian Un Keng, a shrine founded by wealthy Hokkien, is a popular place of worship.

Thonburi's old temples make for rewarding excursions, not only for their antiquity, venerable Buddha images, fine murals and furnishings, but equally because of their relatively tranquil and unspoiled situations. Among the most highly recommended are those built during the Ayudhya period as well as temples of Sino-Thai design either built or restored by Rama III and frequently decorated by local Chinese craftsmen and artisans brought from China. The so-called Rama III temple is simple and solid, with square pillars for support.

Wat Suwannaram (near the mouth of Klong Bangkok Noi), the most impressive Thonburi temple, was built during the Ayudhya period. During the reign of King Taksin Burmese prisoners were brought here to be executed. The temple was renovated by King Rama I and given its present name. The first masonry crematorium was added by King Rama III and it was used as a royal cremation ground for members of the royal family and high-ranking officials until the reign of King Rama V. The architectural style of the temple resembles the Temple of the Emerald Buddha at the Grand Palace. The base is bowed and the lateral walls slope slightly inward from bottom up like a boat; it is a fitting metaphor for the temple is seen as the vessel of Buddhism that carries all sentient beings into the bliss of nirvana. The walls are covered from dado to high ceiling with some of the finest and best preserved murals in Bangkok. Like the stained glass and frescoes of medieval churches in Europe that aimed to instruct and inspire the laymen, temple murals illustrate scenes of spiritual attainment or remind the viewer of the conduct in life that will bring future reward or punishment. These were painted during the Third Reign (1824-51) by two rival artists: Thongyu or Luang Vichit Chetsada and a Chinese master named Khon Paek who used slender Chinese drawing brushes and shading to enhance the naturalism and sense of movement.

The arrangement and subjects of the murals around the Buddha image from Sukhothai follows a standard iconographical scheme. The *Descent of the Sky on the Thirty-three Residents at the Summit of Mount Meru* is illustrated on the wall behind the altar. Key episodes from the life of the Buddha, as well as episodes from the *Jataka* tales of his previous lives, are figured on the lateral walls. The thousand verses of *Vessantara* (Vetsandorn), the tenth and most popular of the Jataka tales, are usually chanted over a three-day period in temples at the close of Buddhist Lent. Prince Wetsandon, the embodiment of charity, is exiled by the king after he gives away the kingdom's white elephant which has the magic power to cause rain to fall. He then gives away his servants, children and finally his wife.

The upper part illustrates the Maravijaya—the name given to the Buddha figure seated in *bhumisparsha mudra* (Earth witnessing gesture). He overcomes Mara, the Lord of Worldly Delusion and Desire and his army (demons of delusion and attachment) through the intercession of Mae Torani (Mother Earth). Maravijaya has called upon the Mother Goddess as witness to his purity. She has stored up all the merits of his past lives as water droplets in her hair which she twists and rings, causing a deluge that inundates Mara's army (including blond Dutchmen with their fashionable three-corner hats). Gautama attains enlightenment and is henceforth known as the Buddha, or Enlightened One.

The extraordinary emotional range of these murals is enlivened by intimate scenes of contemporary life in Bangkok during the first half of the nineteenth century prior to the dramatic transformation that followed the

Bowring Treaty of 1855. There is a remarkable freshness to this world, unconstrained by the controlling illusion of western perspective, and by the juxtaposition of sacred and profane. Figures of Buddha, deities, monks and royalty are interspersed with charming vignettes of ordinary Bangkok people flirting, gossiping, relaxing or working. (Note the interesting unisex hair style fashionable during the reign of Rama III that intrigued the British writer George Windsor Earl: "Both men and women have their hair shaved from their heads, with the exception of a small round patch which is left between the crown and the forehead. This being brushed up, is made to stand on end, which gives them a scared appearance.")

Wat Molilokayaram, the oldest temple in Siam, also dates from the Ayudhya period. Stucco sculptures of French soldiers evoke the memory of the former garrison. Good Buddhists had no past.

Wat Hong Rattanaram is an old temple restored during King Taksin's reign. Its hallmark features are the fine carved doors and pediments, a Sukhothai Buddha (in the walking position invented there) and an important library of Buddhist scriptures.

Wat Raj-Orot, off Klong Bangkok Yai on Klong Dan, is a quiet nineteenth-century temple begun by King Rama II's son who later became King Rama III. It was the first Sino-Thai temple in Bangkok. Its traditional Siamese carved and lacquered wooden pediment was replaced by Chinese floral designs in stucco that were often studded with colourful porcelain pieces. The panels between the windows show Chinese religious offerings, pavilions and lotus clusters. The gold leaf mural paintings are highly detailed and the exquisite mother-of-pearl doors of the *ubosot*, among the best in Thailand, reward the effort of getting there.

Wat Thong Nopakun, built during the reign of King Rama IV, has a theatrical aspect strangely reminiscent one of Bernini's rhetorical Baroque ensembles in Rome. One enters through a door fashioned like a *chada* (the Siamese pointed head gear worn in the *Ramakien*). On the opposite wall fictive curtains have been pulled back to reveal Buddha who is flanked by angels. Risqué scenes on the back walls were removed at the order of King Rama IV, but an amusing cat and a dog give some hint of the playful fun that was suppressed by royal decree.

Wat Rakhang Kositharam, a little north of Wat Arun, is the last major temple built by King Rama I and has one of the most exquisitely-shaped *prangs* in Thailand. The temple was named after a valuable ancient bell (*rakhang*) that was dug up there and later moved to the Wat Phra Kaeo. It is an elegant and richly embellished structure with fine stucco work on the exterior. The interior exhibits some of the earliest examples of Rattanakosin School murals painted during the Third Reign.

Behind the temple is a group of three finely crafted traditional wooden houses that were the residence of the king when he was still a general in Taksin's army; they were later donated to monks and then converted into a library to house Buddhist scriptures. The very fine murals in the pavilion were painted at the behest of King Rama I by a masterful monk-artist named Phra Ajarn Nak and became the prototype for temple decoration during the First Reign. Chao Fa (Celestial Prince) Chim, son of King Rama I and an accomplished artist and poet, was ordered by his father to convert the family's humble home into an elaborate scripture library. Prince Chim, who succeeded his father as Rama II, personally sculpted the entrance door panel which can still be seen today.

Wat Si Sudaram. The famous poet, Sunthorn Phu (1786-1855), attended school at this temple and his life-size sculpture faces the Bangkok Noi canal. He wears a top-knot, a sign that he has not reached puberty, an amulet for protection and holds writing implements and paper. An image—the largest in the country—of his headmaster looms over him; though probably unintentional, the great variance in scale of the two figures provides a metaphor for the overwhelming presence of the headmaster in the boy's life. Sunthorn excelled at the *nirat* form of poetry that uses a journey as a vehicle for emotional release: "My boat drifts with sorrow into/A wide canal at Bangkok Noi district."

Five

RAJDAMNERN AVENUE
(RATCHADAMNOEN* AVENUE)

SANAM LUANG TO THE DEMOCRACY MONUMENT

With map in hand, you can trace the zig-zag route of the three-pronged boulevard (Rajdamnern Nai or inner section; Rajdamnern Klang or middle section, Rajdamnern Nok or outer section). It runs north from the Grand Palace, east to Sanam Luang, past the Democracy Monument, Wat Rajnadda, Wat Thepthidaram, Mahakan Fort, and then due north once again to the Royal Plaza with its beaux-arts Ananda Samakhom Throne Hall.

King Chulalongkorn returned from his first Grand Tour of 1897 with a new vision of modern European boulevards, impressed by the fashionable Avenue Louise in Brussels and the handsome Champs-Elysées in Paris. Civil engineers were recruited from Italy to carve out a new district and create a royal parade route in central Bangkok. This was an immense undertaking that would profoundly affect the development of the city. "Immediately after the new site [for the king's palace] was selected, a veritable land 'boom' took place in the surrounding district," wrote J. Antonio in the *Traveller's Guide to Bangkok and Siam* (1904), "and the clearing of the jungle and the filling in of the swamp took place with astounding rapidity for Siam. Roads were planned in all directions and buildings sprang up like mushrooms." A vast area of marshy wasteland had to be drained; loads of city rubbish were hauled in for landfill.

A banner headline in a local newspaper from 1899 announced the near completion of a "splendid boulevard... to be called Rajdamnern, or King's Parade." Bangkok would soon have its own tree-lined esplanade with a central carriage way and wide flanking paths for smaller vehicles. This long boulevard (three-quarters of a mile in length and over two hundred feet in width) linked the king's new complex, comprising the summer palace called Suan Dusit (The Garden Palace in Dusit Heaven), with the Grand Palace on Rattanakosin. Princely villas of late Victorian design surrounding the palace were decorated with *objets d'art* bought in Europe.

From the founding of Bangkok in 1782 the Chao Phraya river had been a floating ceremonial path for royal pageantry. In an age of colonialism and of modernity a new urban route of western inspiration was more suitable for pomp and circumstance. For the next thirty years the road served as a symbolic extension of the reigning monarch's absolute grip on the conduits of power.

When Somerset Maugham first visited Bangkok in 1923 he found the modern architecture in such a "strange, flat, confused" city like a royal stage set:

> What they have aimed at you see in the broad avenue, straight dusty roads, sometimes running by the side of a canal, with which they have surrounded this conglomeration of sordid streets. They are handsome, spacious and stately, shaded by trees, the deliberate adornment of a great city devised by a king, anxious to have an imposing seat, but they have no reality. There is something stagey about them so that you feel they are more apt for court pageants than for the use of every day. No one walks in them. They seem to await ceremonies and processions. They are like the deserted avenues in the park of a fallen monarch.

The new King's Parade was put to good use by King Chulalongkorn. No expense was spared his fiftieth birthday celebrations in October 1903. An English writer in Bangkok described the three-day festival: "Ships are wreathed in flowers and bunting, banquets are given, receptions are held, and salutes are fired. At night, the palaces in the city, the vessels in the river, every house by the side of the road or on the bank of a stream, are ablaze with light. Night is turned to day, and earth becomes a fairyland."

The royal elite refashioned themselves, both as individuals and as a social group. "By contemplating themselves in their new clothes, new domestic settings, and new urban spaces, the Siamese court ended up convincing themselves, above all, of being modern," writes Maurizio Peleggi. The king hosted nocturnal automobile rallies for the large tribe of royal sons on his new road. Crowds were thick to watch the fashionable new spectator sport on what was then described as the "finest street" in the capital. One of the king's sons acquired a car in 1902; by 1908 there were more than three hundred in royal hands.

Cycling soirées along King's Parade hold great imaginative appeal. I like to stand at the intersection of Rajdamnern Avenue and Tanao Road and picture the royal cyclists—dozens of smooth-faced young aristocrats in colourful Siamese garb gliding silently by like water hyacinths on the river. Softly blurred forms are dusted by the incandescence of the wrought-iron streetlights held aloft by the elegant bird-women *kinarees* of Hindu epic.

Largesse and pomp were wedded in the magnificent procession in honour of the king's return from his second tour of Europe in 1907. The event was well choreographed and aspects of it could have been staged by a triumphant Roman emperor. The king entered the city in a European motorcar; then passed through nine ceremonial arches built by ministries competing for prominence. At each arch, government officials recited speeches on the contribution of their ministries to the "progress" of Siam. The Irrigation Department had organized a hundred people to walk in close formation holding up paddy stalks to simulate a productive rice field. A float presented by the Department of Health included a cardboard hospital with giant replicas of surgical instruments, medical bottles and medicinal herbs. To put this in context, we should remember that modernization and the introduction of western ideas and technology were the kingdom's principal defences against annexation by European colonial powers.

Queen Victoria's Diamond Jubilee in 1887 had set the fashion for monarchic display in an age of colonialism and King Chulalongkorn followed suit. The fortieth anniversary of his coronation (1 October 1908) was celebrated along King's Parade with great pomp and circumstance. The king unveiled an equestrian monument in the Royal Plaza that had been paid for by public donations and cast in Paris by a French sculptor. This imposing equestrian monument showing the king dressed in a mid-Victorian field marshal's uniform quite intentionally evoked the Sun King's monument at Versailles.

Democracy Monument to Mahakan Fort

The Royal Hotel (formerly the Rattanokosin) at the corner of Rajdamnern Nai and Klang (inner and middle sections) was built by the military government in the early 1940s. Its prime location near government and military offices along with its reputation for the best food in Bangkok made it an ideal meeting spot. Diplomats, spies, coup planners and mistresses slipped in and out of its elegant marble lobby.

Walk—or rather drive—down Rajdamnern Klang and right in the middle of the road you will be confronted by the Democracy Monument (1939) designed by Mew Aphaiwong. You cannot miss it: this vast fascistic monument resembles nothing so much as a *War of the Worlds* spaceship: "a huge pile of cement in the middle of a busy and hardly accessible street with obscure meanings... in a grotesque and tasteless style," laments a Thai historian.

This first major monument of the new military government of Field Marshal Phibul made a bold break with the absolute monarchy. It crudely severed the symbolic link between the Grand Palace where the king's oath was traditionally taken and the Ananda Samakhom Throne Hall. Four concrete wings of freedom enshrine the first constitution of 1932. The reliefs exalt the active role of the Thai people in overthrowing the absolute monarchy, illustrating their filial piety, nobility of purpose and absolute dedication to the welfare of the modern state. In truth though, the coup was carried out by the armed forces on behalf of the commoners, most of whom were still intensely loyal to the monarch, not to abstract principles.

Unfortunately the brief flicker of democracy was followed by more than half a century of strict authoritarian rule under the generals. The relatively peaceful transfer of power belied violent struggles between rival political groups in the years ahead. The National Assembly became a puppet body and, apart from brief interludes, military authoritarian rule dominated the political scene in Thailand through to the 1950s and 1960s. Emboldened by the student protests of the late 1960s in Chicago and Paris, the Democracy Monument played centre stage for protests in October 1973. Witayakorn Chiengkul, one of the most influential Thai writers of the period, mobilized students through his writing. During a heated debate between a father (who is a government bureaucrat) and his university-age son—in his *Novel of a University Man* (1969)—the former quotes Sunthorn Phu's famous adage, "To know how to survive is the greatest good."

Students were the inspirational and driving force against the military dictatorial rule, but a groundswell of opposition arose from every sector of Thai society. During a five-day sit-in, subsequently remembered as Black October 1973, thousands of students gathered peacefully at the monument. They demanded the restoration of constitutionalism and an end to the autocratic regimes. When their protests turned violent troops opened fire on them from tanks and helicopters. Scores were killed, thousands were wounded, and the elegant lobby of the Royal Hotel became a makeshift hospital. The king finally intervened; the military leaders stood down, and thus begun a short-lived fling with democracy from 1974-76.

A second bloodbath took place three years later on 6 October 1976 after students at Thammasart University protested against the assassination of a prominent young activist. A well orchestrated media campaign propagated the slogan *Kwai dai Sai* (Right Conquer Left), branding student activists and their allies as "burdens on the land" and "scum of the earth". Civil society broke down when right-wing mobs lynched students. Others were brutally beaten and massacred by police, hired hooligans and right-wing fanatics.

An exhibition called *History and Memory* (now installed at the Queen's Gallery) challenges the dominant discourse of Thai history. Sutee Kunavichayanant's installation *History Class* (*Thanon Ratchadamnoen*) displays fourteen old school desks engraved with texts and pictures. The viewer is invited to make crayon or pencil rubbings as souvenir prints. One of the most disturbing texts is a famous interview with a right-wing Buddhist monk that appeared in *Chaturas Newspaper* on 29 June 1976.

> Chaturas: Is it wrong to kill leftists or communists?
> Phra Kitti Vutto: I believe it is the right thing to do. Even though Thais
> are Buddhists, we do not consider this action as murder. Any one who
> is trying to destroy our nation, our religion, and our monarchy is not
> a whole human. We must focus on the fact that we are killing demons.
> This is every Thai's duty.

Many aggrieved young writers of the time voiced desperate frustration at oppressive military rule. When I pass the Democracy Monument I sometimes hear their voices rising like a Greek chorus. Knomthuan Khanthanu's *Beggar's Chant* is a plaintive revolt against the rule of might.

> lazy we were not
> servile we were not
> we tilled and ploughed
> we farmed the land
> and reaped the debts

the rich are big brothers
we owe money we the dogs
our tongues hang out
our bellies rumble
rice farmers begging rice from others
can anyone understand
can anyone understand

On 17 May 1992 a popular uprising took place at the Democracy Monument against an unelected prime minister named General Suchinda Kraprayoon. The protestors were dubbed the "mobile mob" since a large number were middle-class students. Yet once again violence tragically erupted as soldiers fired automatic rifles from a convoy of army trucks onto thousands of defenceless protestors. Thai journalist Pratya Sawetvimon describes the scene in an article "After the Night of the Generals" in *Asiaweek*.

> Here a peaceful protest turned ugly as troops and civilians confronted each other in nervous tension. Bottles of gasoline were thrown by youths whose love of peace was less defined than their love of democracy. Volleys of rifle shots punctured the tense night standoff. Here fell the dead and wounded. Along this elegant avenue marched soldiers firing M-16 automatic rifles into the air. On these sidewalks three thousand people were brutally shoved into army trucks. And here was destroyed the image of Thailand as a sophisticated modern nation where things like this do not happen.

The Democracy Monument finally merited its name after this bloody student protest, as Australian scholar Marc Askew writes: "it was the nature of the groups involved in the May action, the martyrdom of ordinary Thais, combined with the characteristic cultural propensity to sacralize space, which transformed the meaning of this monument from the emblem of a small minority of coup-makers of 1932 to a genuinely meaningful popular symbol, much more sacred than secular."

In 2001 the 14 October Monument was inaugurated nearby. A ceramic casing of the *stupa* has engraved on it the names of the dead. The ceramicist had hoped that people would make rubbings of them but that has not been the case probably because Thais are terrified of the ghosts of those killed violently.

WAT RAJNADDA

Further down Rajdamnern Klang (intersection Thanon Maha Chai) you will come across a metal palace, a large square-based structure framed by thirty-seven iron spires that symbolize Buddhist teachings. The interior contains beehive cells for the monks' meditation and its summit is reached by a winding staircase of 318 steps, a feature that Siamese architects adopted from European buildings. In 1842 King Rama III sent a delegation to Sri Lanka to acquire a model of the famous third-century metal palace that he had heard about from traders. Bangkok's version of the Loha Prasat was built shortly afterwards in the grounds of the temple dedicated to his favourite niece, Rajnadda, who became briefly King Rama IV's queen, for she died a young mother to her royal husband's deepest grief.

Suchit Wongthed's short story *Lord Buddha, Help Me?* (1969) features Phra Mahaa Bunman, a young Buddhist monk who lived at the temple for ten years. He had climbed to its summit many times for a panorama of a city that was still largely free of skyscrapers. After a sudden decision to abandon his calling the monk confronts contemporary reality on the street. Upon exiting the temple gate, he wanders like a lost stranger around a familiar neighbourhood that he sees, almost as if for the first time.

> He walks on aimlessly... His body trembles [from hunger]... His flesh, his veins are all trembling.
>
> Mahaa Bunman stops walking to wipe off his perspiration. He is crossing the bridge over the canal between Wat Theptidaram and Wat Rajnaddaram.
>
> Feeling weak and dry, he walks passed the Chalerm Thai Theatre. He looks angrily at the poster in front of the movie house. His jealousy is awakened by a young couple sitting in an air-conditioned restaurant. A girl strolls toward him displaying her knees and thighs, and he feels embarrassed, but he can't keep himself from glancing at them.
>
> Why the hell did I leave the monkhood?
>
> Should I commit suicide?
>
> The more he thinks, the more uncomfortable he becomes. He starts feeling sick to his stomach. He smells the stinking car exhaust. He can't

stand the dust rising from the street. Maybe it would be a good idea to pass out so that he would be taken to a hospital, where he would be fed.

The city is full of products that have caused the loss of the country's trade balance. It is full of places of entertainment that are excessive and unnecessary, places of sex that are the cause of vice and crime.

He is at wit's end, totally overwhelmed by the din and chaos of the westernized and secularized city. "There's nothing attractive about Rajdamnern Avenue today," he sighs. With this dark view swirling in his head, Phra Mahaa Bunman slowly traces his steps back to the monk's quarters at Wat Rajnadda. He has neither the money nor the qualifications to function in a complex, technological society.

WAT THEPTHIDARAM

If you find yourself at the intersection of Thanon Maha Chai and Trok Wat Ratchchintda, you will come across a little bridge over the Klong Wat Theptida connecting the Loha Prasat to Wat Thepthidaram. King Rama III built the complex in the 1830s as a gift for his favourite daughter, calling it Thepthidaram, "The Temple of the Angelic Daughter". It was the only temple in Thailand to house *Phiksunee,* or Buddhist nuns, but for only a short period of time. Thereafter it was more closely associated with the famous poet, Sunthorn Phu (1786-1855).

Upon entering the monastery from Maha Chai Road one crosses a large empty area that was formerly used for temple festivals and public gatherings. The monastic complex (religious buildings, the monks' quarters and common grounds) were built to face the canal (now hidden behind later buildings) and Wat Saket with its magnificent Golden Mount. Despite considerable alteration of the surrounding neighbourhood the monastery has not changed much since Sunthorn Phu described it in 1841.

I walked in the evening breeze
Within the temple walls to see:
The prangs stood at four cardinal points,
The Chapel, the Buddha's House, and the Sermon
Hall were painted in gold;
The gable was cast in Cantonese style,
Describing various birds in motion;

Glazed tiles held the roof firmly,
Two pavilions stood just outside the wall;
Chinese lions were frightful to look at,
Shaking their bodies and showing their fangs.

A pleasant path lined with flowering tropical trees leads from the cultic buildings to the monks' quarters where Sunthorn resided. A little cell exhibits articles said to have belonged to him, but his words more powerfully evoke his world.

Outside like a fence, there were flower trees, some in bloom,
Some fading, to prolong the fragrance day and night
Rose apple trees stood in line, laden with fruit
Hanging down in clusters to tempt.

Sunthorn's greatness lay in the range of his literary output, his imaginative powers and the naturalism of his poems that anticipate a less religious worldview, grounded more in actual experience than in Buddhist notions about experience. He was a commoner whose genuine language, passionate sincerity and stirring realism appealed to people outside the court who thereby constituted a new reading public. A few translations have been made of his works but he remains largely unknown in the West.

Sunthorn spent his early years in the Forbidden City of the Grand Palace where his mother was a wet nurse to a princess. After the standard temple education at a monastery, he became a government clerk. But he had a great passion for poetry and the promise of genius that an early poem confirms. His ardour for a woman named Khun Chan, who would greatly influence his work, inspired his first great poem and his first disaster. Khun Chan was a palace lady, a woman strictly off-limits to commoners, and Sunthorn's lover. Their passionate affair was a heinous offence; when discovered both were thrown into the palace prison.

Upon his release in 1807 Sunthorn left Bangkok to visit his father in Muang Klaeng, a township in the province of Rayong. During this month-long boat journey he wrote his first "Nirat of love, In witness of my broken heart on parting" from Khun Chan. This first great poem entitled "Nirat Muang Klaeng" is marked by the strong realism that would characterize his work.

The *nirat* genre, which had made its first appearance in the early Ayudhyan period, is composed of descriptive travel poems encompassing movement and separation. (Imaginary voyages permitted another escape from the harsh realities of life.) Longing is always the key theme of the work, especially in the poet's lamentation of his separation from the beloved. Place-names en route frequently remind the poet of the loved one to whom his heart belongs. Reminiscences in *nirats* sometimes give rise to witty, philosophical, self-referential reflections. A British literary scholar has noted the affinity between the Thai *nirat* and the wanderer genre of Old English poetry in which a travelling minstrel laments lost customs and changes in people. While the English bard assigned these changes to "fate", the Buddhist poet Sunthorn ascribes them to "impermanence" (*annicam*).

But Sunthorn personally struggled with demons that seem to have taken permanent hold of his spirit.

> From alcohol I could safely escape, it did not destroy me.
> It would be absurd not to go near it pretending to look away.
> Not alcohol alone makes us drunk, but love makes us drunk as well.
> Should thoughts of love be suppressed, I wonder?
> Drunkenness with alcohol, day or night, is passing
> But the heart is drunken with love every night on end.

Sunthorn and Chan did marry but his fondness for rice whisky led to many quarrels. Although Chan eventually left him for another man she had already been immortalized in many of his works. One of the most beautiful is a poem called "Nirat Phra Bat" (1807) in which the sights observed on the way to a Buddhist shrine cause him to reflect upon their marital differences in a strikingly modern way.

It was not long before Sunthorn attracted the attention of King Rama II, himself a poet of great talent, who appreciated his lively wit and named him court poet. The two poets had an extremely fruitful collaboration. When the king was in the process of composing an abridged version of the *Ramakien*, the Thai national epic, Sunthorn was always nearby to assist with versification. But Sunthorn's drinking problem incurred the wrath of the king who heard of a violent tussle with an uncle who tried to break up a fight between son and mother. Once again the poet was briefly imprisoned, then pardoned by the king who engaged him as instructor for the royal sons and as chief literary adviser. During this period Sunthorn composed *The Story of Khun Chang Khun Phaen*, which remains a beloved classic of Thai literature.

The death of King Rama II in 1824 deeply affected the poet. At the sight of the royal barge the young poet recalls their memorable journeys to temples to offer garments to monks at the end of Kathin—the Buddhist Lent—during which a constant stream of poetry flowed.

> In front of the wharf I saw the King's boat—
> Tears came to my eyes at the memory.
> When Phra J'muen Wai and I were afloat.
> By the golden palanquin we would be.
> The King was wont to compose poetry,
> Which it was my duty to recite
> Through the long, long Kathin ceremony,
> To his satisfaction and delight.

When King Rama III ascended the throne in 1824 Sunthorn was still smarting from his dismissal and removal from his official residence. He lived first as a vagrant on a boat and later found refuge in Wat Thepthidaram. A daughter of the king was a faithful patron and he continued to write extraordinary nirats and narrative poems. During the reign of King Rama IV he was named Poet Laureate and given a royal sinecure. He continued to write until his death at the age of seventy, including lovely lullabies for the royal children and nirats in which he railed against the bitterness of lost love.

Sunthorn's masterpiece, *Phra Aphai Mani*, is an adventurous, romance-epic that was begun in prison and completed in mid-life. It is highly recommended for anyone who is curious about Thai identity, philosophy and the traditional way of life prior to the rapid westernization ushered in by the Bowring Treaty of 1855.

MAHAKAN FORT TO KLONG SAEN SAEP

If you walk along Rajdamnern Nok for ten minutes you will see Mahakan Fort. It is one of two surviving octagonal watchtowers built by Rama I to protect the city wall (the other is Phra Sumane Fort at the end of Phra

Athit Road in Banglampoo). Mahakan Fort was named after the Hindu God of death, a warning of the fate to be met by any enemy attempting to breach the gate.

Adjacent to the fortress is Klong Saen Sap—the canal of "one hundred thousand stings"—a reference to the swarms of mosquitoes that plagued the Chinese workers who dug the waterway from 1837 to 1840. The canal, which extends for almost forty miles, transported boats from the original walled city to the Bang Pakong river, then to the Gulf of Siam and beyond. It also had an important strategic function: to protect the city from the east in the event of military trouble with Vietnam via Cambodia, then a Thai vassal state. Vietnam was a real threat before the French colonial occupation.

The population along the canal largely comprised Lao and Malay slaves together with Thais and Chinese. A nineteenth-century American missionary travelling along the canal at that time was surprised at the method farmers on the banks used to protect crops from hungry birds. "Platforms six or eight feet in height are placed in various parts of the field, upon which men, women, and children stand, raising their voices to the highest pitch, in order to frighten the various flocks of birds as they are about to descend. The striking contrast of voices, some so hoarse they can barely be heard, and their dark and diminutive bodies in the distance, contrasted with the so glistening fields, made it a remarkable sight to the first beholder." He was less bemused when the locals refused to accept his evangelical tracts claiming that they could not read (which was probably true).

Trade was booming by the early twentieth century and Klong Saen Saep was one of the busiest waterways in the capital. A system of locks introduced in 1904 to irrigate the rice paddies and to control floods was built under the present Rajadamri Road. The area, known today as Pratunam (water gate), quickly developed as a major transfer point and commercial centre.

The canal was also notorious famous for its rollicking night life. The floating brothels (known to locals as "water babies") were paddled by discreet boatmen and curtained for protection. Contacts were made under bridges and at secluded landings. Toward the end of the 1960s the police cracked down and the "water babies" of the Klong Saen Saep were finally put to sleep.

River taxis run from Makahan Fort to Soi Ekkmai—change boats at

Tha Pratunam (Pratunam Pier). Board the boat at the end of Soi Thong Lor (Soi 55) at the pier (Tha Thong Lor). If you want to see anything you have to sit at the front of the boat or stand in the middle as two plastic curtains are raised when the boat is in motion to protect passengers from the murky canal water. The route, which stops at all of the nodal points, is crossed by two overhead expressways, a train track, numerous bridges and the Sky Train, but the ride is an unforgettable experience as Old Bangkok comes alive in a hundred spots along the way. It is a running film of kaleidoscopic impressions—a mishmash of traditional Thai water dwellings, tumbledown shacks, sleek high rises, bland office blocks, temples, mosques, outdoor warehouses and what must be the largest amount of laundry hanging out to dry outside Naples.

ANANDA SAMAKHOM THRONE HALL

During his first visit to Turin in 1897 King Chulalongkorn met with a fellow stamp collector, Queen Elena of Savoy, who also helped to put a new stamp on Bangkok. She helped the king to recruit talented architects, engineers and artists from the Piedmont region. They were largely responsible for the European design of some of the most beautiful buildings in the city.

From 1907 to 1915 a team of Italian architects collaborated on the design for the marble throne hall. Supporting such a weighty structure on the soft sandy subsoil was a significant challenge. It led to the introduction of reinforced concrete supported by a pontoon that was a water-tight basement built on piles. This ingenious construction system would have a huge impact on the subsequent vertical growth of the city. The Dane Kornerup first saw it during the rainy season of 1921 when it "is mirrored in a lake" and "its bold cupola stands among slender palm trees in Dusit Park."

An official guidebook compares the Throne Hall to St. Peter's in Rome, St. Paul's in London and Queen Victoria's Monument in Calcutta—monuments to Catholic, Protestant and imperial sovereignty—but the scale is tiny by comparison. The Thai Throne Hall glorifies the modernized monarchy of Thailand and the interior is an original synthesis of European ecclesiastical architecture and Asian forms. The frescoes show key episodes from Thai history, particularly the triumphs of the Chakri Dynasty. The central image by the Italian Galileo Chini of *King Chulalongkorn Abolishing Slavery* was inspired by the great Venetian illusionist

Tiepolo who specialized in monumental fresco decoration. Painted at right is a fictive worksite showing Siamese carpenters finishing off the lofty dome of the throne hall, completed in 1915. After 1932 it became the official seat of the National Assembly but the kingdom has had eighteen coups since then. Reflecting on the most recent government that replaced the ousted Prime Minister Thaksin Shinawatra in 2006, the current telecom minister told a journalist, "Basically we are not politicians. I think we have different approaches to life."

At the annual opening of Parliament, MPs bow before the revered King Bhumibol Adulyadej, who has presided over an extraordinary revival of royal authority during his sixty-year reign. He sits in an elevated throne in what would be the equivalent of an apse in a Catholic church. This sacrosanct area has traditionally been reserved for the high priests and for the divinely-appointed kings who wielded ultimate power over their realms.

NOTE:

* The old spelling, with its Sanskrit root, is "Rajdamnern", meaning "King's Way" or the equivalent of "King's Parade". In recent time, the official romanization of names and place-names tend to replace the previous spellings with Sanskrit roots. Thus "Raj" becomes "Ratcha" which sounds like a bad sneeze. As for "noen", which is unpronounceable in English, the sound is actually "nern". Banishment of the Sanskrit root harks back to the 1940s when, under a jingoist fever, the written Thai language ignored its roots and became nonsensical.

Part Two

CITY OF TEMPLES AND SHRINES

Six

WAT ARUN

Of all the hundreds of temples in Bangkok the most beloved is Wat Arun (Temple of the Dawn) on the Chao Phraya river. It cannot be missed, not only because it is the tallest religious structure in the capital (its *prang* is 220 feet high), but also because of its brilliance. Its surface decoration is a veritable *horror vaccui,* a kind of Neapolitan birthday cake with a stucco frosting. In it are imbedded countless bits of multi-coloured Chinese porcelain (called *benjarong*), broken crockery formed into the shape of flowers, and seashells. British writer James Kirkup described it in 1968 as an immense monument "roughly glazed with a riotously pretty crackle of broken crockery ... The whole effect is of overwhelming charm and prettiness; of all-inclusive, ravishing miniature detail of decoration on a colossal scale, its splendid vulgarity is both monumental and gay, earnest and frivolous, matter of fact and artificial—combinations of all the qualities I most revere."

Singaporean artist Chen Wen, who visited the monument in the mid-1950s, was much taken by its exuberance and the rhythmic play of the roof gables. They seem to contract and expand like an accordion, an effect he captures on canvas in a vibrant and musical painting on display at the Singapore Art Museum.

Even the few snooty continentals who disdained the decorative use of cheap materials praised unanimously the "indescribably wonderful" effect of the sunlight on the rich incrustation. When bathed in the pure light of early dawn the temple was a "mass of brilliancy", an effect that was quite intentionally sought. For an early twentieth-century British traveller, an Orientalist's dream had come true:

> In the grazing rays of the setting sun, despite its decay and its neglect, the monument with its varnished tiles encrusted in the mortar, with its not yet faded gold on the symbolic ornaments, with its tangle of baked earth on which the vegetation gets hold, forms a grand, magical spectacle, more beautiful than nature, because it is the palpable realization of the most extravagant visions which can haunt you after the troubling reading of *A Thousand and One Nights*.

The earliest foundational myth of Bangkok as capital mentions King Taksin's breathtaking sight of the first blush of sun shining over a magnificent temple in Thonburi. This spectacle at sunrise was a key factor in his decision to found a new capital there in 1767. Taksin built his royal palace adjacent to the temple complex. He fulfilled his vow to restore the temple and installed the famous Emerald Buddha (later moved to new Bangkok across the river by King Rama I).

But it is a life-size statue of King Rama II on a marble pedestal that overlooks the "tumbling and rushing" river near the temple pier. This monument celebrates the rich cultural legacy he bequeathed to the Thai nation and to the world. UNESCO formally recognized the varied achievements of this deeply Buddhist king, poet and musician by naming him World Cultural Leader in 1967. The king began a major restoration of the royal temple when he was still crown prince. When he came to the throne he set to the task of building the towering Khmer-style *prang* with its four smaller satellites. His son, King Rama III, actually implemented the *prang* complex, and when completed it was consecrated as the Temple of the Dawn.

The temple is a symbolic Mount Meru in microcosm, an earthly version of the cosmological Hindu mountain with its thirty-three heavens where all the gods reside. The traditional thunderbolt, the weapon of the Hindu god Indra, seemed to rise "from a nest of turrets, and shoot upwards like a single column rounded off into a cupola at the summit: from thence a bronze gilt arrow extend twenty crooked arms that pierce the clouds," a European visitor pleasurably observed in 1868.

The pyramidal base of the temple rests on a floating foundation. This consists of a raft of logs resting on tightly packed giant water jars placed upside down to trap air inside them. The whole sub-base thus literally floats on the muddy bank of the river. Pavilions at the bottom of four monumental staircases located at the four cardinal points (representing the four continents) contain images of Buddha in the four key events of his final life (birth, meditation under the shelter of the seven-headed naga serpent, preaching to the first disciples and nirvana). They lead in turn to three narrow terraces with small *prangs* on the corners. Architectural sculpture consists of caryatid angels in high relief and the triple-headed white elephants of Indra. Gargantuan statues of Yaksa, those fabulous mythical giants from the *Ramayana*, which are also found at the Wat Phra

Kaeo of the Grand Palace compound, stand guard before the old temple.

With its ingenious engineering, rich history and imagery, it is no wonder that the temple has fired the imaginations of travellers and writers for centuries. An enthusiastic reaction came from the pen of a French scholar Lucien Fournereau writing in 1904. "Let's hurry to say this," he wrote:

> upon arriving, one is royally rewarded for one's efforts by the splendid panorama which stretches out at one's feet: the entire city appears, following the curves of the river, with the spires of the royal palace and its crenellated belt; the countless pagodas threaten the sky with their pylons and like in a gigantic green velvet casket which is the vegetation of Bangkok, shine and sparkle the thousand red, blue or gilded fires of the countless porcelain jewels which are the dress of the Siamese monuments.

For Japanese author Yukio Mishima, coming across the temple at dawn was an overwhelming experience; he saw the symbolic repetition of the layers in a Freudian context as the architectural expression of a complex multi-layered dream sequence. *The Temple of the Dawn* was the last novel of a tetralogy that takes place in Bangkok just before and during the early years of the Second World War.

It was still darkish, and only the very tip of the pagoda caught the first rays of the rising sun. The Thonburi jungle beyond was filled with the piercing cries of birds... The repetitiveness and the sumptuousness of the pagoda were almost suffocating. The tower with its color and brilliance, adorned in many layers and graduated toward the peak, gave one the impression of so many strata of dream sequences hovering overhead. The plinths of the extremely steep stair were also heavily festooned and each tier was supported by a bas-relief of birds with human faces. They formed a multicolored pagoda whose every level was crushed with layers of dreams, expectations, prayers, each being further weighted down with other stories, pyramid-like, progressing skyward... With the first rays of dawn over the Menam River, the tens of thousands of porcelain fragments turned into so many tiny mirrors that captured the light. A great structure of mother-of-pearl sparkling riotously... The pagoda had long served as a morning bell tolled by its rich hues, resonant colors responding to the dawn. They were created... to evoke a beauty, a power, an explosiveness like the dawn itself.

The keen visitor will wish to see the temple at different times of the day, but it is generally accepted that the most beautiful view is from the Bangkok side of the river at sunset when the mellow rays tease the muddy water—after the golden globe suddenly dips behind the horizon at just about 6 p.m. Minutes later the artificial lights go on. Often the glowing monument can be seen against a sky broadly swathed in pure hues like a Rothko painting and the river turns to wine.

Seven

WAT PHO

Picture for a moment a reclining Buddha 150 feet long and 50 feet high; picture further his right arm supporting his head with its tight curls resting on two box-pillows of blue, richly encrusted with glass mosaics. His long left arm seems to catapult directly to the swirling whorls on his toes. Then consider his face with his silver eyes, neither in repose nor asleep; he is finally entering nirvana after 555 previous lives. Visitors to Thailand are told that the feet of mortals must never be pointed at the Buddha because they are ritually unclean. But the Buddha's feet are different: here the mother-of-pearl inlaid feet are the most highly revered features and they are in your face—ten feet high and fifteen feet long. The ebony wood soles are divided into 108 neatly arranged panels, all decorated with peonies, which display the auspicious symbols by which the Buddha could be identified: rocky crags, shells, altar accessories, lotus flowers, dancers, rare birds, white elephants, lions, dragons, horses, peacocks, cranes, tigers, and phoenixes, ships with three sails. As you marvel at this colossal statue, which seems cramped in the huge but sombre space like a child in a cot he has almost overgrown, you realize why Wat Pho is so famous.

The irrepressible Marquis de Beauvoir actually climbed on top of the statue when he visited in 1867 and left this close-up report.

> We looked like Lilliputians surrounding Gulliver, and when we tried to climb upon him we entirely disappeared in his nostrils; one of his nails is taller than any of us. We stood amazed before this Titanic work, of which the architecture can only have been paid for by the treasures of Croesus. No creed ever saw such a display of wealth, for all this enormous coating of the purest gold must be worth thousands of millions; each sheet of metal, and there are thousands, is nearly two square feet in size, and they say weighs 450 ounces of gold.

Wat Pho is named after the monastery in India where the Buddha is said to have lived. A temple, probably sustained by a prosperous Chinese merchant community, existed on this site when King Rama I came to the throne. He felt compelled to enlarge and renovate the temple, and there were joyous celebrations when the magnificent temple was completed. What we see now is, of course, rather different from that original complex; many alterations and extensions have been made in the 260 years since then—in fact, most of the Wat Pho structures are the result of an extensive building programme sponsored by King Rama III.

Not surprisingly, at more than 25,000 square feet, the Wat Pho temple complex is the largest in Bangkok. The main entrance is in Thanon Chetuphon, the road that separates the sacred temple buildings from the monks' living quarters. In the continuous wall surrounding the complex, there are a further sixteen gates, guarded inside by Chinese giants carved out of rock. One of them is said to be Marco Polo; others are reputed to be Chinese warriors and yet others Dutch traders in Ayudhya.

The sense of enormity begins in the outer cloister, which is presided over by 400 Buddha images. These are artistic paragons, selected from more than 1,200 images brought by King Rama I from provinces all over the country for their conservation. Following restoration they were mounted on matching gilded pedestals; then placed on marble plinths in the arcade. Although the images are stylistically varied, the repetitive effect of the entire ensemble is something like the intercolumniation of the cloister at Mont St. Michel which was arranged to induce meditative pause. A slow walk through the temple cloister has a similar calming effect and for those who read Thai, the sacred inscriptions on the columns of the outer and inner cloisters are meant to enrich the condensed spiritual pilgrimage.

The main temple (*ubosot*) itself is raised on a marble platform and nearly wholly enclosed by a white marble wall punctuated by gateways protected by mythological lions. You are reminded once again of the centrality of the *Ramakien* to Thai culture as you come across the exterior balustrade, illustrated with reliefs containing something like a hundred and fifty dramatic episodes of this great epic. The drama unfolds in a continuous narrative from right to left and it is suggested that the devotee should observe these episodes before entering the temple in order "to enact a transcendence from secular to spiritual dimensions," as one writer has put it. For many years tourists could buy stone rubbings of the figures from art students; these were made on mulberry paper using socks stained with black ink, a practice that was fortunately later discontinued to protect the finely carved figures.

There are further episodes from the *Ramakien* on the exterior doors; these are in precious mother-of-pearl inlay. Inside the main house of worship, one is overwhelmed not by size nor by profusion but rather by a sense of great beauty—of both the architecture and of the finest Thai craftsmanship. The traditional lacquer-work decoration of birds and flowers displays an exquisite sense of pattern and symmetry. Diamond-shaped crowns on doors and windows signify a royal monastery. No one can remain unmoved by the extraordinary animated effect caused by the play of light on the fine patterns and iridescent surfaces.

The grand hall lives up to its name, with its great pillars and bronze chandeliers. It is dominated by a venerable Buddha image from Thonburi with relics stored inside. Ashes of the royal family were later buried in the elaborate, gilded pedestal so that the public could pay homage and make merit. Most of the original mural painting has been lost and the decoration now includes an eclectic array of scenes taken from the life of the Buddha, deeds of eminent monks, folk tales and yet more episodes from the *Ramakien*. There are also charming scenes of daily life and customs in nineteenth-century Bangkok. A mural to the left of the entrance door

shows a cityscape of Chinese architecture; the intimate domestic scenes within the walls (including a woman giving birth) have the liveliness and freshness of observed experience.

Yet what is arguably the most beautiful edifice in the country is the Scripture Hall (Hor Trai or Phra Mondop), built by King Rama III. It is a tetrahedron with a crowned gabled roof surmounted by a diadem-shaped crown. However, the sovereign had a vision that encompassed not only beauty and the devout: he was intent on making the temple a place of true enlightenment, a place of study open to all Siamese men, irrespective of birth or rank—he effectively founded Thailand's first public university here. Very few books were in circulation at the time, so the king had narrative pictures made of specialized subjects not taught in local monasteries. A pictorial encyclopaedia was engraved on granite slabs; these covered aspects of Buddhism, history, geography, medicine, astrology, poetry, botany, history, geography, biographies, fables and even nursery rhymes. Visual aids sometimes explicated the "texts" and sculptural representations frequently accompanied literary compositions.

Of particular interest in this "library of stone" are maxims composed at the king's command by a Siamese prince-poet in emulation of verse forms at Ayudhya. They advise men how to comport themselves in a world where things are often not what they seem. "Don't judge a book by its cover" has rarely been rendered with such evocative visual imagery as in the maxim: "The fig, when it is ripe and beautiful from the outside, but inside is full of worms, is like wicked men who look good to all appearances." The Thai Ministry of Culture is pressing UNESCO to recognize the inscriptions in the Memory of the World Programme.

It was firmly believed that physical well-being could be improved by emulation, and the "health parks" in the complex show just how. King Rama I had eighty sculptures made of hermit monks in contorted yogic positions that had been found to relieve stiff muscles and pain following long periods of meditation. Unfortunately only a few dozen of the statues remain today. The policy of public health education was furthered by King Rama III who had two pavilions built for use as an open-air school of traditional medicine and massage. Human anatomy, physiology, child health-care and massage techniques are illustrated in stone on the pavilions in front of the four great pagodas. The Scottish diplomat John Crawfurd observed with interested scepticism the sight of "human figures, thrown into attitudes the most whimsical, distorted, and unnatural that can well be conceived… for the cure of certain diseases."

Since 1962 the Wat Pho School of Traditional Massage has taught traditional acupressure and herbal body massage in two of the pavilions. Mindful of the reputation of Bangkok's massage parlours with a "happy ending", practitioners are careful to tell you that "it's the real thing."

Today, as noisy crowds of tourists deprive the temple of its due reverence, I cannot but think back rather longingly to the atmosphere described by a French visitor just a century ago: "Great silence reigns in its paved courtyards and chapels, frequented by the occasional visitor, by a monk fond of solitude, by an old woman with a shaved head who has come to eke out her widowhood in the shade of the monasteries." "I have often mistaken a living Siamese for a statue, especially in these calm and tranquil *wats*, where no noise is heard, where everyone walks gently, with bare feet, furtively," the Belgian writer Emile Jottrand added.

Eight

WAT SAKET AND THE GOLDEN MOUNT

Bangkok's Wat Saket was founded during the Ayudhya era and restored by King Rama II who liked to stop at the temple to bathe on his return from the battlefield. The consecration ceremony that took place in November 1801 was a splendid affair funded by the royal treasury. A European visitor was quite taken by it: "the crackling of burning sheaves and the joyous tumult of the crowds swept the clouds away, and the moon, appearing under her white parasol, was charmed by such a spectacle and halted in her path to observe it." Numerous flowering berry trees were planted in the temple grounds for the inauguration and silver coins were hung from their branches. Fireworks illuminated the Klong Mahanak and surrounding canals that had been recently dug.

The king watched the week-long public festivities from a specially constructed pavilion on the new canal, which had been excavated at his command as "a place where the people could go boating and singing and reciting poems during the high-water season, just like the customs observed in the former capital of Ayudhya." Boating festivals at the end of the monsoon season featured special boat songs; their internal rhythms were devised to accompany the timing of the oarsmen. Many praise birds, flowers and fish. Others sing of the beauty and the desire for young women.

The monks who lived nearby strove to rid themselves of all desire. The orderly disposition of their large colony of cells (*kuti*) is reminiscent of the famous medieval plan for the Monastery of St. Gallen although the Swiss dormitory was a fraction of the size. Every ordained monk has a private room at Wat Saket with a small patio in front. Prior to the arrival of electricity in the late nineteenth century, foreigners found nighttime views of the *kuti* especially picturesque. Each window was hung with a small lantern that "sways up and down like the shaving mugs of our barbers," remarked Jottrand in 1898. To his great surprise, "In one of these houses, I saw a starkly illuminated portrait of William II."

PLACE OF DEATH

Wat Saket holds a popular annual fair in November when the public pays respect to special relics (a copy of the Buddha's canine tooth is displayed that, through special consecration, is believed to have the same votive value of the real tooth). The mount is aglow with light. It is a Buddhist funfair in a place that once reeked of death.

Since cremation was not permitted within the city wall Wat Saket encompassed a government-sponsored cremation ground for the poor and destitute of Bangkok until 1904 when the practice was abolished for the sake of hygiene. Its records chart the crowded city's public health crises. Disease was rampant. There was no water supply (except at the royal palace), no form of modern medical control, and people threw everything in the canals. The mortality rate among young children was especially high.

Cholera victims (and others who had died unnatural deaths) were usually buried for a month or more before cremation to prevent their spirits from haunting. This was also good sanitation. As a local newspaper noted in 1899, "Earth is the most potent disinfectant known." But during the terrible cholera epidemics of the nineteenth century burial was impossible. In 1873 alone 6,600 deaths were reported. Great numbers of corpses were brought to the courtyard of Wat Saket where they were left exposed to packs of pariah dogs and hordes of vultures. Indeed, burial or the abandonment of the body to dogs or vultures inspired a particular horror in Buddhists who believed that the body must then pass through countless forms of the lower orders of creation before it could again occupy a human body.

A Buddhist cremation is generally a rare combination of ancient ritual, festivity and sometimes largesse as well. Jottrand, who attended a royal cremation in 1898, wrote in his diary.

> We went to glance at the diverse courtyards in which there have been all sorts of celebrations for the last three days, theatre, dance, dinners, etc. Then, like the others who had been invited, we shake hands with the master of the house who, seeing us empty-handed, gives us all a small lemon in which there is a lottery ticket. With that we are sent into the house where, higgledy-piggledy, a mass of gift items comprising the most astonishing collection are found. European trash, umbrellas, betel spittoons, rice platters etc. We are given Siamese jewels made of old money

in the form of small ingots. We express gratitude for them and then leave.

But the indigent brought to Wat Saket were less fortunate in death. The young French Marquis de Beauvoir, who had visited in 1867, left an eye-witness account.

We stood some twenty yards off, so as not to interfere with local super-stitions, and this is what we saw. The body, wrapped in white linen, was taken from the coffin and placed in the kiosque on three rows of dry fagots. The Chao-klein-balat, or chief priest of the talapoins, lighted the funeral pile; the flames arose, and its light added to the first clouds of thick smoke hid all from our eyes; gradually the flames ceased, the smoke disappeared, but the fire continued; then the corpse was seen at the summit, and the flesh crackled horribly amidst the reverent silence of the spectators. But as death had only taken place the night before, the nerves and muscles quivered beneath the roasting fire; the arms worked, the joints moved, the legs contracted and pushed against the fire. If it were not a recognized fact in physical science that a dead cat placed over a fire jumps about like a live frog, we should have thought that the unhappy man had awoke to life. And I must confess that the corpse, rising and throwing about its limbs in convulsive efforts, and seeming to faint away under the agony of the scorching fire, curdled the blood in my veins. Oh! No, I will not die here.

The charnel house was equally macabre but the Marquis was still young enough to leave in good spirits. Back in Paris he had heard tell of a humorous invitation to attend a cremation that was extended to a French-man by the Siamese Ambassador: "Pray come tomorrow punctually at eleven to see my uncle broiled." Now he had seen at first hand that "death produces a very different impression with these people to what it does with us, and all the relations, friends and mutes smoke and chat, joke and laugh while following the procession."

Moving on to the *ubosot* (ordination hall) of Wat Saket, one finds visual pleasure in beautifully carved and mirror-decorated gables. The Chinese-style enclosures for the *bema* stones (that demarcate sacred space) are a festival of pastel colour. The most interesting parts of the interior decoration are the murals on the rear wall depicting the *Maravijaya* (the Buddha who vanquished Mara). Heavenly peace and order dominate the upper half which is divided by two *nagas* surrounding a medallion view of Mount Meru. But all hell breaks loose below where bearded Europeans with three-cornered hats, members of Mara's evil army, are drowned by the flood unleashed by Mae Torani.

Horrid examples of hellish torture on the lower portion of the front wall are a graphic counterpart of the imaginative repertoire of the medieval European monk-painter Hieronymous Bosch. The illustrations are gruesome and their didactic aim was quite explicit, as Jottrand exclaimed: "Without doubt an advertisement for cremation!" For him the air itself was often an unpleasant *memento mori* : "We are rather close to Wat Saket, and when the wind directs the smoke of the pyres in our direction, we are sometimes inconvenienced by it."

Foreigners often went up to the Golden Mount for fresher air. Had this huge structure been constructed in England it might well have been classed as a folly. But not in flat Bangkok where the ersatz hill, with the temple looming on top, is imbued with historical and religious significance. King Rama II determined that the Golden Mount should replicate a similar landmark in Ayudhya and he appealed to faithful Buddhists to make donations of timber logs for its foundation. Although several thousand of them were solidly laid, the soft, marshy ground broke under the weight of the large structure which collapsed before it was completed and the grand project was abandoned. King Mongkut later had a small *chedi* housing a Buddha relic built on top of the mud and brick mount. The last reconstruction was undertaken at the command of King Rama V as a fitting chamber to house a precious relic of Buddha brought from a site near Lumbini on the Nepalese border where the Buddha was born. A Siamese monk, Phra Jinvaransa (formerly Prince Prisdang Jumsai), by chance made a pilgrimage to the site in 1897 soon after it was excavated by an English farmer who owned the land. The relic, comprising pieces of charred bones, was kept in an urn on which a Pali inscription clearly states that it contains the Lord Buddha's remains which belonged to his family, the Sakya. The errant monk, who had previously been accredited to the Court of St. James, had no qualms in writing to the British government in India with a request that the holy bones be presented as a gift to His Majesty of Siam as head of an independent Buddhist nation.

VANTAGE POINT

The Golden Mount marked the entrance to the old royal city precincts guarded by a watch tower (Pom Mahakan). Its strategic advantage prompted anxious nobles to urge King Rama V to demolish it in 1893 so that it could not be seized by the French during a blockade of the river. Their alternative idea was to mount it with cannons that could, if necessary, be volleyed onto the foreign ships in the river. Rama V wisely desisted but ordered watchmen on the mount with flags and a signal to send the alert if any enemy approached and to block access to anyone without a special permit. For the next five years foreigners were denied vertical escape from the flat city provided by its only hill and the wide-open views to the "jungle-clad" interior of the east and the Gulf of Siam on the west that it provided.

After the Golden Mount was once again accessible the Belgian legal advisor Jottrand, who lived nearby, liked to go up for the view.

> From the hill... which we climbed two days ago, the city looks like a forest with a tree-cover through which the many roofs emerge here and there. Towards the countryside, the vast rice and sugar cane fields extend, crossed by buffaloes that walk with a heavy gait and reflect the air of a hippopotamus—mounted behind their necks one sees their keeper seated on their backs.
>
> The stream divides the city by a majestic curve. An immense waterway where traffic is as intense as in the streets and likewise bordered with stores, workshops, banks, offices, consulates and legations. Countless klongs end in it and form a close network of small waterways on which one sails past an uninterrupted series of houses on pillars, or floating houses that are often stores with properly aligned displays. Chinese junks, small rowing barges, rowboats, steam-launches and sampans cross, avoid each other, join, and overtake, just like in any street with heavy traffic.

The hillock of the Golden Mount, originally covered with bricks and plastered, gave the appearance of "a great rock" overrun with trees and vegetation. In 1957 it was finally girded in a thick mantle of concrete, but moss-covered vestiges of the earlier foundation give it an antique feel. A twin stamp set issued by the Thai Post Office in 1960 shows the Roman Colosseum, an ancient masterpiece of engineering, and its Asian counterpart: Bangkok's Golden Mount.

Although it has been humbled by a towering cityscape since the 1960s, a climb up the wide spiral stairway to the top is highly recommended. Almost immediately you feel as if you are on a hallowed pilgrimage route leading past rock gardens, a small waterfall, niches protecting statues of Buddhist ascetics, Chinese memorials with ashes of the dead and old frangipani trees sheltering the *nok gaw gaw* bird (note that speakers along the path transmit interminable taped lectures by the abbot of the temple).

After climbing 320 steps up to the entrance, the interior may seem a bit disappointing but the draughts blowing through the large windows lining the walls provide welcome relief from the heat. At the centre, directly under the great *chedi* on the top floor, lies the reliquary surrounded by a circular passage. Its surface is encased by layers and layers of thin gold leaf applied by the devout for more than a century.

A narrow stairway leads to the summit where one is almost blinded by the reflection from the thousands of small gold mosaic tiles that cover the huge *chedi*. The 360-degree view from the four sides of the terrace gives a more human panorama of the city than any view from the skyscrapers. Most of the landmarks can be identified on a clear day but it helps to have binoculars.

North: Klong Mahanak, Wat Saket neighborhood, government/UN buildings, King Rama VII Museum, King Rama VI Suspension Bridge, Hua Lamphong Train Station

South: Wat Rajnadda, Loha Prasat, Giant Swing, Wat Suthat, City Hall, National Theatre, National Museum, Amulet Market, Sanam Luang, Temple of the Emerald Buddha and Grand Palace, Wat Pho

East: Wat Saket with monks' quarters (running L-shape from east to west), Chinatown, skyscrapers of Sathorn business district, high-rise hotels on the river

West: Shophouses, Klong Ong Ang, Mahanak Bridge, Rajdamnern Avenue, Queen's Gallery, Democracy Monument, Chitralada Palace.

Nine

ERAWAN SHRINE

Popular animist culture, Hinduism, Buddhism and the sex industry overlap in Bangkok like the folds of an elephant's hide. Every evening young sex workers from the Turkish baths at the end of my *soi* proffer gifts of jasmine garlands and other small items at the colourful spirit house adjacent to the dull building. The Thai belief in guardian spirits is a strong part of the national culture. Spirit houses called *San Phra Phoom* abound in Bangkok in all types and material. They propitiate and honour the guardian spirits (*jao tii*) of the land that have been displaced by construction works.

Most of these miniature Thai temples consist of a shoe box-like room and an outer platform set at eye-level on a single post. At the rear of the inner chamber is a standing angel, a *devada*, with a leaf-shaped halo of light around the head. Symbolic effigies of the land gods are included as well as little figurines of elephants and dancers for their entertainment. Apartment owners or shopkeepers often take turns supplying the spirits with gifts—incense sticks, flowers, candles, sweets, Mekong Whisky, soft drinks. In all of my wanderings throughout Bangkok I never saw a single abuse of cultic sites. "Disbelieve but do not disrespect," is a well-heeded Thai admonition.

Other types of good spirits inhabit the natural habitat—mountains, forests, caves, water and trees. My preferred shrines are the old *bodhi* trees wrapped in multi-colour gauze. Locals bring offerings to the spirits, not only food and drinks, but also lingams—symbolic phalli—associated with the Hindu god Shiva and said to bring fertility and good luck in business. Should you be near the Intercontinental Hotel on Wittayu Road, follow a brick garden path lined by knee-high wooden phalluses to the tree shrine of Goddess Tuptim encircled with pastel gauze. A mini-Stonehenge of phalluses of various sizes has been erected around the shrine. Most are made of wood; some are as high as ten feet. A number of the grandest are supported by two wooden legs that have large "testicles" hanging like ripe jack fruit. Garlands of flowers, soft drinks and toiletries are left by the favour seekers.

Religious ceremonies, royal rituals and everyday activities have shaped Bangkok, continuing to provide a certain sense of community and continuity. While it is true that the globalizing market economy and modernity have dislocated social relations, common memories are still attached to physical sites that ground residents in time and history. Urban sociologist Richard O'Connor sees Bangkok as a "patchwork of named places" for its Thai residents. Their mental map gives the city its everyday popular image, in contrast to the official, bureaucratic one, or the tourist itinerary. "Wherever people congregate—whether to live, work, shop, travel or make merit—that area is a noted place. It is not that activity comes first and prominence later, but that the two feed on each other and so make places busy, active and alive."

A widespread cultural disposition to sacralize places believed to be imbued with intrinsic power is evident throughout the city. A visit to the revered shrine of beautiful twin sisters on *soi* Suan Phlu draws many Thais heading to the immigration office as they are said to help with visas and to bring good luck in the lottery. Of course, age confers great importance on certain cultic sites. So does the association with royalty. Popular belief that King Chulalongkorn returns to earth two days a week draws regular crowds to his equestrian monument in the Royal Plaza to petition for help and pay their proper respects with candles and fragrant flowers.

RELIGION: THAI FUSION FASHION

Kukrit Pramoj once explained that Buddhism would never have been adopted in Thailand had it not been for Hinduism. The subtle balance between the two was like a good martini, he said, "You call it a dry martini. And then you wash the glass with martini, wipe it dry and just drink the gin."

Much of the Hindu mythology of India was adopted in Buddhist Thailand, as seen in the numerous images of mythological creatures, such as the elephant Erawan, Brahma's mount. But mythology was popularized in Thai fusion fashion. "The Hindu gods have become characters in fable and drama to the Thai," writes a distinguished manuscript scholar," but none the less potent characters of great renown. Brahmanic rites have been retained from ancient times and amicably coexist with Buddhism. As a Bangkok voice explains, "...since Buddhism places emphasis on the ultimate transcendence of earthly cares, there is scope on the popular level for a multitude of beliefs and folk customs that can be relied upon to address more mundane matters."

Drivers raise their hands in a *wai* (bringing the palms together, as in prayer, to show respect) to the statue of Brahma at the famous Erawan Shrine (intersection of Ploenchit and Rajadamri Roads). This is one of the most celebrated corners in Bangkok. On the opposite street the posh Gaysorn Plaza shopping mall looks sterile by comparison, though a gilded divinity blesses it from the roof. The nearby Central World Plaza is also under protection from sinister forces. When it was first built in the mid-1980s a Feng Shui consultant suggested appropriate protective features for the businesses in the building—a large mirrored pyramid, an open spatial zone before the building, a shrine to Phra Siam Devathiraj, guardian spirit of the king and the country. Every major building in the area has a shrine to a divinity, seeking to placate land spirits displaced when foundations were laid.

For locals, a dark shadow was formerly cast upon the Pathumwan area by its grim past. Prior to its transformation into a bustling crossroads of commerce, shackled criminals were put on public display in the area. It was also a detention centre for prisoners brought in by boat from the vassal state of Cambodia.

When the government decided that the city needed a large deluxe hotel for a big international conference in the early 1950s, the offer to build was put out to tender but there were no takers and the government took it on. Construction of the Erawan Hotel was plagued by a host of misfortunes that rattled the superstitious workers—accidents and inexplicable delays. Finally, after a shipload of Carrara marble from Italy was lost at sea they refused to return to work until the land spirits were suitably appeased. A famous Brahmanic astrologer was brought in for consultation. After calculating that the foundation stone for the hotel had been laid at an inauspicious time, he recommended that the site be placed under the protection of the Brahma, the most important Hindu deity. A sculpture was made of the finest materials and installed under an ornate gilded canopy. Construction of the hotel then proceeded without a hitch. Each of Brahma's four faces represents one of his special virtues—kindness, mercy, sympathy and impartiality—which the public seek to enlist in gaining a personal favour.

Not everyone is convinced of the efficacy of the Brahma of the Erawan Shrine. Wanit Jarunggidana's short story *Michigan Test* (1974) describes the absurd adventures that befall him in his quest for a passport and student visa to join his brother in California. Officials at the American Embassy in Bangkok inform him that the visa is conditional upon his passing the "Michigan Test" for language proficiency. When a friend advises him to seek help from the Brahma, he responds: "He's been standing there with his four arms in the air for God knows how many years, and he still can't wiggle them. How could he possibly be any help?"

Many Bangkokians would simple smile at Khun Wanit's blasphemy as their approach is one of gaiety, reverence and hope: tables are stocked with teak elephants and fragrant Thai wreaths as offerings. Bargaining with images "suffuses the Thai world view" as Marlane Guelden writes. If a wish is granted, grateful supplicants must fulfill vows. The shrine is considered an auspicious place to gain merit and devotees purchase lottery tickets and release little sparrows from their cages (they are usually recaptured).

Another sign of gratitude for a wish granted is to hire dazzling dancers dressed like Siamese angels to dance for Brahma. Ernest Young, a British educator in Bangkok at the end of the twentieth century, did not understand traditional Siamese dance but was greatly impressed by their contortions.

The ladies go through a series of posturing evolutions euphemistically called dances. They are nothing more than extraordinary contortions of the body accompanied by equally strange motions of the limbs. The fingers are bent backwards from the joints, and the arms backwards from the elbows in a way no untrained person could possible imitate. From early childhood the fingers and arms are daily bent out of place until finally they become, as it were, double jointed. The actresses whiten their faces with powder and do not relieve their ghostly appearance with any touch of colour. They fasten on the finger-tips artificial gold finger-nails of abnormal length.

It is said that the Hindu god appreciates topless dancing that takes place late at night, but this is an urban legend as the dancers all leave before midnight. For the past twenty years they have come from Trok Nang Ram (Lane of the Dancing Ladies) near Thanon Lan Luang, a community of performing artists founded by Rama III. As the market for shrine dancers is very limited, competition is intense among troupes. Slim figures and elaborate costumes have to be well kept. But for those who dance at this little corner of the world, the significant financial rewards are worth bearing the heat, heavy costume and tedious replay. Dancing for a god is a very unusual way to earn a living.

If you're in Las Vegas, visit the 8,500-pound replica of the shrine outside Caesar's Palace, dedicated in 1984 by Buddhist monks. Thai dancers were brought in to give an extra boost to gamblers' luck.

Part Three

CITY OF MERCHANTS AND MISSIONARIES

Ten

SAMPHENG LANE

The near complete destruction of the Kingdom of Ayudhya by the Burmese in 1767 had shattered and scattered the population of Siam. When King Taksin founded the new royal capital in Thonburi he welcomed immigrants from the south-eastern seaboard of China—he was himself of Chinese Tiochiu ethnicity. Poor Chinese were a reliable and cheap source of labour; and enterprising Tiochiu merchant families, who prospered on a prime piece of riverfront on the east bank of the Chao Phraya river, generated welcome revenue for the war chest. Their leader, Phraya Choduek, one of the king's top men, was the chief officer responsible for foreign relations east of Siam, principally China.

They were asked to move in 1782 when Rama I desired that land to build the Grand Palace, a symbol of his new dynasty. The population of about five thousand received a ribbon-shaped allotment along the riverfront in exchange—Sampheng, a very small area of land (about three-quarters of a square mile). That area is the rich commercial vein of the oldest and most prosperous of the world's Chinatowns and arguably the most authentic. Although the Chinese superficially adapted to their host culture, and their collective history with the Siamese is tightly intertwined, many aimed to preserve their distinct ethnic integrity. A number of Chinese merchants and entrepreneurs were, however, absorbed into the upper echelons of courtly society. Following age-old practice, the wealthiest of the merchant lords offered their nubile daughters as royal consorts with the hope of titles of rank as reward. A court poet in sixteenth-century England might have been pleased to claim as his own a lovely sonnet composed by King Rama III for one of his favourites (translated by Edward Van Roy).

> Lovely, fragrant Chinese flower,
> You have wealth as I have power.
> Though my courtiers all may glower,
> 'Tis my heart that you devour.

Rama III was enamoured with all things Chinese, and Sampheng became the major port for Sino-Thai maritime trade during his reign, an era of rapid economic development in Siam. During the 1820s it was reckoned that about 7,000 immigrants began to arrive annually. Peasants from what are now the Fujian and Guangdong provinces in south-eastern China migrated to the kingdom where they found unparalleled opportunities as merchants, shopkeepers, artisans, craftsmen, planters and sojourners. The British envoy John Crawfurd observed that migrants were "the most valuable importation from China to Siam".

King Mongkut encouraged Chinese immigration to meet the manpower demands of the new, western-oriented trade system that followed the signing of the Bowring Treaty. Even so, he barred Chinese women with the apparent aim of injecting more energy into the more languid Siamese bloodstream. In 1889 the abolition of bond serfdom or debt slavery further increased the demand for cheap Chinese hired labour.

By the mid-nineteenth century Bangkok's Chinatown had become the nodal point for trade with the outside world. With a steady influx of immigrants expanding to meet the volume of trade, Sampheng Lane became a major centre of trade and capital investment in Southeast Asia. After 1862 it was linked up with New Road via Songwat Road, and this area quickly mushroomed to encompass a myriad of stores stocked with gold, hardware, cheap clothing and fabrics, toys, stationery, traditional herbal medicine and expensive oriental delicacies. Indians and Muslims set up shops nearby and built a Sikh temple and a Sunni mosque.

Locals called Chinatown Yaowarat, the name of a thoroughfare created as a third arterial in 1891 following a huge conflagration. Fires regularly swept through the clusters of crowded wooden houses along the river; caused either by carelessness in cooking or by acts of arson from those anxious to make insurance claims before debts were due at the end of the Chinese lunar year. A foreign resident gives a vivid eyewitness report of a fire in 1898 published in *The Bangkok Times Weekly Mail.*

> The fire, spurred by the wind, advanced almost before our very eyes, on both sides of the road, like a battle order. Everywhere, Chinese and Siamese ran away in panic from their houses, carrying with them as much as they could, pushing or transporting the most diverse objects, without proper judgment: rich pottery and old planks, furniture and iron fences, pigs with their four legs bound together, ducklings clutched tightly, tattered clothes, full or empty bottles, in one word, their every

possession. In the street, an agitation as in an ant's nest reigned; a jumble of things and moving people, turning in all directions.

The sporadic conflagrations continued until General Sarit Thanarat, who was prime minister from 1958 to 1962, had a culprit summarily executed in the grounds of a temple before a huge crowd of spectators. The incidence of arson diminished dramatically afterwards.

TRADE, DIVISION OF LABOUR AND IMMIGRATION

The Siamese aristocracy enjoyed a system of land tenure with royal approval. This was a clever system of abstract land tenure which accompanied a title. The titled person did not actually own the land, as in feudal Europe, although he may have had a document indicating nominal ownership of a surface area. All land belonged to the king until the Fifth Reign when title-deeds came into being.

Most of the Siamese people were wedded to cultivation and disdained commerce. Men were compelled to provide the state with four months' annual *corvée* labour. Exempt from this were monks, slaves, all public functionaries, fathers who had three sons of serviceable age and Chinese (who paid a triennial poll tax instead). Trade in Bangkok was wisely left to the Chinese commercial genius and capacity for hard work. Until 1912 when queues—pigtails—were officially done away with in China, Siamese subjects sometimes grew them to avoid higher taxes, though the government had penalties for these "fake Chinese".

The division of labour once strongly reflected regional lines that can still be detected today. Hokkien, the first Chinese to arrive, were carpenters, odd-job labourers, proprietors of retail shops. Tiochiu, the largest Chinese dialect group in the city, were mostly vegetable wholesalers and hawkers. Goldsmith shops, restaurants and teahouses were run by the Cantonese. Hakkas ran shoe stores and apothecaries.

Chinese merchants and hired labourers were valued by the Siamese aristocracy for their ability to procure and transport valuable commodities. They also were the middlemen between western firms in Bangkok and the indigenous population, acting as purchasing agents for tin, rubber, shellac and agricultural goods and often becoming very rich in the process. Nearly all the bilateral trade was in Chinese hands; their homeland was Siam's biggest trading partner. Siam exported rice, pepper and sappan wood to

China and imported tea, copper and luxury goods such as silver, silk and porcelain for the king and wealthy Chinese merchants in the city. Chinese boat builders were recruited to build junks since these could be made more cheaply in Bangkok than in China or India because of the abundance of hard wood. Chinese blacksmiths supplied eastern India with large quantities of *quallies* or iron pans. They also dominated commercial mining and the production of sugar, rice and alcohol and controlled the lucrative franchises controlling gambling, opium, alcohol and the lottery for the government.

The Chinese financed their commercial ventures with gold; it was secure, portable and easily convertible. Gold hoarding was a favoured method of saving for the Chinese who did not trust the banking system. Dozens of identical-looking gold shops that look like clothes pegs on a line have been passed down from one generation to the next. The Gold Traders Association, located in the Gold Trade Centre building along Yaowarat Road at Talaat Kao, provides the standards of purity fixed at 96.5 per cent but the industry is rife with stories of adulteration, deception and "blood" gold.

Already by the start of the twentieth century Bangkok was a city dominated by the Chinese. *The Bangkok Directory of 1904* estimated the population of Bangkok at 400,000-500,000 divided as follows:

Chinese 200,000
Siamese 150,000
Peguans (Mons) 80,000
Malays 30,000
Cambodians and Annamites 20,000
Laotians 15, 000
Indians, Klings, Pathans 4,000
Burmese 3,000
Europeans, Americans, Japanese and Koreans 400

Chinese dominance of commerce and marketing, from watch repair to prostitution, was fully sealed by this date, as an English writer confirmed.

They are everything and everywhere. The greater part of trade and much of the industry, large and small scale, is in their hands. We have seen them as printers and jewellery salesmen. They are also cabinet-makers, blacksmiths, watch repairmen, electricians, pharmacists, physicians, dentists, restaurant owners, laundry men, tailors, and shoe repairmen. There is no employment in which they are not found, and no way of making money they do not attempt. They are in the state administration, the post and telegraph offices, the Customs House, the railway, and the penitentiary services. They form the majority in the banks and European commercial concerns. They work as cooks, valets, and coachmen. They drag rickshaws. They are universal. Some speak English. Almost all of them quickly learn the smattering of Siamese needed for daily use. Their children attend the schools open to them and easily take first place.

In 1910 five hundred opium dens were closed; during the same year Chinese workers conducted the first-ever strike. The police were unable to restore order and the army was called in to quell riots. Crown Prince Vajiravudh was deeply distressed at the ineffectual police response and so he devised an unlikely exercise that he called "Catching Chinese", which took place in the gardens of the Saranrom Palace. Royal pages were divided into two groups: the "Chinese" and the "Police". The Chinese went out to mind miniature shops that he had built in the garden. If there was an infraction the police brought the lawbreaker to the Magistrate, the role played by Vajiravudh. If convicted, the defendant would be sent to a nearby "jail" on the premises.

Apart from King Rama VI, who was crowned on 23 October 1910, the Chakri dynasty never tried to hide its Chinese blood; the royals had always kept on good terms with the Chinese community in Bangkok. The king, who seems to have contracted the fear of "Yellow Peril" from his British allies, is alleged to have penned a notorious pamphlet entitled "The Jews of the East" (1914) in which the Chinese were castigated for their alleged love of money, restrictive trade practices and refusal to adapt to Thai culture. During the next decade the king ordered the government to extinguish the flames ignited by Chinese nationalism. Chinese newspapers accused of inflammatory and Bolshevik tendencies were closed down by royal edict. Ethnic Chinese were denied access to twenty-six professions designated exclusively for the Siamese.

At the same time the king instituted Cheng Men, the Chinese Ancestral Worship for the Court, a ceremony which continues down to this day. He also stipulated that when he died he wished to have the full Chinese funeral ceremony in addition to the traditional Hindu-Buddhist one.

Nearly forty thousand Chinese are recorded to have arrived in the city from 1936-37. Their junks passed a city of royal power—the Royal Palace and Wat Pho—and a city of promise—the new railway bridge built by King Rama V, infantry barracks, manicured trees along New Road. A few minutes later, after thousands of miles at sea, they finally arrived at Sampheng. We can only imagine their response to their first sight of a place that was described by a visitor as "a confusion, a rabble of houses, a piled-up, wholesale display of hovels, huts, boxes, and soldiers' huts under Chinese roofs with Chinese gables and glazed tiles."

After the Japanese devastation of southern China during the Second World War most Chinese immigrants who flooded into Thailand arrived with nothing but "a mat and a pillow" (*seua pheun morn bai*). Seventy per cent of the immigrants were women and children. This reversed earlier processes of assimilation and reinforced the ethnic and economic strength of the Chinese community in Bangkok, thereby generating more concern in government circles. Anxiety was exacerbated by the communist revolution of 1949 that led to a huge influx of Shanghai Chinese. In 1950 there were estimated to be over three million Chinese in Thailand, or roughly 17 per cent of the total population.

Increasing Thai nationalism during and after the war led to the introduction of aggressive discriminatory legislation and economic harassment of the Chinese, despite the fact that most Thai families claimed Chinese ancestry. Prime Minister Phibul himself was of Chinese descent. Ethnic Chinese were urged to adopt Thai surnames. Chinese schools and newspapers were closed, Chinese political parties were prohibited, and the government forbade the raising of funds for China's nationalist resistance.

But Chinatown remained the undisputed emporium of the city. When Germaine Krull, post-war proprietor of the Oriental, set out to find refubishments for her tattered hotel, she immediately headed over to Sampheng, "one of the richest streets… [in Bangkok and] fortunes amounting to millions are accumulated in its tiny shops."

SHRINES AND TEMPLES: SAN JAO SIEN KHONG AND WAT TRAIMIT

Chinatown is dotted with numerous bright and colourful ancestral shrines to the Chinese pantheon of household gods. Prows of vessels display an image of the seafaring goddess *Mazu* (Respected Great Aunt), revered as the protector of sailors. Soon after arrival the immigrants would visit her shrine bearing offerings—flowers, incense, mandarins—in gratitude for a safe journey. More expensive gifts were given on her birthday in the third lunar month including performances of Chinese opera.

If you walk along Songwat Road down soi Phanurangsi and left just past a small Chinese shrine you will come upon a large temple honouring San Jao Sien Khong or the Town Deity. Like most Chinese temples, it is painted bright red and has lavish gold altars decorated with peacock fans, gaudy statues of warriors, grimacing ceramic animals in high-relief, bright Confucian images, incense and horoscopes, lanterns and candles. Until the end of the nineteenth century families of wealthy Chinese who wanted their corpses sent back to China brought offerings to this shrine to request a "spiritual passport" for their deceased relative. This guaranteed that the soul would be unperturbed by other spirits on the sea journey back to China. Final send-offs could be quite impressive, as a local newspaper reported in 1892.

> Some stir was caused this morning by a Chinese funeral procession on an unusually elaborate scale. The wife of the teak merchant Lam Sam died a couple of years ago and her body is now being taken back to China for burial. At the Oriental Hotel landing the coffin was placed on a funeral barge amid the deafening noise of bands and cracker firing, and the procession was continued by water, the funeral barge being followed down the river by a number of boats, with no end of bands and banners.

For prosperity in this life, many Chinese also invoked the Lord Buddha at Wat Traimit (The Three Friends), a small Thai-Chinese temple, squashed between the junctions of Yaowarat, New Road and Hua Lamphong train station. This temple houses one of the wonders of Bangkok— a gigantic Buddha figure weighing five and a half tons that was reported by the *Guinness Book of Records* to be the largest Buddha image made of gold in the world. The story goes that workmen extending Bangkok's port in 1957 found a huge stucco image of Buddha, dating from the period six centuries earlier when the Thai capital was in Sukhothai. As it was being moved it fell to the ground and cracked, offering a glimpse of the gold within. The thick plaster coating was carefully peeled away by the workers, and the monks who had assembled were astonished when the exquisitely formed figure emerged. Another chance discovery—a key in the base— showed how ingeniously it was constructed. It unlocks nine parts of the body for removal including the neck, the arms and the Flame of Knowledge on top of the Buddha's head.

The temple's carnival atmosphere suits the Chinese tourists who flock here to make oblations. Religion and commerce being lock and key in Thailand, the temple has its own currency exchange and three or four ATM machines.

VICE "FARMS"

Commerce and vice separated the day from the night in Chinatown. There simply was not much else to do after sunset. One area of Sampheng came to be known as the Green Light District after the green lanterns hung before "tea houses" offering girlie shows and cheap sex, mainly procured from Cantonese women, but there were prostitutes for every ethnic group in various lanes. After 1913 new legislation, aimed at preventing rampant venereal disease, brothel owners had to pay a fee to register their premises, to keep an official list of all employees and to display the house's registration number next to the glowing lanterns.

Alexander MacDonald, former US intelligence officer in Bangkok during the Second World War, stayed on after the armistice because he felt drawn to the city's sensual pleasures. One of the most famous brothels was owned by Old Lady Faeng, as Macdonald called her. This famous procuress wanted to make merit for her next life and received permission from King Rama V to build a temple, Wat Kanikaphon, just off Yaowarart and Thanon Plabplachai, which originally bore her name. The city council later changed the street name, apparently incurring the wrath of her spirit, which supposedly still haunts the place. Old Lady Faeng can be visited today on the opposite side of the temple entrance where her bust is enshrined in a small niche with a Thai *chada* (head-gear) to hide her baldness as the effigy is actually that of an old Buddhist monk disguised to look like her with make up. She is an ageing beauty draped with accordion-pleated red and gold scarves, fake garlands and shiny baubles.

The notorious *Tuek Kow Chan* (Nine-Storey Building) at the corner of Yaowarat and Thanon Mangkorn promised a hedonistic adventure that beats anything Hugh Hefner ever invented—as far as I know. After an "apéritif" on the ground floor, the sybarite ascended to further sensory pleasures, each one more provocative than the last. Ultimately he arrived at the summit, a "heaven" and a zone of carnality one is left to imagine.

Birds' nest and shark's skin soup and sex with virgins were the anti-age treatment for wealthy Chinese, especially the opium barons, and still have a powerful draw. Despite legislation introduced after the mid-nineteenth century banning the sale and consumption of opium, rival secret societies smuggled opium grown in India and sold by British merchants who were immune from prosecution.

King Mongkut abolished the royal monopolies that had provided the fiscal basis of the royal administration in 1855. To fill the coffers he auctioned off franchises to trading syndicates formed by Chinese merchants—opium, the lottery, gambling and alcohol (but he did not aim to control prostitution). These "farms", strictly forbidden to ethnic Thais, generated between forty and fifty per cent of all government revenues in the latter half of the century. In 1883 there were 263 opium dens in Bangkok. In 1907 the government knocked out the Chinese middlemen and took over management of the opium trade. By 1917 there were 3,000 dens and shops in the whole country which suggests that the government was making a windfall profit.

Opium (*chandu*) could be found anywhere in Bangkok, from rich Chinese mansions to decrepit back rooms. Chinese labourers lived in cramped and squalid conditions, often without proper sanitation or ventilation. Opium offered some relief after a long day's slog, easing aches and pains and lulling the user into a narcotic daze. "For the price of a pipe they get company, entertainment, café service, a bed and brief oblivion from the drab, exhausting labour of the day," wrote Australian writer, Norman Bartlett. He describes a flourishing opium den in Chinatown in the late 1950s.

> The entrance is through a narrow shop front in a busy street. The ordinary passer-by would never notice anything out of the ordinary about the shop or its customers. Beyond the screen at the back of the shop you step into another world. There are three huge floors, one above the other, with four hundred couches in narrow cubicles divided by busy passages. Each cubicle accommodates four smokers who lie on smoke-browned cane mats polished by years of use. The smokers are mostly Chinese but Thai girls frequent this popular divan to massage the clients or to tell fortunes with cards. The whole area is subdued bedlam. There are no soft lights or silk hangings or oriental serenity. An endless process flows along a gangway between the cubicles, customers, boy selling cool drinks, offering flowers, brandishing books of lottery tickets, noodle-sellers and other food vendors, fortune-tellers, *naklengs* [hoodlums] on the look-out for likely victims and disguised policemen all ears for useful information. Radios blare and you can hear the rattle of mahjong sticks and the rhythmic whine of an itinerant *likay* show.

Seven or eight thousand smokers per day provided huge revenue for the licensees. And there was a coin to be turned almost everywhere.

Swatches of cloth used to wipe out the opium pipes after use were sold to the very poor for a pittance and placed under the tongue for a mild high.

Traditional rivalries between different provinces represented in Chinatown led to numerous hostilities as well as regular conflicts between Chinese opium dealers and the Thai state. International opposition gradually forced the government to close its opium houses but they persisted in Chinatown until the early 1960s.

Gambling was the favourite pastime in Chinatown; sixteen licensed houses were assigned to concessionaires by public auction and tax farmers generated great sums for the government. The main gambling houses at Pratoo Sam Yod were open day and night. From all reports they were grubby places, devoid of comfort. Charles Buls went inside one during his sojourn in 1901:

> We enter a gambling place. It is a vast, grubby hall, the roof of which is supported by wooden poles. Petroleum lamps hang from the beams, lighting an oval mat of 5 to 6 meters diameter around which all the ethnographic specimens of the world are squatting, but especially Chinese and Siamese. A large cross divides the mat into four quarters, marked from 1 to 4. In front of the banker, sits a quantity of beans or cowries. He randomly takes a handful. Meanwhile the gamblers have put their bets in the quarter of their choice. Rien ne va plus! The banker starts putting down the beans, four at a time; then counts the numbers remaining. The quarter number corresponding to the number of beans remaining wins. The banker takes the bets from the quarter opposite the winning game and the others neither lose nor win. The winner has its stake doubles... The Chinese loses or wins without showing the slightest emotion. The Siamese laughs or makes a gesture of disappointment.

This was not a new vice. Three centuries earlier the Jesuit Abbé de La Loubère had observed at Ayudhya that "the Siamese love Gambling to such an Excess as to ruin themselves, and lose their Liberty, or that of their Children: for in this Country, whoever has not the wherewith to satisfy his Creditors, sells his Children to discharge the Debt; and if this satisfies not, he himself becomes a Slave."

Writing in 1854 Bishop Pallegoix also signalled his frequent distress at the sight of people losing everything they had and then continuing to play for the very clothes they were wearing. But the Chinese were incorrigible, as Paul Morand, a French writer in Bangkok at the end of the century, was quick to note: "Gamblers come to pawn their jewels, their silken robes, their pipes. The more the pipes have been smoked and filled with opium, the more they gain for them. Lotteries, cockfights, fish fights, betting on Shanghai races, ten days journey from here; all are played. Bets are even placed on the number of pips in a melon! It is reported that naval officers, under arrest and confined to their boats continue to play at sea, by signal!"

Gambling had an unlikely impact: stolen goods found their way into some western museums. "When their own property has been squandered they take that belonging to other people, thus producing an endless succession of daily thefts," observed Ernest Young in his *Kingdom of the Yellow Robe* (1898). "The city is full of pawnshops, some streets containing scarcely any other form of business. It is in these places that the Europeans hunt for their frequently stolen property, or search for the curios that are afterwards presented to friends or sold to museums at home."

Chinese New Year was the only day they allowed themselves to close shop. A local journalist wrote an account of 1934's holiday for *The Bangkok Times Weekly Mail*. Following age-old custom, elaborate offerings of Chinese food were offered for the spirits of the ancestors—numerous small bowls filled with all kinds of dishes, dominated by a boiled pig's head or a large joint of pork and duck or fowl on long trays. For drinks, they were presented alcohol made from soya beans. At 3 p.m. homage was paid them in silent prayer. But due to the danger of fire no more fire-crackers were let off as in the old days. The feast was followed by 72 hours of free gambling and when night fell all the gambling houses on Sampheng Lane were illuminated by kerosene flare lamps.

To redress the balance, let me quote from Botan's famous epistolary novel *Letters from Thailand* which, even though it was written in 1969, reflects the traditional view that a *jek* (the pejorative Thai word for a Chinese man) was often welcomed as a spouse because of his earning capacity. Upon hearing of her daughter's plans to marry, a Thai mother exclaims: "Good for you, daughter! Marry a *jek* and you'll eat pork every day; you won't eat dried fish and chase ducks round a pond all your life, like your poor mother."

Grandfather Tan Suan U, in the same novel, vehemently defends the reputation of the Chinese by pointing the finger at the Thais.

> The idea that all Chinese are loud and coarse is as false as the notion that Thais are always smiling. If you live among them you know that is not so. There are sullen pouting Thais, plenty of them! And Thai thugs who hang around bars and coffee shops all day and night hoping for a fight, any excuse to spring at a stranger, and kill him without reason or pity... Yet people praise Thailand as a land of peace, of endless smiles and yellow-robed Buddhist monks; of people whose culture is deeply engrained, and who follow the five moral principles faithfully.

Even the poet Sunthorn Phu in the early 1800s rued this preference:

> At Bang Luang on the small canal, many Chinese are selling pigs.
> Their wives are so young, fair, pretty, and rich it makes me feel shy and small.
> Thai men like me who asked for their hand would be blocked as if by iron bars.
> But if you have money like those Chinese, the bars just melt.

SIGHTS, SMELLS AND SOUNDS OF CHINATOWN TODAY

If you can brave elbow-to-elbow crowds, the hot foul breath of air, porters with laden carts and teetering boxes of merchandise, mopeds on your heels, and an utterly bewildering confusion, you will discover one of the most authentic Chinese communities outside mainland China. The rhythms of daily life can be most closely observed in postage-stamp neighbourhoods in the dense rabbit warren of narrow, crowded streets. Teeming markets (*talaat*) and a profusion of alleyways (*trok*) are crammed with people who live a communal life that does not award high value to personal privacy.

Chinatown has been arguably successful in preserving its identity because it is barely penetrable and very clannish. Extended families of three generations live together in the multi-functional shop-houses that line the streets. During the day the family uses the ground floor where business is done. The upper floor is a mezzanine for sleeping. Residents of the older buildings that once relied for ventilation on circular metal holes drilled

through the walls, now have fans and sometimes air conditioners for relief from the often torrid heat.

Chinatown is still spectacularly deafening both night and day, though it is machine noises that now generally prevail. Travel back a century and it is noise of a different kind that disturbs the sleep of a resident foreigner: "After midnight the successful numbers [of the lottery] are shouted through the streets by Chinese criers, who rival the pariah dogs for making the night hideous," he complained. Piggies who went to the market in the morning gave quite a squeal, as Ernest Young describes.

Their two feet are tied together, and then their hind feet are similarly fashioned. A stout piece of wood is passed under the two loops thus formed, and the pig is carried by two men, each bearing one end of the pole. The animals generally object very strongly to this form of motion, and signify their disgust, and perhaps their pain, by the most heart-rending, ear-piercing shrieks. Thus another set of discordant sounds is added to the medley that roars from morning to night.

The pigs found their way to one of Chinatown's crowded fresh markets. The oldest is Talaat Kao (Old Market) on the opposite side of Talaat Charoen Krung (New Road) from the Talaat Mai (New Market). King Rama I designated the area as a Vietnamese settlement. As waves of Laotians and Cantonese Chinese arrived, the neighbourhood expanded to Bang Rak and the Vietnamese established their own ethnic enclave in Samsen. The Old Market is now Crown Property.

Another famous Chinatown institution is the Thieves Market (Talaat Weng Nakhon Kasem) where stolen goods once changed hands. "According to Siamese law if you shot a thief *you* went to jail and this encouraged the profession," Carol Hollinger wryly reported in 1963. "At night all downstairs windows of middle-class homes were heavily barred and shuttered and many of the finer houses employed Indian night watchmen. Eternal vigilance was the price of too many valuables…" Now the market is awash with cheap electronic merchandise, watches and mobile phones spread out on the street like dry leaves after a sudden storm.

Chinatown by day is best imagined as a huge open-air department store. The aisles are crowded streets and alleyways. The counters are city blocks, fronted by stores crammed to the rafters with an incredible variety of merchandise: cheap textiles, tennis shoes, fake watches, costume jewellery, domestic hardware, automotive parts, plastic toys, traditional medicines, moon cakes, steaming noodle soup, ancient traditional medicines, squirming fish and foodstuffs spilling from jammed stalls.

Soi Charoen Krung 16 (also known as Trok Issaranupha), which leads from Songwat Road to the Talaat Kao, a daily food market for the past two centuries (near the Mahayan Buddhist Wat Mangkorn Kamalawat), is not to be missed. The perfume of star anise rises from huge soup cauldrons. Fish wriggle in big plastic vats. Ambulant clothing dyers balance a cauldron of burning charcoal and a pot of liquid dye. Vendors hawk gooey Thai sweets. Chestnuts roast in fiery stone-filled vats. Smelly dried shrimp spill out from giant plastic bags. Clouds of incense form. Chinese paper lanterns graze the head. Groups of young porters lean on dirty metal dollies and chain smoke. Ancient herbalists sip tea from tiny, chipped cups.

At certain spots along the way you might be tempted to consider Mark Twain's famous quip in *The Innocents Abroad* (1869) about the dank, narrow streets of an old European town. It was a blessing, he said, that the malodorous places were not any wider for if they were, they would hold more. Imagine his olfactory shock had he been in Chinatown in the late nineteenth century. Foreign residents downstream on the river front grumbled regularly in local papers about the rank stink that rose from goose and duck farms, the piggery on Suriwong Road and the buckets of fertile "night soil" collected for sale as manure by poor Chinese from the seventy-nine public latrines in the city. A British resident was almost bowled over by "the most unsurpassed of smells, to which dead dogs, diseased Chinamen, or festering drains all give their contribution."

Captain Lunet de Lajonquière, the French soldier-turned-scholar who visited Chinatown in 1904, remarked upon its robust smells and how "the scent of flowers and fruit, the strong smell of pharmaceuticals, of joss sticks, of food cooked in the open air mingle with these whiffs of rot and with the miasma that rises up from the infected mud at night." It was also the only place in the world where lepers with hideous sores were permitted to beg openly, as a local journalist for the *Bangkok Times Weekly Mail* noted with repugnance at that time.

The rapid modernization of Bangkok around the turn of the century gave a great jolt to the Chinese mercantile families. The disappearance of the junk trade, government closure of the lucrative tax-farms and lack of western expertise made it incumbent to syndicate into other business ventures. Some of the most successful built rice mills, founded shipping companies and banks, invested in land development projects along what remained of the old canals. By 1912 only one of the eighty-four rice mills was western-owned; the Chinese owned more than half of them.

Many of the mills had moved from the outskirts of Bangkok to the city "centre" on the west bank of Thonburi. Their tall chimneys blackened by thick smoke from burning rice husks were like ugly industrial stalagmites that jarred many visitors who had come to see glittering temples and golden palace roofs.

By comparison with the upward expansion of Bangkok Chinatown is still on a linear vector, although the horizontal ascent has begun with a number of major high-rises under construction in the area. To Bangkok native Suthon Sukphisit, "they seem like forest vegetation pushing even higher to gain access to the retreating sunlight."

Eleven

NEW ROAD

"Cities are by origin, nature and development un-ecological entities," writes Singaporean geographer Victor Savage. "As artifacts of human endeavour, cities are engineered landscapes developed for human comfort, activities and interests." His observations are borne out by the dramatic changes to the natural landscape in Bangkok after the Bowring treaty opened Siam to international trade at mid-nineteenth-century.

By that date Bangkok had a population of about 400,000 but no major thoroughfares. Shortly after the treaty foreign consuls petitioned King Rama IV for "a place to take the air of an evening." *The Royal Chronicles* for 1861 recorded:

> In the third month the foreign consuls all signed their names to a petition which they presented to the King. It said that the Europeans were used to going about in the open air, riding carriages or riding horseback for pleasure. These activities had been good for their health and they had thus not suffered from illness. Since their coming to Bangkok, they found there were no roads to go riding in carriages or on horseback for pleasure and they had all been sick very often.

The king saw that the royal capital "was greatly overgrown with grass and climbers; our pathways were but small or blind alleys; our larger pathways were dirty, muddy, or soiled, and unpleasant to look at." He commanded that a proper street be built with modern shops flanking it. New Road traced the former path of an elephant track and extended four miles from the Grand Palace to an area called Bang Kolem. After passing through the rice-mill district; it terminated at Land's End (Thanon Tok) close to the abattoirs.

Laying out roads was problematic, not only because the alluvial mud solidified but also because bricks were scarce and had to be imported from China. King Mongkut was especially disturbed at the discomfort to holy people—monks, nuns, Brahman priests—who often went barefoot. To lend a Buddhist dimension to a public works campaign, he enjoined public donation of bricks either "in good condition, in broken pieces, in large or small quantity" as a meritorious act. They were laid on their sides horizontally and layers of sand spread over them. But the sacred soles were not protected when wet weather turned the bricks into quagmires of thick red clay and the dry season produced thick dust.

King Mongkut's sponsorship of New Road (Charoen Krung) was meant to encourage cordial relations with the growing diplomatic and mercantile community but, as owner of all land, he actively shaped the city to promote economic development. New Road was a purpose-built commercial strip in a burgeoning area, convenient to the Customs' House, European legations, warehouses and mercantile firms. By the end of the century the handsome neo-Palladian headquarters of the East Asiatic Company stood as a landmark at the foot of Oriental Lane. Further downstream were docks, sawmills and rice mills up to Bang Kolem. This direct road also circumvented the river's broad bend so that goods moved more rapidly by land to the Royal District.

The king authorized another innovative feature: the construction of nearly half a mile of continuous blocks of rentable commercial premises along both sides of the road. Chinese shop-houses, the basic unit of commerce and industry, attracted speculators and led to Bangkok's rapid expansion at the end of the nineteenth century. They were multi-purpose buildings with arcades that followed the shop-house plan: two storeys, about fifty feet deep, divided into frontages of about twenty feet, roofs of Thai or Chinese tiles. The formula was versatile: ground floor—shop, office, warehouse; upstairs—sleeping area. Those with river frontage had entrances from both water and land. A small number of shop-houses were purely residential; others were used as gambling dens, brothels, meeting places for mutual associations and guilds. They generally lacked basic amenities (toilets, fire escapes, ventilation) and very few of the Singapore-style building survived the rapid urban renewal that began in the 1960s.

The establishment of New Road as a major transport artery changed the amphibious character of the original city. Villages (*bang*) of tradespeople and rice farmers had planted settlements linked by paths (*trok*) that led off from river banks and canals through dense vegetation but the road network decisively established a pattern of growth inland. Straight roads were cut inland at right angles, carving the residential parts of the city into nearly rectangular plots. Many tropical trees were felled to make way for this development. This first public road was a harbinger of the inevitable destruction of the floating city in a garden, the natural habitat of the Siamese that had been so greatly admired by countless foreign visitors.

Soon after the construction of New Road, rickshaws were introduced from Hong Kong and Singapore. A contemporary painting by a Chinese artist called Lertjak is one of two large pictures that have probably hung on the wall of the old Ia Sae Coffee Shop on Padsai Road in Chinatown since it was built in 1926. The first customers were Chinese labourers and rickshaw drivers to whom the coffee house gave temporary escape from the very hard work that is somewhat idealized in Lertjak's picture. By 1901 they clogged the city roads and a law was passed limiting their number. The police impounded 700 rickshaws in 1905 because of "their habits of slovenly uncleanliness and other evil ways", reported a local journalist. By

the mid-nineteenth century cycles were added to the carts. Chinese merchants regularly used them but a sensitive Chinese man in Botan's *Letters from Thailand* (1969) tells his mother that he could not even bear the thought of getting into one for "it is too painful to watch a hungry man struggle... no job is so deforming of the body, or of developing those starved knots of muscle."

King Mongkut had sewn the seeds of modernization—English education at the Palace, diplomatic missions to France and England and appointments of honorary consuls in Europe. His son, Rama Chulalongkorn faithfully carried on the process. During his reign whole sections of demolished city walls were used as road foundations. A journalist reported in 1889 that, although the road had been tarred, it was still quite a rough ride due to the "mass of enormous rocks, and half or whole bricks, amongst which the vehicles jolt and flounder to the injury of wheels and springs."

In the dry season Chinese labourers splattered canal water on the thick dust of New Road from wooden buckets balanced on their shoulders. But New Road was always "in a chronic state of filth, wet or dry," a visitor wrote in the 1880s. A few years later Lucien Fournereau dismissed the so-called "great artery parallel to the river" as a dirty, stinking road with fifteen bridges "bulging like an ass's back". By 1925 New Road had been asphalted and was "freed from the menace of a thick cloud of dust" but it quickly turned into a canal during the rainy season as it was right at river level. Fortunately, the harshness of the road diminished at night when the "phosphorescent glow" of scores of fireflies lent it a soft bluish cast that a French visitor liked.

In this formerly aquatic city walking day or night was a life-threatening exercise, especially on New Road where there were no sidewalks to speak of. The diarist Emile Jottrand, "an amateur of pedestrian strolls" in late nineteenth-century Europe, gave up completely once and for all when he understood that the rules of the road in Bangkok are size and power—rules that are still fully operative today. The whip was the master of the road, as he wrote:

> … a leisurely drive by carriage is wonderful: one rushes others off their feet instead of being run over! What is amusing is to see the superiority derived from using one or the other category of equipage: the rickshaw (or pull-pull) is content to chase the pedestrians, so they often despise them. The Siamese coachman races the push-push off his feet, dealing blows with the whip. The Malay coachman, who steers the elegant victoria of a European, rushes into the Siamese carriages, insulting them as he overtakes, while on the other side he administers blows of the whip to the Chinese rickshaw-pullers. Finally on top of this, the buggy, driven by the master himself, who does not give way to anyone but bothers everyone—pedestrians, trishaws and victories—arrives. He advances by repeatedly dealing blows of the whip and overtakes by out doing all those who had been in front of him without anyone daring to protest

against the white man who drives himself, not against his colored, bare-footed and quaintly dolled-up bellboy who bundles himself, in the back of the car. From time to time, the road climbs bridges which overhang *klongs* or canals with a rather strong curvature. When descending it, one has the sensation of being on a roller-coaster!

A British reporter for the *Bangkok Times Weekly Mail* confirmed Jottrand's view that Bangkok was not a city for walkers in a piece that appeared in December 1890. He noted the encumbrances on New Road: traditional charcoal braziers, old furniture and packing cases. But the biggest nuisance was a large western stove in a sidewalk kitchen. A Frenchman was more aware of the fragmenting forces of modernization on a people "whose spirit no longer has time to reconcile itself amidst the reforms which are each day introduced to public institutions and every facet of practical life, amidst their crumbling superstitions, their broken traditions, the interesting metamorphosis of their streets where the electric trams make their way in between pagodas and scared elephants, where bicycles run into noblemen's palanquins, upsetting every movement known to them."

NEW ROAD YESTERDAY AND TODAY

The first urban transit system in Bangkok, inaugurated along New Road in 1887, consisted of an iron tram pulled along twin rails by a four-horse team. Seven years later a resident Irishman named Shea introduced electrified trams installed by Danish engineers, making Bangkok the first Asian city to introduce them. Locals were initially bewildered, as Ernest Young reported in *The Kingdom of the Yellow Robe* (1898). The remarkable adaptive powers of Bangkokians showed then, just as they do now, and, "In less than a week, the cars were packed every journey."

The high demand for electricity meant that circuits could easily overload. Until the late 1920s almost every light in town blinked at 8:00 pm when electricity was momentarily suspended. Toasts were raised at the *8:00 Wink* by westerners; it was a "boon to club men and hostesses," wrote a local journalist for the *Bangkok Times Weekly Mail*. Certain parts of the city lost the wink after 1925 but the lamps still flickered throughout the Oriental Hotel and the Bang Rak area for some time until circuits in the area were improved.

By 1900 the new tram ran along a route of thirteen miles from Bang Rak to the City Pillar Shrine (Lak Meuang). A second tram line was set up during the reign of King Rama VI to connect Charoen Krung and Pratunam through the residential district of Silom. Visitors riding the tram brushed shoulder-to-shoulder with the locals but rarely had real contact with them. Danish writer Ebbe Kornerup, who road the tram in the early 1920s, and left this vignette.

> Then we drove down New Road again—the enormously long main street of Bangkok—while fireworks crackle from the low Cantonese houses. The Chinaman is dressed in white or black, the Siamese, on the other hand, in a blue, red, brown, or green *panung*, or white European dress. There are also white-clad Tamils from southern India, keeping guard with turban and staff over their property. Shops with plate-glass windows twinkle in the lights, stone bank buildings, government buildings, consulates, legations, small hotels, theatres, many klongs spanned by bridges... and it goes on.

A rather less romanticized reaction came from a local journalist reporting at that time. The smells, he said, were overpowering. Two particularly offensive odours came from the indigo drycleaner "smack in the center of New Road" and the tannery at one of the crossing stations of the tram that "emits such offensive effluvia that it almost suffocates the passengers."

Elderly Bangkokians who lived in the Silom area remember the trams differently. During the summer flowering Burmese rosewood blossoms fell on the tracks "like a long, yellow, feathery trail", recalls a wizened local. Another recounts how kite-flying enthusiasts placed glass on the tracks so that the tram would pulverize it. The crushed glass was used to make the "cutting" strings used during the winter kite fighting season. Muslims in the area would reportedly catch the many snakes that plagued residents. Believing that the snakes were emissaries of Satan, they beat them, then pinned them to the rail so that they would never return.

By the late 1960s the enormous growth of bus, private car and taxi transport made streetcars obsolete and the few remaining trams had their last run. The sister lines of the Bangkok Tramway carried passengers for more than a seven decades. The tiny yellow and red trams were retired in 1968 and the tracks were paved over. This was a nostalgic moment for the trams had not only popularized new areas but had also provided informal social services, as writer Sornsarn Phaengsapha recalls:

> Bangkok tram services ran from 05:30 to 23:30. Tram drivers on the last rounds (around 23:00) would driver very fast. However, the last round of feeder lines such as the Ratchawongse line would be 18:30 since the last round of boat services would be about that time. The Ratchawongse area was the place to have fun for those who had money to burn at first-class restaurants like Hoy Tian Lao (AKA- Lard Fah Restaurant).
>
> The tram officers were generally people of good heart...volunteering to help people who lived along the tracks, asking adults to give up their seats for students, sending drunkards from bars back home, helping to set up funeral rites...

Although New Road was the artery of the Central Business District its heart was in the vibrant cosmopolitan communities in the perpendicular *sois* and *troks*. The street changed character from the more official section leading off from Thanon Sanamchai, to the predominantly Chinese section running parallel to Thanon Yaowarat (which could easily be mistaken for an old street in Shanghai). Then it ran through the more western commercial area from Thanon Songsawat to what is now the Saphan Taksin Skytrain stop (locus of the British Dispensary, famous general stores like Kiam Hoa Heng's and Nai Lert's which introduced ice in the 1899). It finally ended abruptly after a long stretch of shops at Land's End.

Somerset Maugham was not impressed with New Road; it was "lined with houses, low and sordid, and shops, and the goods they sell, European and Japanese for the most part, look shop-soiled and dingy." Although all of the old shops are gone, we can still enter the fictional Karachi Store that was once opposite the General Post Office with the heroine of Margaret Landon's novel *Never Dies the Dream* (1949). Angela, the young American wife of a Thai prince, goes shopping for dress fabric. "The Karachi Store on New Road into which she turned was one of several run by Indian merchants, who had almost a monopoly on the sale of yard goods in Bangkok. Some of their shops were hardly more than holes in the wall with bolts of cloth piled to the ceiling. The Karachi Store was spacious and catered to the foreign trade. It offered for sale many things hard to find elsewhere:

embroidery cotton, silk hose, English linens and voiles. There were also brass trays, rugs, carved ivories, and ebony elephants for tourists."

A lot of money changed hands on New Road and by 1936 many of the most important exchange banks were located on or nearby it: the Hong Kong Bank-Shanghai Bank and la Banque de l'Indochine. English was the language of business along the street and signs translated into English were often comic. A Chinese laundry advertised *Chai Wan Washes Man* and the *Randez vous Club* offered the well-sudsed bodies of young women. Bangkok has always been a place where everything is for sale and New Road was the city's first inland entertainment area, a place where sailors liked to carouse.

Sexual services could be had for a song. Somerset Maugham was most inappropriately handed a card by a tout that read: "Oh, gentleman, sir, Pretty Girl welcome you Sultan Turkish bath, gentle, polite, massage, put you in dreamland with perfume soap. Latest gramophone music! You come now! Miss Pretty Girl want you, massage you from tippy-toe to head-top, nice, clean to enter the Gates of Heaven."

Although New Road has been almost completely westernized since 1861, its social texture has been preserved in neighbourhoods that have not yet succumbed to the developers. Some of the most deeply rooted communities of Old Bangkok can be explored by walking south from Saphan Taksin Skytrain stop along New Road to Thanon Tok. Stop first at Wat Yannawa, a 140-feet junk commissioned by King Rama III who feared that the memory of the Chinese junk would be forever lost in the new age of the steam ship. There are two pagodas and sacred objects on the stern and a monastic building that is a memorial to Rama III. Along the route are: Buddhist temples that are congeries of the most incongruous objects, animated by free-roaming ducks, and dogs and cats, guardians of quiet monks' quarters, corners framed by brilliant bougainvillea, Victorian-style mosques, shops stacked with richly gilded coffins and gleaming inlaid mother of pearl, grimy Chinese shop-houses stocked from ceiling to floor with auto and industrial parts (presided over by thin, bared chest Chinese elders who seem as inert as the objects), massage parlours, two-chair hair salons, vendors of Chinese house shrines. In all likelihood you will see old fishermen on stinky canals that have been partially covered.

Get lost. Take a detour down Charoen Krung (New Road) 85 Yaek. This extraordinary ramshackle old neighbourhood contains traditional

Thai wooden houses and huts. Food vendors and card table merchants proffer a festival of food. Follow the street parallel to it through a maze of roads and lanes parallel to New Road as far as you can to exit at number 89. Imagine the heroine of Anchan's *A Pot That Scouring Will Not Save* (1990), a Vermeer-like figure cloaked in silence, until her reflections are interrupted by the "*jawk-jack* of sparrows in the mango tree outside. A flock of them descended into the tree every morning, causing the branches to brush against the eaves of the house and the window of their bedroom."

Should you one day chose to sit and watch the world go by from a coffee vendor on a side street in the New Road area, take a little notebook to record the sounds. Be on the look out for a bright-eyed kid in a worn, old T-shirt who alerts the whole neighbourhood that the Chinese noodle man is on his way by beating on a pair of wooden blocks. He trails a few feet behind pushing his steaming noodle wagon—a two-wheeled Rube Goldberg contraption with piping cauldrons, pantry and sink all built into one. The *satay* vendor uses a cha-cha tempo; the sweet seller has a syncopated beat. The man shaking the maracas has a cart full of brooms and brushes. The junkman cometh rattling chains and peddling an open-bedded cart. Listen for the lady with the tom-toms whose shoulders support a wooden pole from which two blackened containers dangle, their glowing coals keeping sticky rice warm. Other marketing noises are bird whistles, clown horns, bicycle bells and soft drink caps strung on a wire. This noisy market-in-motion gives theatre-like glimpses of ordinary but exuberant Thai urban life for which you may have a free, front row seat.

Twelve

STRANGERS IN A STRANGE LAND

Fewer than two dozen westerners lived in Bangkok prior to the Bowring Treaty of 1855, most of them missionaries. The Presbyterians particularly were ill-prepared for the chaotic life of a bustling Asian city. An elder wrote of a young missionary who had arrived in Bangkok in 1843: "Like the rest of us with New England ancestors, [he] took exception to the dirty streets, the constant noise, and the difficulty of mastering the language." Visitors had an insight into their day-to-day problems as George Windsor Earl complained in his traveller's tale (1837). "It is very inconvenient to walk in the town, not only on account of the mud, but from the number of dogs, these brutes appearing to consider Europeans fair game," he wrote. "During two or three excursions in this swampy town, I was attended by two of the boat's crew, armed with paddles, and we were therefore enabled to keep these troublesome animals at bay."

Not all westerners reacted so negatively to the city—some thrived. Robert Hunter, Scots trader, swashbuckler and opium dealer who lived in Bangkok for two decades (1824-44) and became fluent in Thai, was one of those. Initially he occupied a floating house near Santa Cruz church; then in 1831 King Rama III awarded him a royal title as well as permission to put up the earliest foreign residence on land. Hunter built "a very fine, large prominent home" which welcomed "every stranger", one of them wrote. A small sketch shows an ersatz two-storey brick colonial style

house with louvered windows that set a standard for foreigners' residences in the city.

Mr. Hunter's balcony overlooking the river gave visiting Europeans a moving panorama and locals an open window into foreign ways. In his lively and humorous journal *A Narrative of a Residence in Siam*, which was compiled in the 1840s, F. A. Neale provides rare glimpses of both. His observations are unique as he was residing in Bangkok before the signing of the Bowring Treaty that would so dramatically transform it.

European Day
5:.30 A.M. Wake Up. Cawing of Crows.
6:00 A.M.   Sparrows Chirping Madly. Squirrels Begin Sharp and Piercing Cries.
6:30   Swim in the Cool Waters of the Chao Phraya.
10:00   Breakfast at Mr. Hunter's, followed by a stroll on his balcony.
11:00   Excursion on the river to visit foreigners, to inspect the dockyards, to chat with a prince, to shoot or to fish.
12:00   Lunch time.
13:00-3:00 Siesta.
3:00   Arrival of sea breeze.
3:00-6:00   River watching.
6:00   Short dull twilight.
6:30   Impenetrable night.
            Dinner.
11:00   Bed time.

Siamese Day
6:00   Saffron robed Buddhist monks collect offerings of food from people on the river banks... Betel nut vendors do a brisk trade... a Chinaman sells pork... a fish monger has fried and stewed fish... the baker's girl hawks bread and hoppers (a cake of rice flour and cocoanut milk)... then floating vendors stream by with raw commodities: sea and river fish, goats' meat and poultry, fruits, vegetables... [the vendors] bought and sold, smoked and drank strong tea without either milk or sugar, paid a business visit to merchants and

captains of junks, made balance-sheets and received money due to them.

10:00   A stout, old Chinaman stopped by Hunter's to console him for the penance exacted by his religion that required him to walk along the balcony in such great heat for "in their estimation, that man must be a lunatic who would walk half a mile, when he might be comfortably paddled the same distance, luxuriantly seated in a canoe."

12:00   Loud trumpet signals mid-day meal.

1:00-2:30   Perfect silence reigns.

3:00-6:00   River is animated by more boats... people throng to floating houses... shipping vessels arrive and depart, load and discharge...

6:00-10:00   ...the long row of lights in the floating-houses give symptoms of wakefulness and of supper being under way... the occasional snatch of a Chinese carol... by degrees this sound would cease, and save the low mournful cry of some hapless young vendor of fish or fruits, who dared not seek her home before disposing of a stipulated quantity, for fear of chastisement from her ruthless master, nothing disturbed the solemn stillness of the night.

Dr. Dan Beach Bradley, an American missionary who lived next door to Hunter, kept a wary eye on the balcony as well. After attending a New Year's party at Hunter's home, he opined that "dinner parties conducted by Europeans in the East... are too powerfully efficient in fostering intemperance both in eating and in drinking and a host of consecutive evils..." Bradley was the antithesis of Hunter; he was effectively the Dr. Schweitzer of Siam—schoolchildren are still taught about his laudable contributions to public health, especially modern surgery and vaccination against smallpox. His first residence in Bangkok was briefly located near Wat Samphanthawong in Chinatown, until King Rama III had him moved near the church of Santa Cruz across the river where he could be supervised by the Minister of Trade and Foreign Affairs. Bradley's career in Siam was multifaceted. In addition to his medical work, he acted as unofficial American ambassador and government advisor. He also brought the local news to Bangkok by establishing *The Bangkok Recorder* (1844-67), the first fortnightly newspaper in Siam (in English and Thai), from a press he had shipped from Singapore. Furthermore, he founded an almanac called *The Bangkok Calendar* (1860-72) and played a key role in publishing the first Thai-English dictionary in 1873.

Robert Hunter's gregariousness won him many friends. King Pinklao, second-in-command as deputy king during the Third Reign, had a great fondness for him. He and writer Neale were guests at an extraordinary Christmas party that King Pinklao hosted for about thirty Europeans:

> The invitation included the officers and mates of all the merchant vessels then in the river, and the American and French missionaries, these latter, however, declined the invitation, and it was well they did so, for all of the carousels I have ever witnessed [...], I never saw one to surpass that at Bangkok... Among the crews of the English vessels we mustered a couple of fiddlers, a hautboy, a flute, a fife, and a drummer, and with this *magnificent band*, commenced the business of the day with the British National Anthem. Everybody joined in the chorus, and though the music was execrable, and the singing alarmingly out of tune, we got through it on the whole remarkably well. The ladies, or rather princesses, had a place portioned off, through which, by aid of eyelet holes, they were spectators to this, to them so novel a spectacle; and it was worth a great deal to see the cats in the palace, tearing about, tail up in the air as the first burst of our dissonant orchestra fell like a thunder-peal on their astonished and alarmed ears.

At about one o'clock "a glorious spread of *déjeuner à la fourchette*, [was] laid out in the court-yard under the cool shade of a pandal, a species of temporary balcony consisting or a lot of dried grass introduced between a trellis-work of split bamboos... Champagne ad libitum was poured down our throats, and though it was not frappe it was deliciously cool, from the process adopted in India of standing bottles in salt-peter and salt and water." After a tipsy game of leap-frog that amused the prince and brought "ill-suppressed titterings" from the ladies behind the screen, a game of shuttlecock, then a Chinese theatrical performance, "dinner was announced and we were introduced into an apartment which none of us had ever before witnessed, and which surpassed in splendour our utmost expectations." A sumptuous Christmas feast was laid out accompanied by copious libations; the toasts began and the party continued until the early hours of the morning when the king sent the merry guests home on his state barge.

Hunter's fame eventually came from a very different direction, as a result of his shrewd if dubious entrepreneurial skills. His neighbour, Dr. Bradley, reported how Hunter's eye was caught by a strange object moving through the waters of the Chao Phraya river: "It was a creature that appeared to have two heads, four arms and four legs, all of which were moving in perfect harmony. As Mr. Hunter watched, the object climbed into a nearby boat, and to his amazement he realized that he had been looking at two small boys who were joined together at the chest." He had by chance discovered the original Siamese twins, Chang and Eng. Hunter quickly saw the commercial possibilities of exhibiting the twins and, after some persuasion, their mother and Siamese authorities allowed them to be taken abroad. They left Bangkok in April 1829 and never returned to their native land; though millions of westerners first learned of the distant kingdom of Siam through them.

Over the next forty-five years the boys travelled extensively in Europe and the United States. They appeared before enthusiastic crowds, and the great showman P. T. Barnum made them circus stars. During this time they learned to speak and write English fluently and generally impressed all who met them with their charm and intelligence, not to mention the extraordinary co-ordination with which they performed athletic tricks. The twins eventually became American citizens, married two sisters, Sarah and Adelaide Yates, and settled in North Carolina. Their unconventional marriages were, by all accounts, happy; Chang and Adelaide had ten children in all, while Eng and Sarah had twelve. They lived in separate houses a mile apart and for 25 years the twins alternated between the two, spending three weeks at each home.

Chang developed severe bronchitis in January 1874 and died five days later. Eng succumbed a few hours afterwards, before a planned operation to separate them could be performed. They were buried in the Baptist cemetery in White Plains, North Carolina. The Siamese twins have about a thousand descendants still living in the United States, some of them still in the same area where ancestors spent their last years.

Cosmopolitan Life in Bangkok

"A new class of citizens began to populate Siam after the opening of trade relations with the West in 1856," Bradley wrote. "Adventurers came from all over the world to pursue their fortunes, some of them with wooden legs." Many found the local women irresistible, like New England businessman George Virgin who purchased a string of mistresses and never returned home. "Being men and lonely for women, they sometimes used the smooth, slim women who crept into their beds," writes Norman Bartlett while admiring their chivalry as they "did not exploit them in bad novels or mention them in their ponderous reminiscences."

The Bowring Treaty was a watershed that opened Siam to international trade and made important concessions to encourage foreign investment. Extraterritorial jurisdiction was granted to European consuls; foreigners had the right to own property, to establish residence at Bangkok, and to travel freely throughout the kingdom. But there were some limitations which were addressed a year later when King Mongkut issued an edict "Concerning Treaty *Farangs*" decreeing that French, British and American nationals could "reside permanently in the Divine City within a distance of 24 hours' journey at which ordinary boats of the country can travel." In fact, the westerners who arrived in Bangkok in the second half of the nineteenth century settled alongside the locals; they did not create a protective enclave as in other bustling Southeast Asian colonial towns and cities such as Rangoon, Batavia [Jakarta], Saigon and Singapore. They lived in close proximity to the locals but their large bungalows were palatial by comparison—"verandahed houses, flagstaffs, tennis-lawns and flowering trees"– strung out along the Chao Phraya river adjacent to a floating community of local inhabitants. British miner H. Warington Smyth found Bangkok pleasingly cosmopolitan: "At one table would be seated Danes, Germans, Italians, Dutch, Belgians, American and Britishers."

Most westerners opted for Bang Rak village, located at the juncture of New Road with Silom, Suriwong, Sathorn and Siphya Roads, where a western-style central business district had emerged after the digging of a canal and roads in 1861. Warington Smyth noted that there were almost no Frenchmen "except one or two officials of the consulate, who generally held aloof, and one popular trader, who, with the conspicuous gallantry of his race, long held the only French mercantile house in Siam above water."

Pas de surprise. An ominous confrontation in July 1893 bringing

French gunboats up the Chao Phraya to anchor outside their legation had sent shudders down the national backbone. King Chulalongkorn took to his private quarters, refused medication and wrote a poem of heartbreaking misery from his sickbed. Fortunately the situation calmed down after the king "negotiated" to settle the territorial claims of France over areas that had been ruled by the Siamese. The monarch ceded extensive territories in Laos and Cambodia; then in 1904 he was forced to comply with further demands as a protection against French expansionism. Charles Buls, former mayor of Brussels who was in Bangkok as a legal adviser, saw through *casus belli* colonialism. "In the East, France is ever ready to seize the smallest pretext to justify an armed intervention and the theft of a few stretches of Siamese territory."

The British had a monopoly on three-quarters of the trade in Bangkok, especially timber and tin. A few wily French traders attempted to counter British influence by feeding the local press misinformation about their shoddy expertise. Newspapers ran headlines such as this one: A NEW CROOK HAS LANDED THIS MORNING. A LOT OF ADVISORS BUT LITTLE REASON!

By comparison, the Italians were regarded much more favourably and following King Chulalongkorn's trips to Italy in 1897 and 1907, even more immigrants were invited to Siam. They established Little Italy in Thanon Pan, a narrow *soi* connecting Silom to Sathorn Roads, and jobs and honours followed. By 1909 two dozen Piedmontese artists, architects and engineers were listed in the Official Directory of the Ministry of Public Works of Siam. Italian journalist Salvatore Besso described an al fresco meal enjoyed in the company of fellow *compadri* in a "fresh and verdant quarter on the banks of the river, where in a sumptuous Siamese palace that was formerly occupied by the Minister of the Interior, lives Galileo Chini, our magnificent ornamental painter, who brings honour to all of Italy due to the commission the King of Siam has given him to paint the vault of the new audience hall."

The year before *The Bangkok Times* reported that the engineer Carlo Allegri (who directed the Department of Public Works) was justly honoured by the conferral of the 3rd Class of the Most Exalted Order of the White Elephant and of the Crown of Siam. He had worked for nearly two decades "to transform Bangkok from a city of canals with few roads, into a city of roads [that were] much more important than the canals. All the new arteries were surveyed and made by him, together with the bridges and many other improvements." Giuseppe Canova, who had designed the first rail line and Mario Tamagno, architect of the Throne Hall at Dusit Park, were also honoured for their lengthy service.

The Italian Club, founded in 1891, was one of many social clubs that kept the gossip mill turning. "Bangkok is a great place for gossip and scandal," an American missionary noted, and there was plenty of social life to provide grist for the mill: receptions at foreign legations, sporting competitions at the Royal Bangkok Sports Club, dances at the Bangkok United Club, dinner at the Oriental, and frequent royal events, elegant occasions where men dressed in tailcoats or smoking jackets and women donned long white gowns. A European guest was entranced by "the charm of these balls in hot climates, half in the open air, half in the salons and under the verandahs, with the breeze, the perfume of the flowers, the boatmen who bring the guests, all the languages which one hears and the picturesque contrast of couples walking in dreamlike lawns, while the illuminated dance hall resound with music and the dancers spin about."

"Now and again a newcomer proposes the formation of a philosophical society, or a debating club or some of those half-intellectual half amusing pastime [but] there seems to be only one method of enjoyment and that I need not specify," wrote a discreet English resident in a local newspaper (1903). By the turn of the century there were about a thousand Europeans and Americans living in the city. Many were members of the sixteen expatriate clubs listed in a Bangkok guidebook, mainly for sports: polo, clay pigeon and rifle shooting, cricket, an eighteen-hole golf course and one of the finest race courses in the East.

But for many foreigners, whether drawn by avarice, adventure or duty, daily life in Bangkok could take a real toll, though the aristocratic types generally seem to have fared better—"resolute in cork topees and immaculately laundered." Dr. Bradley was candid about the strains of expatriate life in a profoundly Buddhist country that had kept most westerners at bay until 1855. "Superficially these foreigners appear, for the most part, to have led the normal, uneventful lives characteristic of their various vocations, but the records indicate that their existence became increasingly complicated by psychological pressures imposed on them in a distant land within an alien culture." Those who "went native" with flamboyant disregard for western manners and customs were "absorbed whole, like wasps in amber, and finally regurgitated with perhaps a touch of cirrhosis on their livers and a dash of cayenne in their tempers."

Like those who went native, second-generation *immigrés* tell a different story from the glamorous but burdened one of the expatriates. In 1904 the French scholarly team of Lajonquière and Finot took a boat across the river to the home that Dr. Bradley had inhabited for decades. Being carried across the river and down a moss-covered quay, they came to a modest house that appeared to be deserted. When they were eventually admitted to the salon they were genuinely surprised at what they found.

> It was the restrained, heavy, and thread-bare décor of some old provincial holier-than-thou transported wholesale to the tropics. It made an odd effect between the wooden partition walls of the apartments and the large window-doors open to the outside, now vibrating in the sun. No less odd was the mistress of the house, the reverend gentleman's daughter. Tall and skinny, with huge yellow teeth in a horsy face, she came toward us laughing, shook hands vigorously, and excused herself for speaking Siamese because she had completely forgotten her mother tongue. Our request to buy some of the works published by her father occasioned another burst of laughter, and she went out to seek out from the corner of the dining-room buffet a dozen fragmentary copies. After having more or less put together from this hodgepodge of debris what seemed to be interesting, we paid and requested a receipt. There was another burst of laughter. The tall skinny girl went to look in some old boxes to take out some green letter paper with silver initials embossed on it, but she declared that she no longer knew how to write and in fact painstakingly signed her name while spelling it. There indeed was the conservative Anglo-Saxon character, the life of that woman, born far from the land of her ancestors, completely separated from her roots, living wholly apart from her compatriots but having carefully preserved around her those furnishings from another country and age that were the sign of her nationality.

The numbers of westerners living in Bangkok increased with time but the problems confronting them did not diminish. March, April and May were known as the cholera months, a disease that ravished the population until a proper water system was installed in 1907. The poor drank from the river or canals; foreigners stored rainwater in giant earthenware jars and fretted. Europeans were not spared, despite their precautions. British Consul Wood describes their grim litanies. "At the United Club one would ask in the evening: 'Where is Jones?' and be told he was dead of cholera. 'And Brown?' 'Dead too.' 'And Robinson?' 'Laid up with cholera.'" A British doctor with twenty-five years of practice in the city noted that foreigners who succumbed to cholera were often teetotalers.

A high-ranking British general who visited the city during the same year also recommended frequent tippling: "A certain amount of alcohol is more necessary for one than in England. It helps out the less nourishing food, and turns the mind from trivial worries, which are often unduly magnified by the heat and mosquitoes of tropical life."

For some, opium was the drug of choice. "The British in Bangkok didn't smoke opium, but many of the French did," remarks Gerald Sparrow who was a British judge in Bangkok for two decades. He befriended a French architect named Monsieur Nicot, who "was not old but gave the impression of being ageless... His hair had thinned from a high forehead and his face was mobile and sensitive. His features were fine, but the skin was tightly drawn over the cheek bones and his under lip had the weak, tremulous protrusion I came to associate with all ardent smokers." Nicot invited Sparrow to his home on Sathorn Road, called *Le Mirage*, a place "easily recognizable as the home of an opium smoker, for even in the driveway one was assailed by the sweet, sickly, cloying smell of opium." On his third visit Sparrow met Nicot's beautiful Siamese wife Rada.

> She was lissome and elegant, quite young and, though she wore Siamese dress, a Continental veneer was suggested by her make-up, her earrings and her few words of broken French. She smoked Turkish cigarettes from a long ivory holder, but these were not all she smoked. Her husband had persuaded her to be sensible and companionable and to join him in his chief delight. She had been reluctant at first, saying that she was afraid the drug might claim her as a victim, but he had laughed aside her fears, so she had succumbed—a puff at the initial stage, then a pipe, then rather more.

After a tour of the well-appointed residence Rada unlocked the door to the opium den.

[It was]… a charming light room which was richly furnished with the same good taste as the rest of the house, but more richly. Monsieur Nicot had here collected his favourite treasures, including a fine head and shoulders of the Virgin Mary… [his] tastes were religious but catholic. There were some remarkable statues of Buddha in bronze and one small gold statue of the 'starving Buddha.' A superb etching of Rheims cathedral caught my eye. In the centre of the room was a divan large enough for two persons, and beside this stood a Chinese blackwood table, intricately carved. On the table, neatly arranged, were seven silver-handled opium pipes and the little flame burner and pan used for preparing opium for smoking.

After they were under the spell of its "pristine magic," Sparrow stole out into the windy street.

SNAPSHOTS OF FARANG LIFE

Extra-territoriality rights conferred by treaties had encouraged economic growth in Bangkok but limited the authority of the sovereign. Foreigners had the privilege of governing and judging themselves independently of native officers and tribunals. Moreover, foreign consuls (many who seem to have been inept) had to make a wide variety of judicial decisions from the simplest police ordinance to the regulation of opium. Judge Sparrow turned from dealing with opium addicts to other realities in 1940 when Thailand became a Japanese base overnight. Just a few hours after the attack on Pearl Harbor the Japanese demanded the right to move a force of troops across Thailand to the Malaysian frontier. After a brief skirmish with the Thai army Field Marshal Phibul ordered an armistice. Shortly thereafter Japan was granted free passage, and a few weeks later Thailand and Japan signed a military alliance with a secret protocol wherein Thailand undertook to assist Japan in her war against the Allies and Tokyo agreed to help Thailand get back territories lost to colonial powers.

Sir Josiah Crosby, the elderly British consul, summoned his co-nationals to the British Club as quickly as he could on 8 December 1940 and then gave them some bad advice. "Sit tight. That is what I am going to do." British nationals in Bangkok were rounded up and interned "for four long years of horror and torture," as Sparrow reported.

When Sparrow first arrived in Bangkok with his English bride in 1930 they had taken a room at the Royal Hotel on Sathorn Road, "an immense rambling place, with a half a dozen towers and turrets, surrounded by a tropical garden with giant palm trees." The hotel "was a happy blend of Chinese and European architecture, conveying no hint of its tragic beginning or the horror and intrigue it was one day to house," Sparrow wrote a quarter of a century later. No one had told him as he had his morning tea that the wealthy Chinese owner had experienced a disastrous financial reversal and hanged himself by a red silk cord from the ornate carved roof of the dining room. A British guest who arrived a decade later (1940) was driven through the utter chaos of Chinatown into the lovely grounds of the Royal.

> Soon after, I am sitting in my room; the folding doors to the garden are open, an intoxicating scent of gardenia and orange pours in, the air is soft and warm, and beyond the balcony fireflies twinkle among big dark trees, flicker brightly, and go out again. The strange mystery of the tropics, the sound of chirring grasshoppers, croaking frogs, ticking geckoes, fills my ears with music; it is pleasant here, this is a free place, and I feel at home at once.

A year later the Japanese Imperial Army commandeered the hotel as a torture chamber. During the Cold War years it was occupied by the Soviet Legation and "Russian activities in South-east Asia are now largely directed from the rooms that seemed so gay and pleasing to us," Sparrow glumly wrote.

During the post-Second World War boom years, the Bangkapi suburb became the chic new quarter for foreigners but some opted to live in more traditional settings. Writer William Warren describes the incommodious features of canal side living, noting that they were common to most of Bangkok at the time.

> Dogs, cats, mosquitoes, lizards, and occasional snakes had free access to the ground floor rooms and took ample advantage of it, especially in the rainy season when the *klong* rose and sometimes flooded the garden. There was no telephone, no air conditioning, no hot water, and no gas; we cooked on a charcoal stove, and when the water supply failed (as it

did regularly if two taps were turned on at the same time) we bathed with a dipper from a large jar, shouting *pit nam* ("close the water") to anyone who might be listening. Two or three times a week the electricity went off for several hours, nearly always at night; even when it worked the slightest overload, like turning on a spotlight to illuminate the garden, promptly blew all the fuses. The refrigerator, an ancient pre-war model, barely chilled: we bought blocks of ice daily and kept them in a large chest, along with any food likely to spoil soon. During the dry months, from November through May, the *klong* became a sinister trickle that smelt of sewage and dead things, floating a few feet from the dining room. Just beyond the back fence was a swamp, overgrown patch of wasteland; most of our mosquitoes and reptilian visitors came from there and so, late at night, did frequent banshee wails from an elderly drunken hag who had built a squatter shack in the shrubbery and who was said by the servants to be a witch.

Although they cohabited peacefully, westerners rarely penetrated the surface, as H.W. Smyth had earlier noted. American writer Carol Hollinger experienced the "social incest" of expatriate life in the 1960s.

There was good reason for the huddling instincts of the American in Thailand. After a few safaris out among the Siamese I realized that integration had its hazards. Not in danger, but in a bewilderment so intense that you had to give with the culture or avoid it. Adrift in a muddle of six feet wide shops, festivities only dimly comprehended, towering, colorful heights of unintelligible din, the American has the sensation of struggling through a nightmare where all familiar symbols have vanished. In this environment a search for a paper or a bobby pin is as harrowing as an effort to keep your self in heroin would be in America. No road is straight in Bangkok and the most ordinary pursuit has the habit of ending in extraordinary chaos. Americans complained and despaired and were made neurotic by this aspect of life in Bangkok. It was the part that I enjoyed most.

For their part, the Thais have always had a highly ambivalent attitude to foreigners that continues to this day. They have had good reason to be wary of *farangs*, itself a mildly pejorative term that conflates Caucasian race and western culture, for they remembered the French gunboat threat of 1893.

There is an old legend that *farangs* once inhabited a distant region called the outside kingdom (*muang nauk*) and their eccentricities are described in a Thai chronicle, the *Nya Phuum*. "They are exceedingly tall, hairy and evil-smelling. They school their children long, and devote their lives to the amassing of riches. Their women, though large and round, are very beautiful. They do not grow rice." *Farangs* sometimes appear as villains or comic figures in Thai literature, such as *Phra Aphai Mani* written by Sunthorn Phu during the Second Reign. Mural paintings in temples from the Third Reign depict Europeans as followers of Mara, the God of Evil, who led an onslaught to tempt the Lord Buddha before his Enlightenment. Sometimes they are caricatured as sinners being cruelly and grotesquely punished in hell. French and Portuguese soldiers, diplomats and priests are joined in the Lower World by demons, ogres and semi-human or sub-human beings.

Belgian legal adviser Jottrand's memoirs mention the banning of a princess from the court and from Siamese society in 1899. This was due to her "too accommodating an attitude in giving Europeans the chance— through herself, her friends, or others—to form intimate alliances with them." Some years later national poet Ankham Kalayanapongs denounced the moral decay and horrid traffic of the capital, placing the blame squarely on politicians for their acquiescence to the agendas of the foreigners.

> A new animal: A miracle!
> Half human, lovely
> yes but also
> half automobile
> and note the integrity of the whole
> See the *farang* give it "thumbs up!"
> Good for you, Thailand
> Countless autos radiating sex
> female, male,
> drunk, voracious
> crawling, squirming
> in the streets,
> in transports of fornication

tasting the bliss, licking the rapture,
the delicious garbage of Siam.

There are a number of colloquial expressions in Thai that show con-tempt for the "other" especially in matters of social etiquette. The old debate about the meaning of *siwilai*, a Thai translation of "civilized", which began in the first quarter of the twentieth century, is taken up again in a manual on Thai social etiquette published by the Ministry of Culture in 2004. *Farangs* are presented as complete boors who flout Thai manners. Drawings illustrate four of the most serious transgressions: groping, picking, squeezing and scratching of the body. The manual concludes: "If you understand our general etiquette and the deeper structure underlying it, you will not find it hard to gain lifelong Thai friends." For a free copy of the book, please contact the Office of the Permanent Ministry of Culture and don't forget to say *khob khun kha* for ladies and *khob khun krab* for gentlemen.

Thirteen

THE ORIENTAL HOTEL

Tourists flock to Thailand, over fourteen million last year, and all bar a very few will expect to rub shoulders with glamour in one form or another. The temples, the food, the heat, the tropical vegetation—something exotically "other". In one form or another you will probably find something strangely different. If you are wealthy enough, you can even buy into the mythology of the city, the legendary history—you can become part of the stream of the great and glorious who have stayed at the Oriental Hotel, the writers, the royalty, the movie stars, the outright flashy, the eccentrics. You can stay in the legendary Authors' Wing, with suites named after Noel Coward, James Michener and Somerset Maugham. Joseph Conrad's pleasure in drinking at the Oriental bar was memorialized by the hotel's seafood restaurant named *Lord Jim*. From the full-length windows of the Joseph Conrad Suite one can still imagine his farewell salute to guests breakfasting on the lawn as his ship, the *Otago*, finally left port.

Amidst the plush surroundings of this five-star hotel, guests will find no hint of its origins, which were dull and tawdry, or of its periods of disrepute, or of the enormous effort a handful of indefatigable managers have put into keeping it a focal point in Bangkok; nor should they, for a grand dame survives and indeed flourishes despite the vicissitudes thrown at her by history.

Go back to 1855 when the Bowring Treaty, in opening up Siam to international trade, not only allowed foreign ships into Bangkok but also the sailors and the adventurers who came with them. Foreigners inserted themselves into the crevices of the city, some dubious, some seeking a better life. Along the unwholesome morass of the riverfront they set up hostels, rough and tumble places where heavy drinkers were prone to the "pot-house shindies" that Joseph Conrad had witnessed at first hand. One British hotelier drowned while crossing the Chao Phraya after celebrating his acquittal on charges of shooting a Siamese with a pistol. Another, a black American who ran a boarding house and saloon named Cottage Home, was attacked by drunken British sailors. Down the lane and across a canal was Captain Dyer's Oriental Hotel run by Dyer, an American master mariner, with his partner J. F. Barnes. This hotel did not fare much better, being razed in a disastrous fire in 1865 that destroyed almost seventy buildings in the burgeoning area of hastily thrown-up consulates, teeming markets and ramshackle commercial buildings.

A team of enterprising Danish steamer-captains had a new hotel up and running a few years later. They advertised "Hotel and Club Rooms: Family accommodations. American bar, Billiard Saloon, Baths, Newspapers kept, Boats for hire, Table d'Hôte, Breakfast 9 A.M., Tiffin 1 P.M., Dinner 7 P. M." Their wooden bungalow had a dozen rooms all opening onto a balcony. En-suite bathrooms were small dark cubicles equipped with a large earthen water jar, a scoop for bathing and squat toilets. Many of the guests fell into bed after boisterous drinking games at the bar that often degenerated into brawls. Payment was by "chit", a no-care-for–the morrow system that may have been the reason the Danish owners eventually packed up and left.

In 1884 another Danish sailor by the name of Hans Niels Andersen came to Bangkok and bought the premises of the Oriental for Anderson & Co., a ship chandlery and general story. Three years later he founded the East Asiatic Company, built the fine neoclassical office near the hotel and soon had a large fleet in all of the major world ports of the time. Andersen was also a trader-diplomat who had important international connections. He met with King George, the British Foreign Minister, Tsar Nicholas I, the Kaiser and the German Chancellor in an effort to broker a peace deal during the First World War. The London *Times* mentioned in his obituary of 1938 that he was the only Dane outside the Royal Family to have been decorated with the Order of the White Elephant by the King of Siam.

In his dealing with consulates and international shipping firms Andersen saw the need for a respectable hotel with good accommodation, a western menu and a well-stocked bar. He resolved to build such a hotel and was apparently aided in this venture by the remarkable Prince Prisdang Jumsai. The prince was the first Siamese student to take a western university degree and the last to do so with such sterling results: at his 1876 graduation from King's College, London, with a degree in civil engineering, he took almost every academic distinction.

He was Siam's indefatigable roving diplomat in Europe and the United States during the penultimate decade of the nineteenth century, at a crucial period in the history of the kingdom. He was one of the key architects who devised the country's protective shield against predatory colonialists. He established the Siamese Legation in London and presented his credentials to Queen Victoria at Buckingham Palace on 15 July 1882. But Prince Prisadang ran foul of his cousin King Chulalongkorn, who had commanded a private report from him following Burma's fall to Britain in 1885. In his response he outlined the political and cultural reforms that might stave off the imperial threat, even proposing a Siamese Constitution. Prisdang approached officials at other legations to add their signatures to this document, which was regarded as a breach of confidentiality by the king. He was recalled to Bangkok and his days as a diplomat were over. His energy and expertise were not wasted, however, as he was appointed the first director general of the Department of Posts and Telegraph; then he founded the Department of Public Works and consulted on various construction projects in the city, including a new Oriental Hotel.

While there may be some doubt as to the precise chronology of Prince Prisadang's collaboration in refashioning the Oriental, his very elderly widow Mom Sagniem asserted (according to the then-manager Madame Krull in her memoir, *Bangkok: Siam's City of Angels* (1964)): "The middle of your hotel was his father's palace... and he gave it away to the foreigners just like that." Mom Sagniem went on to explain that her deceased husband wanted "to do something for the poor foreign captains and sailors who came to Siam and did not know where to stay" and overcame his father's vehement opposition through sheer determination to provide a decent hotel for foreigners. Assuming that his father owned land there, the donation of land for hospitable purposes must have taken place prior to his death in 1868.

After 1885 a straight lane was cut from New Road to the river, colonial-style wooden villas were built opposite the hotel and a general store with a European bakery was established that made early morning deliveries of foodstuffs to the foreign community. A team of local Italian architects, Cardu & Rossi, designed the new Oriental Hotel and its construction caused quite a titter among the natives. They thought foreigners would be unwilling to climb up all the stairs; that they would be lodged in the air. As John Crawfurd had already noted in 1824: "These people have an extreme horror of permitting anything to pass over the head, or having the head touched, or, in short, bringing themselves into any situation in which their persons are liable to be brought into a situation of physical inferiority to that of others, such as going under a bridge, or entering the lower apartment of a house when the upper one is inhabited."

The grand opening day of the refurbished Oriental Hotel was 19 May 1887. It boasted forty "commodious and well furnished bedrooms", according to a report on the inauguration that appeared in a local paper with an open invitation:

> We have been asked to say that no invitations have been sent for the opening of the new Oriental Hotel on Thursday, but the proprietors Messrs Andersen & Co wish all to know that they will be welcome on that occasion from 4 p.m. onwards when the fountains of magnanimity will be turned on and rain hospitality all around.

It was a splashy affair. Foreigners and the Siamese elite turned out to admire the handsome Italianate building. The ornamental rising sun on the Victorian pediment announced the dawn of the first luxury hotel in Siam. A painting in the hotel verandah leading out to the river shows it as it looked then. The large central portico was divided into a multi-functional room: lobby, office, reading, smoking and ladies rooms, a billiard room and "splendid new bar" that led into the Blue Room with a seating capacity of fifty. The sitting room had peacock blue divans and matching Brussels carpets. A loggia on the ground floor of the annex led out onto a garden court refreshed by five bubbling fountains. The upstairs bedrooms had large verandahs and were decorated in *fin-de-siècle* chic: mahogany bed sets, Parisian wallpaper and soft furnishings. A spiral staircase at the end of each wing led to the balustraded roof for a river view.

The first major hotel event was a grand banquet in honour of Queen Victoria's Golden Jubilee on 24 May 1888. The Oriental's first chef, fittingly named Monsieur Georges Troisoeufs, and a bartender named Spider, who had been lured away from the French Consulate, teamed up to create a festive menu. After spectacular fireworks and a 101-gun royal salute, the band played *Rule Britannia* and guests danced until early morning. A Siamese audience watched from their boats on the river, captivated by the sight of intertwined couples in formal dress waltzing on the moonlit lawn.

Prince Prisdang Jumsai gave a splendid banquet at the Oriental in the autumn of 1888, the charming Victorian menu of which came to light during research for this book. Guests at that dinner, held in the elegant

179

Regency Room (the original lobby of the old hotel), were members of the Post and Telegraph Departments. One hundred and nineteen years later to the day in 2007 the general manager of the Oriental and his wife hosted the first Prince Prisdang Annual Dinner in the sumptuous interior, recently restored to its former *fin-de-siècle* opulence. Executive Chef Norbert A. Kostner replicated the original menu to the apparent delight of Her Royal Highness Princess Maha Chakri Sirindhorn who graciously presided over the event. It was a rare gathering of eighteen royal clansmen and clanswomen—all descendants of Kings Rama III, Rama IV, Pinklao (the Second King in the Fourth Reign) and Rama V. The guest list also included two lucky *farangs*.

Imagine a full score of handsome, fresh-faced Thai waiters entering a resplendent, glimmering chamber, its dado richly upholstered in soft tufted gold leather and high walls covered with hand-woven silk panels echoing the shade below. Dancing light from two magnificent hand-cut Bohemian chandeliers twinkles in the panes of French windows that give onto the Authors' Terrace. As the waiters glide forth in unison the rustling of their copper-colored silk *panungs* mimics the swishing sound of wind among reeds; their swan-like movements animate the great gilded art nouveau mirrors at each end. Kneeling acolytes serve the smiling princess. Table decorations—gold burnished miniature elephants in ceremonial apparel, great clusters of shiny Italian green grapes, *dok rak* (flower of love) garlands and commemorative menus—capture the vintage look to perfection.

This was no easy fête to recreate, as a beaming Chef Kostner related to a rapt post-prandial audience. When he first received the menu from 1888 he turned *tout de suite* to the classic cook books of French master Antonie Carême, as well as to the "Emperor of Chefs", Auguste Escoffier, who had introduced *service à la russe* (serving each dish in the order printed on the menu). A few phone calls—to Michel Roth, Executive Chef of the Ritz in Paris and to his counterpart Bruno Turbo of the Negresco in Nice—gave him good food for thought and a few measures of *bon courage*. Digestifs began to flow. And the night had an unforgettable golden glow.

During Andersen's period of ownership in the late nineteenth century great quantities of alcohol were consumed at the hotel. When King Chulalongkorn hosted a dinner there for Crown Prince Nicholas of Russia in March 1891, the German manager Herr Schmidt had *carte blanche* to provide "all the luxuries which modern civilization can offer." The king had personally met the prince at the port of Pak Nam and escorted him to Bangkok. His guest was dressed in a most impressive uniform of the Hussars of the Imperial Guard, his black bearskin hat topped with a white egret. A British journalist reported the unusual visit: "The hotel offered free hospitality to the officers who arrived wearing helmets surmounted by gilt or silver double-headed eagles larger than pigeons. Every drop of alcohol was consumed in no time and the hotel had to lay in a fresh supply for the next day which met with a similar fate."

But the evenings could be unbearably dull for more cultured types. Lucien Fournereau was quite bored, as he describes in a brief essay written in 1892.

> Distractions? None. Here one does not even find the equivalent of what one has in Saigon, the rue Catinat, so happy and so French. No cafés, a few more or less shady bars; no theatres, no concerts,... no gypsies, no European quarter, hence no visits to pay; my God, how bored one is!
>
> What is there then to make life at the Oriental Hotel tolerable? Nothing. Two clubs have been set up in Bangkok: one is English, the other German; one cannot go in except by introduction. Everybody lives at home: the married men with their wives, the single men with their boredom. *Voe solis!*

The Oriental Hotel changed hands once more in 1892 when H. N. Andersen sold it to Louis Leonowens, the son of the redoubtable Anna. He had returned to Siam in 1882 and was appointed a cavalry officer by his mother's former student, King Chulalongkorn. He then founded what would become a successful trading company. At the hotel his first action was to install more fountains on the lawn. He threw lavish, sometimes rakish, parties for Thai and foreign friends that would have shocked his prim mother. His manager "Wild Bill" Hurst was a sloppy accountant and blamed white ants for destroying the books. Legend had it that Leonowens rode horseback up the staircase of the Oriental to fire him on the spot.

Madame Maire and Madame Krull

By the turn of the century a rail line brought travellers to the Oriental Hotel from the new train station across the river in Thonburi. The hotel

had become like an informal club for locals; its lawn was the scene of circuses, marionette shows, Thai boxing and cricket matches. They immediately warmed to the "smart dining room" with its newly installed electrical
lighting. A bandstand had been built on the lawn and the Siamese Navy
Band played western music every Monday night that "saved many a one
a fit of the blues," an expatriate reported.

The hotel attracted a variety of guests, some rather more notorious
than others. Count Zalata, for example, had fled the Ukraine after the Tsar
was told that he had raped 72 peasant girls. Another famous escapee was
Marguerite Steinheil, who was dubbed *Pompe Funèbre* (pun of "funeral
industry" and "deadly sucker") after the French President Félix Faure died
of apoplexy in his office, allegedly while she was performing oral sex.

A succession of short-term owners came and went until Madame
Marie Maire took over in 1910. While her husband supported the bar,
she went to work revamping the hotel. She installed a good French chef
in the kitchen, redecorated the rooms and made all concerts free. The following year the hotel was inundated with royalty for the coronation of
King Rama VI. All forty rooms were booked by Prince William of Sweden,
Prince Waldemar of Denmark, Grand Duke Boris of Russia and the
foreign journalists who accompanied them. They were followed by the
visit of Peter Carl Fabergé, the famous *bijoutier* to the Russian court, who
presented a lavish exhibition of Fabergé finery that attracted *tout Bangkok*.
The new king ordered some exquisite pieces, including an image of
Buddha that is now kept in the temple of the Emerald Buddha at the
Grand Palace.

Madame Maire was still manageress of the Oriental Hotel when Somerset Maugham arrived in Bangkok in 1923 following a two-month trek
through the Shan States and northern Siam with his secretary-companion
Gerard Haxton. The writer took respite at the hotel, away from the
streetscape of "dust and heat and noise and whiteness and more dust". He
later recalled his riverfront bedroom at the Oriental as "dark, one of a long
line, with a veranda on each side of it, the breeze blew through, but it was
stifling." Possibly a serious attack of malaria made him dyspeptic, for he
later recounted an ill-natured and possibly embellished account of this
event in *The Gentleman in the Parlour: A Record of a Journey from Rangoon
to Haiphong* (1930):

It was apparently a bad attack, since for some days the quinine had no effect on me, my temperature soared to those vertiginous heights that are common in malaria and neither wet sheets nor ice packs brought it down. I lay there, panting and sleepless, and shapes of monstrous pagodas thronged my brain and great gilded Buddhas bore down on me. Those wooden rooms, with their verandas, made every sound frightfully audible to my tortured ears and one morning I heard the manageress of the hotel, an amiable creature but a good woman of business, in her guttural German voice say to the doctor: 'I can't have him die here, you know. You must take him to the hospital.' And the doctor replied: 'All right. But we'll wait a day or two yet.' 'Well, don't leave it too long,' she replied.

Rather surprisingly, Maugham returned to the Oriental in December 1925, for a bit of sightseeing as well as inspiration, he told a local journalist. Soon he was an habitué, he wrote, of "the unofficial club which meets every day (except Sundays) in the old bar, and which draws its membership almost exclusively from the mercantile houses on Oriental Avenue and Charted Bank Lane... From eleven to noon a good deal of gossip passed over the marble-topped tables and the sound of the dice box was not unknown." But on his final visit to Bangkok in 1960 to celebrate his 85th birthday the famous author stayed in the new Erawan Hotel rather than at the Oriental, where Madame Maire had allegedly nearly evicted him, he told reporters, for fear he would "ruin her business by dying in one of her rooms."

Maugham's negative remarks on the Oriental Hotel, published in *The Gentleman in the Parlour* in 1930, may have influenced Noel Coward to choose the Phya Thai Palace Hotel when he came to Bangkok that year. This beautiful retreat built by King Rama VI was "new and modern, splendid, but in good taste," Coward noted. However, towards sunset Coward headed over to the Oriental Hotel for magical evenings, as he recalled in his autobiography *Present Indicative* (1937): "There is a terrace overlooking the swift river where we have drinks every evening watching the liver-coloured water swirling by and tiny steam tugs hauling rows of barges up river against the tide. It is a lovely place and I am fonder of it than ever".

The Oriental was the meeting place for almost every foreigner who travelled to Bangkok, as well as the social centre for the local foreign community. At the annual Christmas Dance in 1935 a local artist painted a panoramic frieze of Alpine scenery along the walls of the large dining room and a specially laid floor turned the lawn into an open-air ballroom for two hundred guests. But this fantasy life was doomed. After abdicating the throne in 1934 King Rama VII was a royal exile in England. The Japanese were making their presence felt in Bangkok, as were arms dealers who supplied the emerging nationalist movements in Southeast Asia, especially in Vietnam. Military domination of politics fostered militant Thai nationalism that made Europeans in Bangkok uneasy.

During the Second World War the rising sun over the Oriental was almost permanently eclipsed. Madame Maire sold the hotel lease and equipment in 1934 to the Japanese army occupying Thailand. It became an officers' club and locals were forbidden entrance. When the Japanese were forced to retreat, the Thai army locked up the silver flatware and dinner service. The hotel then became a billet for Allied personnel—Dutch, Australian and English—who thought they were destroying Japanese property when they ransacked the place. The porcelain and silver that they stole, bearing the monogram and mark of the Oriental, turned up for years in the Thieves' Market.

Determined to restore its former elegance, a new management purchased the lease and six new partners put up $250 dollars each. There were three Thais—a general, a lawyer and a prince; two Americans who had served in the Organization for Strategic Security and stayed on in Thailand to make fortunes after the war—John Webster and Jim Thompson; and a French woman named Germaine Krull who brought rather unique qualifications to the job of manager that she accepted in 1947. Krull had been sent to Bangkok by Agence France Presse as a war correspondent and photographer. As a photographer she was not unknown (during the 1920s she had done a pioneering series of nude and lesbian studies and taken a famous portrait of Jean Cocteau) but as a manager she became famous.

En route to her first inspection of the place she turned off New Road into what was then called Oriental Store Lane—a "narrow bumpy lane, full of pot-holes, which seemed to lead straight into the river." She then walked from "unkempt lawns and garden" into "the dirty desolation" inside. Her inventory of the ground floor, published in her memoir, records the sorry state of the hotel.

LOBBY. Crude Tudor style. Teak wainscoting, ceiling beams, doors, windows and a horrid fake fireplace all painted soot black. Four over-stuffed English club settees with springs exposed. Rotting carpets but attractive tiles underneath.

KITCHEN. Massive antique European stove. Four tables crowded into corners covered with a welter of dusty boxes stuffed with old newspapers. Broken bits of crockery. Dirty dishes, pots and pans. Old cans. Worn toothbrushes. Rusty razors. Indescribable rubbish.

ROOM NEXT TO KITCHEN. Dark, slippery, dirty. (But the American Air Force officers who occupy half of the hotel don't care; they only eat canned food.)

Then Madame Krull leads us upstairs:

All the hotel guest-rooms were on the first floor [the American second] reached by the wide staircase with its wonderful old carved banisters. Facing the river in front were two large Victorian-style rooms nearly seventeen feet high. They had huge mirrors framed in gold, decorated with garlands held by fat little cherubs and in the middle the sweet profile of good Queen Victoria. Both of these rooms were separated by wooden partitions from huge elegant bathrooms with marble floors and walls and built in marble tubs. The water did not run in these bathrooms and two huge earthenware jars, standing near the doors, had to be filled daily by coolies who carried the water upstairs. An archway separated windows with wooden shutters. Of course there was no glass in any of the windows and the shutters had to be kept closed to keep out the sun or the rain. The furniture should have been in a junk store, and included many styles and colors. These were the hotel's two proudest rooms—the bridal suites.

On 12 June 1947 the hotel opened once again to great fanfare. Krull seems to have been a natural hotelier. She trained the local staff, hired Chinese carpenters to make bedroom sets and Vietnamese university students to paint the walls; she taught the Thai chef how to cook European cuisine. She scoured flea markets for crockery, mosquito netting and provisions, transformed a jungle into a garden. Her industry filled the hotel with "every type from newly arriving diplomats to fortune hunters, adventurers, spies and crooks. Everyone claimed to be a VIP with a heroic war record..." "Lady friends" were spirited in and out, she says. Money was stolen. Jim Thompson quit as partner over a plan to build a new wing. Endless crises occurred.

Loopy foreigners and other eccentrics also came and went. A Frenchman returned a request for payment of his bill by stating that, since he had been "instructed by Television Radio to go and have my meals at the Oriental Hotel and I had done so, am I to be blamed for the deed I had done, and for the bills incurred at your hotel?" It was signed "H. W. Berlandier, Thai Super Natural Extraordinary". A self-proclaimed Latvian bishop and his secretary strode into the hotel lobby wearing flowing red robes; their gaunt, bearded faces crowned by tiaras on top of skull caps. They were there to denounce the *Sodom and Gomorrah* of Bangkok. Krull handled all these events with efficiency and humour, even those occasions when diplomats were caught in embarrassing situations with Thai women at garden parties.

To compete with a new local bar called Chez Eve and other trendy clubs, Krull opened the Bamboo Bar in 1947, which became to Bangkok what Harry's is to Venice except that it had music. It is still one of the best places in the city for jazz and blues. The bar got off to a frisky start when the soprano started throwing ashtrays at the Thai pianist and then at anyone else she thought looked at her in the wrong way. Krull obliged men to wear ties for admission, but *mai pen rai* (never mind) if you didn't have one handy. She had hundreds made from the brightest and cheapest satin available with the bar logo painted on—cocks with flamboyant spreading tails.

In post-war Bangkok the guests themselves were often the best entertainment, Krull recalls:

> We did not need a floor show as we had exotic guests from all over the world wearing fabulous gold and silver embroidered costumes with gorgeous jewelry. Others wore the latest styles from Europe. Sometimes the atmosphere was that of a carnival or Mardi Gras as guests dropped in still wearing the elaborate traditional dress they had just worn to a diplomatic reception. Officers in uniforms covered with medal and gold braid glided by with the tiny wives of their Thai counterparts barely coming above their belt buckles even with the help of elaborate pompadours.

HOME AWAY FROM HOME

During her nearly two decades as part-owner and full-time manageress of the Oriental, Krull transformed it into a modern hotel almost single-handedly. New hotels were more centrally located in the expanding city, but the first hotel in Bangkok had a history and a riverfront location that were unbeatable. Krull feared Thailand would fall to the communists and decided to sell her share of the hotel in 1967. The next owner was the gregarious Italian entrepreneur Giorgio Berlingieri who brought in Kurt Wachtveitl, a graduate of the prestigious École Hôtelière de Lausanne, Switzerland. Khun Kurt, as he is known to the 800-member staff, has taken the hotel into the twenty-first century while preserving the quintessentially Thai graciousness that is evident as soon as you walk in the door. In February 2006, after another major facelift, the grand dame celebrated her 130th anniversary with the proud manager for the last four decades as a beaming host.

Royalty and the *glitterati* are still coming to the Oriental, drawn by the service, style and its reputation. *Travel and Leisure* (August 2007) rated it one of the top ten hotels of the world. Awards garnered over the years are displayed in the Trophy Room adjacent to the Authors' Lounge. Autographs and messages from glamorous guests from every walk in life are on view as well. The Oriental has been home to some of the word's most famous faces. Marlon Brando stayed there when he came to visit M. R. Kukrit Pramoj who had co-starred with him in *The Ugly American*. Yet more names lend glamour: Roger Moore, Elizabeth Taylor, Princess Grace of Monaco, Yehudi Menuhin, Lauren Bacall, Alfred Hitchcock, Audrey Hepburn, Richard Nixon, Sean Connery, Neil Armstrong, Omar Sharif, Henry Kissinger, George H.W. Bush, Sophia Loren, Norman Mailer, Mick Jagger, Queen Sofia of Spain, Jacques Chirac, Vaclev Havel, Pelé, Mel Gibson, David Beckham. Prince Charles and Princess Diana stayed there. "No home away from home has a right to be so luxurious and so human," Sir Peter Ustinov reckoned. "When I leave, I'll already be on my way back."

If you are in the mood, take a short walk down Oriental Lane. Follow the sign pointing to the French Embassy at the heart of the postage stamp *quartier français*. A handsome colonial building was home to the first French legation in 1857 and became the official site of the French consulate during the reign of Rama V. Nearby is the fine masonry building occupied by the Embassy. A visitor in the late nineteenth century was impressed by the view from the second floor: "as the Menam widens in gracious curves, the city develops and takes on an appearance not lacking in greatness."

For a decade or so after the French Revolution, the number of missionaries diminished and the first Catholic Church, The Assumption, built in 1809, had a sinuous Sino-Portuguese façade that was a better cultural fit than the present cathedral—a European building with its imported marble and stained glass. When the indefatigable Bishop Pallegoix arrived in 1830 there were already five Catholic communities in Bangkok. Assumption Camp was surrounded by the houses of the faithful spread out in vast gardens near the church. The famous American Protestant missionary, Dan Beach Bradley, once wondered if the "extreme humidity and heat of this place contribute to a kind of madness that sometimes overtakes the foreign residents of Siam." Not the Frenchmen, who never abandoned their long beards and floor length-black cassocks. They were a valiant lot, especially Fr. Colombet who in 1885 founded Assumption College (opposite the Oriental Hotel), still the most prestigious secondary school in the city.

Bangkok must be one of the only cities in the world where a Muslim residential area is a stone's throw from the luxury suites of world famous hotel. The Haroon Mosque built in 1897 is the centre of a thriving community of about sixty families living in old wooden houses and very simple dwellings as they have for over a century.

Within a few minutes walk is the Church of the Holy Rosary (Wat Kalyanamit), a lovely little cream-coloured architectural doily in neo-Gothic style (1891-98). French Bishop Pallegoix invites us to imagine its earliest days.

> There is a Chinese-style church built especially for novices by means of a subscription made among Christians and even among the heathen. It has replaced an old worm-eaten hall of which the floor collapsed one day when they were baptizing some twenty Chinese. Godfathers and catechumen fell any old way but only got up with many bruises. The priest, who was on a flight of steps, remained at his post as if he hung in the air.

Part Four

CITY OF ART AND FOOD

Fourteen

SILPA BHIRASRI MEMORIAL
FOUNDATION

Once out of the flamboyant Grand Palace complex, walk across Thanon Na Phra Lan. The street contains graceful old shop-houses dating from the reign of King Rama V. Nearly invisible behind a crenellated white wall is the main entrance to Silpakorn University. This institution was founded in 1943 by the Italian-born art professor Corrado Feroci at the behest of King Rama IX, who bestowed on him the honorific Thai name of Silpa Bhirasri, "creator of beautiful art", in 1944. Under his thoughtful and visionary tutelage as dean the university became the cradle of modern Thai art and he is revered as its father. In the past sixty years it has expanded to include numerous faculties and its 7,000 students are spread over three campuses. The compact Tha Phra Lan campus comprises an assortment of nondescript buildings from the 1950s and 1960s, working studios and a beautiful building that was part of a late eighteenth-century royal palace—the Tha Phra Palace, the oldest building on campus and architectural centrepiece of the university.

Tha Phra Palace was a traditional Siamese complex built in the First Reign for the son of King Taksin and son-in-law of King Rama I. It was already connected with the arts from the Second Reign (1809-24) when the future King Rama III, Prince Jesdabordin, resided there and directed a huge building programme for temples. In the Fourth Reign (1851-68), Prince Krom Khun Rajsri (Jumsai), a gifted son of King Rama III, headed the Royal Crafts Department, which included building construction and stonework. The audience hall was a workshop for the carpenters, wood carvers, mosaicists and cloth painters who were employed on royal projects. A sepia photograph in the Authors' Wing of the Oriental Hotel dating from the mid-nineteenth century shows the prince, in traditional Siamese dress; he bears a gold sword and a compass, befitting his role as royal architect under King Rama IV. He designed many important buildings in the Grand Palace and Phra Pathom Chedi, among others, and his sons, including Prince Prisdang, all became artists and architects.

The last royal occupant of the palace was Prince Narisaranuwatti-wongse (Prince Naris), who was one of the foremost artists and architects of the early twentieth century as well as a great patron of the arts. He had wooden structures torn down to make way for three neoclassical European-style buildings. He retained the royal reception hall, but modernized it by adding fluted columns, shutters and awnings. After his death in 1964 his heirs sold the palace to the government, which incorporated it into the Silpakorn campus as the university art gallery.

First Art Professor in Thailand

The choice of Silpa Bhirasri to develop a university devoted to art was a particularly astute move by King Rama IX. Ajarn Sin (as he was known) was an unusual art missionary: he steered a diplomatic and careful course between two traditions, instituting a conversion to western methods while promoting indigenous values to make modern art. Charismatic and indefatigable, he trumpeted this vibrant new visual culture internationally. New Delhi, Vienna, New York and London got a virgin look at modern Thai art. He had a genuine paternal devotion to students, lending money, exacting strict discipline, supporting study abroad and opening up new horizons. Prayad Pongdam, a former student and major artist who is still active today, describes the academic programme that was enlivened by expansive art history lectures.

> Our studies were based on daily practice. The first year we studied anatomy with the human skeleton, the second the muscles and Leonardo's sketches, and the last year we learned about light and shade. Professor (Ajarn) Silpa Bhirasri took us to the sea or to the mountains, and we were happy walking with him and listening to him talk about everything—Romanesque, Gothic, Renaissance art, about styles and tastes of bygone times.

At the request of King Rama VI the artist had left Florence in 1923 to live in Bangkok and assume the role of Official Sculptor. Belying the rather Kafkaesque title he held for nearly forty decades—"civil servant extraordinary #1 of the Fine Arts Department"—Silpa was a remarkable man with a clear mission. He was dogged, passionate, a true *cortegiano*. He made more than eighteen monuments in Thailand and left an invaluable and enduring legacy. Silpa brought the heroic memorial to Thailand; his numerous bronzes illustrated the grand Thai nationalist narrative.

Despite the unique position accorded him, Silpa's dealings with the Thai military regime were not always equable. Field Marshal Phibul who ran Thailand in the 1940s and for most of the 1950s wanted architecture that expressed a martial ethos and sought his collaboration as a sculptor. The Democracy Monument on Rajdamnern Avenue designed by a Thai architect evokes the icy fascism of Mussolini's EUR in Rome as well as Mexico City's grandiose Monument to the Revolution in the Plaza de la República. However, half of Silpa's plaster casts for the relief panels of the monument were rejected by the coup leaders because they did not illustrate the ideological aims of the ruling regime. A model for a relief showing King Rama VII presenting the Constitution to the people was the most contentious because it highlighted his role in the transition to constitutional monarchy. Rather than compromise his own artistic integrity, Silpa asked his students to complete the work.

The Silpa Bhirasri Memorial Museum at the rear of the Silpakorn campus displays a number of the artist's prized works and an array of paintings and sculptures by gifted students. Adjacent to the gallery is what was the artist's daily workspace, preserved without hagiography. The visitor experiences a palpable sense of his creative intellect in the glassed-in bookcases containing European and Asian art books, dictionaries, sheaves of documents, lecture notes, preliminary drawings and watercolour sketches. His regular daily habits are evoked by dusty, quasi-ethnographic objects: plaster models, a terracotta royal bust of the reigning King Rama IX (left unfinished at the sculptor's death), small bronzes, sculptural tools, a fissured blackboard encrusted with chalk, an old gramophone with a scratched recording of Beethoven's 5th, odd bits of rusted, anachronistic office supplies and other miscellanea. On his long teak worktable a bronze bust of his toddler son Romano—now an octogenarian architect in Milan—seems like an improbable, ancient guardian over a vintage Olympia typewriter and a yellowed photo of his father deeply concentrated before it.

The persona who emerges from portraits, photographs and posters shows keen awareness of his professional role as a European artist and as the first academic art educator in Thailand. Yet his cultivated *gravitas* was not primarily intended to advance his personal myth of greatness but rather to exemplify the image of the professional artist for his Thai students.

An exhibition at the National Gallery in 1992 brought together seventy-three former students who paid homage to their master, still loyal thirty years after his death. Unfortunately, their dedication is often lost in the poorly translated catalogue, though sometimes to comic effect. Silpa's repetition of a quip used by Renaissance artists to prick intellectual pretension, "We painters think with our hands," is translated as "Don't paint with your hands and feet, but use your head, too."

In a farewell note to his beautiful young Thai-Danish wife just before he died, Silpa asked that grief be temperate. After all, he had spent his professional life "for something useful as a modest servant of my art." At his death in 1962 his writings comprised over fifty pioneering articles in English and Thai, the fruit of primary research on Sukhothai, Ayudhya, murals, painted cloth banners, lacquer works, wood carvings, monumental bronzes and Buddhist iconography. Against his expressed wishes, he was given a royal cremation but it was a glorious send-off rather than a great solemn affair. Silpakorn students bathed his body with lustral water, dressed him in his white civil service uniform, placed joss sticks and incense under his gilded coffin and consumed great quantities of food. We can guess at the atmosphere from the writer Carol Hollinger's description of death ceremonies (which she preferred to cocktail parties) in *Mai Pen Rai Means Never Mind*: "If you can imagine going to church on Sunday and telling jokes, eating popcorn while your minister delivers his sermon, you have a rough idea of what happens at a Thai religious ceremony. All social events of note are usually religious and all religious events are usually social."

Silpa Bhirasri's birthday is celebrated annually at Silpakorn University every 15 September with a *sanuk*-style celebration that is quintessentially Thai. His life-size effigy in Silpa Bhirasri Square is festooned with colourful bouquets and delicate *malai*—garlands of pale jasmine flowers and miniature roses. This is a measure of his exceptional importance in Thai society that usually elevates only kings, noblemen and monks. Prizes are awarded in his honour and special exhibitions are inaugurated. Cult items—mugs, T-shirts, tote bags, most bearing his portrait—are stacked high. After a typically al fresco Thai dinner, an artsy crowd transforms the marble platform beneath his effigy into a luminous birthday cake with tiny candles placed on dollops of melted wax. Verdi might well have imagined the set design but not the marching band that plays the Silpakorn alma mater and Teodoro Cottrau's *Santa Lucia* sung in Thai-accented Italian.

Following Silpa's death his pupils went "their own ways, far from the field of naturalistic heroics, into abstraction, impressionism, cubism, revival of traditional art and into paths for which names do not come easily," in the view of art critic Michael Wright. Queen's Gallery on Rajdamnern Avenue and dozens of galleries in the Silom and Sukhumvit stretches of the city exhibit the work of the next generation. Traditional Buddhist themes sell well, as do Georg Baselitz-style abstract paintings. Young artists take on contemporary social problems but their moralizing works could do with a shot of satire. Graduates of major urban schools who have gone back to their farmland roots up-country show a hip ecological trend. In his overview of *Modern Asian Art* (1998), John Clark detects irony in the consumption by a city-dwelling market of paintings by "folkway purveyors of an essentially anti-metropolitan attitude to life" in Bangkok. In a huge, polluted mega-city, some locals need escape artists.

Through Ajarn Silpa's exemplary devotion to art, both as *praxis* and as an intellectually grounded activity, he aimed to elevate the collective status of the modern artist in Thai society. The Bangkok Art & Culture Center (BAAC), scheduled to open in February 2008 at the Rajprasong intersection, will give concrete realization to his deep "hope that very soon a new era in the understanding of the importance of contemporary art may start in Thailand and, arising from this indispensable factor, our artists may reach their professional maturity."

Fifteen

M. R. KUKRIT PRAMOJ HERITAGE HOME

To get a glimpse into the life of an aristocratic Siamese, deeply concerned with tradition but also open to modernity, you could do no better than visit what is now known as the M. R. Kukrit's Heritage Home on a quiet lane (19 soi Phra Pinit) off South Sathorn Road.

Kukrit Pramoj (1911-95) was a Mom Rajwongse, a king's great-grandson. His paternal grandfather was the sixty-first child of King Rama II. Unlike European nobility, where one could marry into royalty, the Thai royal family has always been aristocratic by virtue of royal bloodline. The young Kukrit was raised under palatial glittering roofs and educated by private tutors at home until the age of fifteen. He was sent to boarding school in England and then went on to Oxford where he took an honours degree in Philosophy, Politics, and Economics in 1933—a year after the coup d'état ended absolute monarchy in Thailand.

On his return, Kukrit began a remarkable and versatile career as military recruit, banker, professor, classical dancer, movie star, politician and writer. In 1945 he established the Progress Party, the first political party in the country. He starred as an Asian prime minister in the *Ugly American* opposite Marlon Brando (1963) and later served briefly as thirteenth prime minister of Thailand (1975-76). He founded and owned the highly-influential *Siam Rath* newspaper. A suite in the Authors' Wing at the Oriental Hotel is dedicated to Kukrit Pramoj—the nation's foremost modern author of novels, short stories, stage plays, poems and newspaper columns. In 1985 he was named a National Artist in Literature.

Kukrit was a handsome man of patrician bearing who liked to dress in the old Siamese court uniform with a high-collared long white jacket over a beautiful silk *panung*. He could be charming and was a brilliant conversationalist with cultivated Oxbridge English—"as long as you are not a victim of his rapier sharpness," warned Germaine Krull, post-war proprietor of the Oriental Hotel. "Even the most adroit diplomats carefully avoided crossing swords with Kukrit after their first experience with this 'enfant terrible' of Bangkok's social life," she wrote.

Kukrit held salon at the "House on Suan Phlu", his impressive residential compound set in a two acre-garden of tall areca palm trees (from which betel nuts grow). Over a period of twenty years he bought five small authentic teak houses from the central plain of Thailand, some over a century old, to this site. Traditional Thai houses are like living organisms designed for a tropical climate and in harmony with the natural surroundings. They are raised on stilts to protect from seasonal flooding, to facilitate ventilation, and to provide a storage area under the house for animals, farming implements and fishing equipment. During the day the ground floor would often have been used as a reception area where guests could relax on bamboo beds in the shade; or it would have doubled as an open air area in which to produce handicrafts.

The five houses were dismantled for transport; then reassembled in a U-shape. Two teak staircases were added and they were interconnected upstairs by a tiled floor. Kukrit determined that each of the one-room houses should have its own specific function: bedroom, library, official reception room, private sitting room and family shrine. But he did once admit that it was not very comfortable living in these beach-like bungalows, especially during the long rainy season from June to November. He likened it to "a country cottage in a far-off village in England, recently done-up by

a millionaire from London. Although it retains its characteristics, the standard of comfort is entirely different." Furnishings in the rather monastic sleeping area of his personal Thai *maisonette* are reduced to scale—a single bed, a prized Burmese Buddha, photos of the royal family, curio case, stereo speakers and a video recorder. On a narrow table under a carved wooden dividing screen sits an old thermos, a ceramic cup, and a bottle of Metamucil that no one has bothered to hide.

This may be the only private residence in Thailand inspired by a fictional house. Kukrit wanted to recreate a teak compound described in the epic poem *Khun Chang Khun Phaen* by the great nineteenth-century poet Sunthorn Phu. Khun Phaen, the poem's lusty protagonist, lived in a traditional style Thai home in the countryside outside the capital city of Ayudhya. (This fictional place was actually built a few decades ago in the center of the old capital where it can be visited today.)

One moonlit night Khun Phaen gazed from his verandah at playful goldfish whose amorous games amused him.

> Next to the flowers in tubs and fishbowls
> Where goldfish, big and small, swam about.
> Sprouting water, they floated and sank
> Down in pairs, all the more admirable
> Some made their way through the water-lettuce
> To the mountain gaps, biting and fighting,
> Some rubbed at moss or caressed their mates.

The poet then invites the reader to join him upstairs where the elevated floor gave onto ponds and gardens; blessed by southern breezes during the hot Thai summer, it was the perfect setting for Khun Phaen's nocturnal nature-watching.

> Some plants show off their abundant blossoms
> Under the resplendent light of the moon.

But Kukrit's evenings were not so peaceful, at least at the start. One of his night-time "guests" was the ghost of an old lady named Ruen Khun Yai. She had owned the first of the small teak houses that he had had dismantled and reassembled in his garden. It was a real case of house-moving and her ghost came with it. She apparently kept arriving nightly at "Grandmother's House" (it was named after her) in a pedicab she had commandeered. Then she would disappear into her old home and caused all sorts of odd disturbances that the new owner enjoyed recounting.

Some years later this first house was once again dismantled and enlarged to make a formal reception pavilion (*sala*) that is open on three sides for public functions and classical dance performances. Set high on the wall is a portrait of Kukrit like a venerable ancestral god in royal dress that clearly enshrines his own lofty place in the traditional Thai social hierarchy. You may even have an eerie sense that he instructs the grimacing *khon* demon masks behind the glass on the right to keep an eye on you as you wander across an intimate walled sculpture garden to his favorite writing spot just off the informal sitting room under the house.

We see him again in a large watercolour with his beloved beagles Samsee and Sabai. Samsee's disappearance in 1968 prompted a poignant lament by him in *Siam Rath* that apparently shocked his readers for its rare emotional transparency.

> Long ago I rejected ambition.
> Long ago I stopped thinking of rank, admiration, fortune or even the love and understanding of my fellow man.
> Long ago I lost interest in the gossip and criticism about me...
> One black dog. He made my loneliness bearable.
> Every time I went out, he was there to see me off, and whenever I returned home, he was there to welcome me. When I was home, he would stay close to me. He is the only thing I felt close to.

The *Siam Rath* also ran a serialization of Kukrit's novel *The Four Reigns* (1954) where the author aimed to chronicle the "inescapable facts of getting born, falling ill, growing old and dying" against the backdrop of modern Thai history. The long queues forming each day at newsstands for the latest installment testified to his popularity.

To the old Siamese middle class, daily life in royal circles during the reigns of the four kings (1892-1946) was the stuff of high drama featuring aristocratic characters from the hidden world of the Inner Court. Kukrit took readers behind the thick, crenellated walls of the Grand Palace to a forbidden city. He let them overhear the gossip at the "tunnel" where the servants of court consorts and concubines bathed. His work was steeped in nostalgic detail for Old Siam, for the "modes and mores of a disappearing age." It portrayed the kingdom at the crucible of modernization/westernization and the rapid changes as they were largely reflected in the life of the fictional Mae Ploi who was brought to the harem as a ten-year old during the 1880s. She died at the age of 64 on 9 June 1946 from shock and grief at the mysterious death of King Rama VIII. Throughout her tumultuous life she upheld the "old values: unwavering loyalty to the throne, love and responsibility for the family" that were threatened by the new word "politics" that had entered the Thai language in 1932. Even though she is a fictional character, Mae Ploi has been arguably named as the most famous woman in Thai history.

Ironically, the author of more than thirty books addressed his widest audience with a line scripted from *The Ugly American* (1958) by William Lederer and Eugene Burdick. The film version (1963) starred Marlon Brando as a Foreign Service Officer who wears a conservative pin-striped suit and sports a trim little moustache. Kukrit (who was originally hired as the film's technical consultant) plays a handsome, idealistic prime minister of a mythical Asian country. He assures the American that "democracy has been the fountain of my life." Kukrit thought he was a perfect for the role, as he later told a reporter: "Playing a mere prime minister is no difficulty at all. I look my part. That's why I was so convincing." *New Yorker* film critic Pauline Kael agreed, crediting Kukrit with saving "the later part of the action, when Brando's role is dim".

Kukrit became a real-life prime minister in 1975, a pivotal year for Southeast Asia during which South Vietnam, Laos and Cambodia fell to the communists. He visited China, the first Thai head of government to do so since 1949. Nervous cables went back and forth from the big players but Kukrit did not concur with the American domino theory that Thailand would be the next to fall. He closed American military bases in the north with serious political as well as economic fallout. In *Paradise Preserved* (1981), a short story by the Isan writer Khamsing Srinawk, a northerner mocks a brother-owner whose "carnal paradise" crumbled with the "withdrawal of the gallant American troops".

Kukrit tried to juggle somewhat rival dispositions. A royalist by birth, he was an ardent democrat by inner instinct while a pragmatist by necessity. He tried to moderate polarizing forces but a right-wing reaction started gaining momentum even before his election. A bloody uprising in Bangkok in 1973 had led to the exile of the junta, but the students wanted their grievances heard and massed at front gate of the House on Suan Phlu with funeral garlands (improbably made of cut-up plastic flip-flops). Kukrit was not receptive to their demands for radical social change; he was still strongly attached to the traditional social order. Two years later the military and its allies brought down his short-lived government.

For nearly two decades he wrote scores of editorials on a broad range of social, political and spiritual issues in an effort to educate Thai voters. Page four of *Siam Rath* kept a democratic opposition alive during a repressive era of military dictatorships and coups. It took real courage to do so in a country where hit men were (and still are) very cheap. A staff writer recalls Kukrit's somewhat incautious advice: "Try to ridicule them. When the people laugh, they will lose face and lose everything."

Kukrit also became a kind of Thai agony aunt, addressing all sorts of social problems in his daily advice column, *Let Me Answer Your Questions.* If there were any problems with the in-laws the columnist could claim a certain sensibility: his grandmother-in-law lived right next door. Lyudmilla Borsocoff had been a beautiful young nurse whose father was Chancellor of Fine Arts at the University of St. Petersburg. She fell in love with the grandfather of Kukrit's wife, and voyaged alone on the Trans-Siberian railway to marry her prince in Bangkok. She enthusiastically adapted to Thai ways, though she held her own lively salon for the foreign community, especially the Italian artists who found warm welcome there.

Much like Montaigne in his *citadelle*, Kukrit chose to retreat in his garden-home surrounded by books, beautiful objects, a Siamese garden with a famous collection of miniature trees, and a western-style lawn at the back of the house surrounded by fragrant trees and shrubbery. During the final quarter of the last century he was known as "the Grand Old Man"— the undisputed dean of cultural life in Bangkok and the most vocal preservationist of Siamese traditional arts. Life was very informal in Bangkok until the 1980s by which time explosive city growth and traffic jams made getting around a chore. The Grand Old Man held "audience like a nobleman of old to petitioners and visitors who came to talk with him or seek special favours."

One morning he scribbled out a wistful farewell that friends later included in the memorial book presented at his cremation at the beautiful

Marble Temple (Wat Benjamaborphit) designed by Prince Naris. It was an impressive state ceremony for "one of the nation's monuments" presided over by Their Majesties the King and Queen. "Cry not for Kukrit," he had urged his many mourners. "He is not lost." Indeed, Kukrit is still very much at home on Suan Phlu where aristocratic Siamese living is shown at its best. As he once told a journalist, it was "an elegant sort of life, surrounded by benevolent and exuberantly plentiful Nature, with adaptable morals and a serene detachment to the more serious problems of life."

Sixteen

JIM THOMPSON MUSEUM HOUSE

In every great city of the world legends abound of figures larger than life, be they expatriates or refugees or spies or perennial bums—from Hemingway in Havana to Raffles in Singapore; and Bogart as Rick in Casablanca fleshes out the stereotype. Bangkok can lay claim to an equally sensational example in the American Jim Thompson.

His home on Klong Saen Sap, now a museum-house, was a set design for a life of charm, beauty, glamour and intrigue. Thompson lived there for about ten years surrounded by a priceless collection of Southeast Asian art and a lush tropical garden for his dogs, cockatoos and ducks. But it all ended mysteriously after a picnic lunch with friends on Easter Sunday 1967. Thompson took a stroll in the jungle-clad Cameron Highlands of Malaysia and was never seen again. Neither his body nor his fate has yet been discovered despite the huge reward that was on offer for ten years with immunity from prosecution. A host of theories has been put forward, some very dark. His disappearance added another facet to his legendary life.

Vanishing into thin air in a Southeast Asian jungle was an unlikely ending for a man born in 1910 to privilege in Greenville, Delaware, and educated at St. Paul's and Princeton. His early plans to make his name as an architect were compromised when he failed calculus at the U Penn graduate School of Architecture and left without a degree. Nevertheless he worked for a Manhattan architectural firm from 1931 1940 but could not legally practise in the state. He designed a number of country houses on the East Coast, an experience that would later serve him well.

During the 1930s Thompson was a debonair young man about town, thanks to the bequest of a wealthy relative, good breeding and piercing blue eyes. He developed a keen interest in ballet, especially set design, and became a board member of the Ballet Russe de Monaco that Michel Fokine had brought to New York in 1923. On a trip to Paris Thompson picked up a rare edition of costumes by Léon Bakst—a major figure in the formation of the Diaghilev Ballet and famous for his theatre designs and sensual use of complementary colours in costumes. It included oriental costumes for *Schéhérazade* that premiered at the Opéra Garnier in Paris in 1910.

Thompson was a man who hated routine. Not surprisingly, his political views began to sharply differ from those of his WASP family. He became a Democrat; then enlisted in the Delaware National Guard. He wanted action and escape and by the 1940s had been selected for the Officer Training Corps of the US army. His fluent French was soon put to use. In 1942, six months after his marriage to a former debutante and ex-fashion model, he was sent to North Africa to work with French intelligence forces as a member of the Organization for Strategic Security (precursor to the CIA). From there he went to France where he was involved in daring clandestine missions behind enemy lines. After V-E Day in May 1945, he was sent to Ceylon and was about to be parachuted into Thailand as part of the push to liberate it from the Japanese when the war abruptly ended. For a number of months he was OSS station-chief in Bangkok and set up a temporary American consulate with a military friend named Alexander MacDonald who would stay on to co-found the premier-English daily *The Bangkok Post*.

Thompson originally intended to return to the United States but after his wife divorced him he decided to stay, convinced that there were abundant business prospects in post-war Thailand. He became a partner with Germaine Krull, new manager of the Oriental, in a project to renovate the hotel. A falling-out over a proposed annex to the old building abruptly ended this collaboration and he was forced to follow other interests.

Colourful, hand-woven silks had always been prized in Thai culture, but gradually they had been supplanted by machine-made textiles. Thompson began to collect old pieces, and part of the legend surrounding him was his fortuitous discovery of a weaving enclave in Bangrua on the Klong Saen Sap of Muslim (Cham) families from Cambodia. They had been granted royal rights to live there by King Rama I who was impressed by their artistry. Thompson liked the nub of their weave—its "humps and bumps"—that made it more interesting than other regional silk. He persuaded one of the Cham weavers to produce long bolts of the cloth. With several suitcases full of silk he headed to New York where he met with Edna Woolman Chase, editor of *Vogue*. He convinced her to join in his new venture and she in turn enlisted an Italian dress designer to make a gown of pale mauve silk that appeared in the fashion magazine, causing a stir.

Back in Bangkok Thompson tried to drum up local business and obstinately lived in the Oriental for more than a year where he remained on chilly terms with Mme. Krull. He stood in the lobby like an antique sculpture, his left leg bent slightly forward in counter-pose with silk draped on his extended right arm. Customers interested in a purchase were guided to his office-bedroom upstairs where bolts of shimmering material were ready to be unfolded. Thompson founded the Thai Silk Company in Bangkok in 1951 but it took eight years to shape the scattered and independently-minded weaving families into a coherent cottage industry. He gave shares in his company to the weavers he employed and always had an intimate rapport with them despite the fact that he spoke very little Thai.

Ironically, his fame rose as the result of the Rodgers & Hammerstein musical *The King and I*, the success of the film being largely due to the magnificent costumes. Thomson had worked closely with the designer Irene Sharaff, suggesting appropriate historical styles from old Siamese books of the mid-nineteenth century and producing special weights and colours of silks. After the film the orders started pouring in. Thompson's description of himself as a "missionary but with better visual results" was right on target. He had an innate and exceptional flair for colour and pattern (some of his early combinations came from the Bakst ballet costumes) as well as a commitment to keeping his new silk company a cottage industry so that the weavers would work side-by-side in competition and hopefully generate more income. He standardized the production, introducing colour-fast Swiss dyes to replace the traditional vegetable pigments of orange, dark green and magenta, thus making the silk more attractive for contemporary fashion. Weavers were changed to foot-operated looms which increased their productivity. The measure of his success was immediate. Dozens of copycat silk firms sprang up in Bangkok but no one else had the artistic ability to weave the spindle of silk thread into such original and beautiful designs, with incandescent jewel-like colours. Thompson once told a reporter that the murky canal water in which his silk was traditionally washed gave it a special lustre and guaranteed that it could never be replicated.

THE SILK KING

During the early 1950s Thompson began to dream of a private residence that would allow him to showcase his extraordinary collection of Southeast Asian and Chinese art, picked up for a song as there was little local interest in it. He bought half an acre of land across the canal from his Ban Krua weavers. Although the Pathumwan area was busy even then, the street leading down to the house still preserves some faint traces of the quieter, gentler, more harmonious Old Bangkok that must have attracted him. In 1958 he began to build a house that brilliantly fused Thai design with western features. At that time the traditional wooden homes remaining in Bangkok were the preserve of the Thai elite who used them ceremonially or for classical dance performances. These houses were comprised of sections, each section formed by wall panels held between wooden pillars. The typical *ruen ton* arrangement consisted of a group of airy pavilions functioning as separate units but linked by an open verandah with a staircase outside. King Rama V had issued an edict naming it the Royal Preferred style—though he opted to live in the European Dusit Palace. For most commoners the traditional arrangement was old fashioned and impractical as it was necessary to go out of one section to get to another.

Thompson bought six traditional houses from Bangkok and Ayudhya and reassembled them to suit his needs. The largest house, with a slightly curved roof (drawing room area), was brought from across the canal in Bangrua where it had housed several generations of silk weaving families. He aimed to unify the house as a single structure in order to create an open flow of space; and he did so without sacrificing the authentic Thai character despite the structural problems caused by the high-pitched roofs. Hallways were added on to link the house-rooms and doors were cut to permit access. By leaning the walls inward like a house of cards in traditional fashion, he preserved the tapered, more intimate effect. The drawing room walls were reversed so that the fine exterior carving under the window frames was visible from the inside. Another novel feature was an elegant foyer with an indoor staircase. While traditional teak homes were usually unpainted, he had the exterior protected with flat-red creosote. Apart from the indoor bathroom there were few other concessions to modern comfort. During an elaborate ceremony on 3 April 1959 priests blessed and purified the house and a very fine spirit house for the guardian protector was installed.

Thompson's story had great romantic appeal. *Reader's Digest* did a profile on him for an American audience. A surge of journalistic interest followed. *Time* magazine, *Newsweek*, *Life* and the *New York Times* featured him in high relief—the "Thai Silk King" who had revived a moribund industry and moved into an art-filled dream house on a *klong* in an exotic country. He could barely keep up with the silk orders. "In short order, Thompson found himself cast in the role of a colourful character and, soon, as the best-known foreigner in Bangkok and perhaps in all of Southeast Asia," noted William Warren, author of *Jim Thompson: the Unsolved Mystery* (1998). Thompson Thai silk became famous worldwide. Costumes for *Ben Hur* featured it. The prestigious Savoy Hotel in London used it to redecorate suites and Windsor Castle ordered his silk to refurbish its Canaletto Room. French fashion designer Pierre Balmain designed an exclusive wardrobe for the beautiful Queen Sirikit of Thailand to wear on visits abroad from costly silks brocaded in gold.

The Silk King was an almost compulsive entertainer who did not like to eat alone and had guests almost nightly. Many came with a letter of introduction—statesmen, diplomats, theatrical people, art experts, socialites, journalists. Others did not need one: Joseph Alsop, Cecil Beaton, Barbara Hutton, Ethel Merman, Jacqueline Kennedy, John Rockefeller, William Holden, Anne Baxter, James Michener and Truman Capote. Edward G. Robinson, who starred in gangster movies, later wrote to tell him that dinner had been "the highlight of my trip to Thailand". Somerset Maugham was most impressed by his host's sense of interior design. "Not only do you have beautiful things, but what is more rare, you have displayed them beautifully," he commented. He would have noted that the ornate matching mahjong tables used for dining bore the monogram of King Chulalongkorn. These, a gift from the Chinese people living in Thailand, mysteriously ended up on the market after the king's death.

William Warren, also a guest, writes that Thompson put his house together as a "museum theater" best seen at night:

> Thompson's house by day was not really at its best: then one saw the wiring stretched rather crudely across the ceiling, the inevitable dust on the great chandelier, the flaking paint on the antique cupboards. One noticed in the merciless sunlight of a Bangkok mid-afternoon that the weaving village across the klong looked uncomfortably like the dismal slum it would certainly be called in any American city, and that unspeakable objects were drifting past in the murky water. Thompson,

however, was almost never home during the daytime, and with evening, enchantment set in, as it does when the lights dim in a theater at curtain time. The deliberately soft lights might not have been good for reading but they made the bold colors of the drawing room glow and picked up the dull gilt of the pawnshop doors leading to the bedroom. The over-grown jungle garden became a place of luxuriant tropical mystery with its dangling creepers and its carefully illuminated statuary. The weaving village became exotic, with its spicy scents and its waterfront houses that glowed like little stages presenting scenes from an alien culture.

Thompson had some very unpleasant encounters with that culture in the early 1960s. State authorities accused him of dealing in illegal antiq-uities after the stolen provenance of five limestone heads was confirmed. In a letter to the head of the Fine Arts Department he stated in his defence that Thailand was his permanent home and that he was so "deeply inter-ested in the archaeology and preservation of the beautiful things" of the country that he had written a will donating his home and its contents to the Siam Society. (This will was later changed to give the house and its collection to his nephew.) The official response was a blistering rebuke, aimed not only at his willingness to be completely upfront and to estab-lish his home as a museum but also at his almost single-handed revival of the silk industry. He made a very painful decision to sell his collection of Thai Buddhist art, but kept a few prized pieces. During the period that ensued he began collecting Chinese porcelain and added a charming little picture gallery to the canal side of the house to display his recently pur-chased nineteenth-century paintings of traditional Thai life that had been commissioned by an American missionary in Bangkok.

DISAPPEARANCE

Thompson had always been a vigorous man, trained in jungle survival, but his health began to decline when he was in his late fifties. After several gallstone attacks he was advised to keep a supply of medicine on hand for emergencies. Friends found him tired. He was glad to accept an invita-tion from an old friend to spend the Easter weekend of 1967 in an isolated cottage in a tranquil colonial resort in Malaysia. Following a picnic lunch at which he seemed uncommonly restless, he told his housemates that he was going for a nap but he never returned. Footsteps going down the gravel path leading to the road were the last that was heard of him. He was a chain smoker but left his cigarettes behind as well as his "jungle box" of pills, as he called it, in case of a medical alert that could render him helpless.

The massive manhunt that followed was like a scene out of Conrad's *Secret Agent*: "They swarmed numerous like locusts, industrious like ants, thoughtless like a natural force, pushing on blind and orderly and absorbed..." The story of Thompson's disappearance was sensational and made the front page of newspapers around the world.

Then came an avalanche of theories, each more bizarre than the other. He had been eaten by a tiger, fallen into an animal trap or been the victim of a bungled robbery. One psychic said he had been abducted by communists. There was a report that he had died his hair red and was working as a fortune teller in the Ipoh area of Malaysia. A British mind reader with a nightclub act in Bangkok said that he had gone to the jungle like an elephant in search of a place to die. A Malaysian businessman suggested that he had been kidnapped by a love-sick aboriginal woman in the Highlands area. More pragmatic minds said he committed suicide, probably slipped down a precipitous ravine or was run down by a car.

Some people believe that Thompson had never ceased to be a spy; that he was a non-official CIA member, whose kidnapping and death was part of a political conspiracy. The year of his disappearance was the height of the American conflict in Vietnam, a war Thompson vociferously opposed. Cynics theorize that in the playing fields of espionage his position was an intolerable betrayal. But a former CIA agent interviewed by Warren said that contacts had continued during his early years in Thailand but the agency later thought his views were too liberal. Conspiracy theorists note the fact that the American army risked sending helicopters to join the manhunt even though they were entering a neutral country's airspace during wartime without permission. Warren's tantalizing account of the disappearance is the most thorough to-date and he believes the truth will never be uncovered. In 1974 Thompson was declared legally dead.

In the year of Thompson's disappearance the company he had founded grossed one and a half million dollars and employed more than 20,000 weavers. The Thompson Silk Company is now the most famous silk emporium in the world with offices in Suriwong Road, retail shops in major hotels and malls all over the city as well as abroad and a state-of-the-art

factory in Khorat. And you can perhaps spot Jim Thompson himself, or rather a wax figure of him, in a sky blue silk shirt with his pet cockatoo, Cocky, sitting on a park bench on the first floor of the Center for the Arts adjacent to his museum-house.

Seventeen

THAI FOOD

This book began by noting the contradictions that have always made Bangkok an extraordinarily alluring, yet equally enigmatic place. All these tensions are resolved in world-famous Thai cuisine, though it was only after the 1960s that its true complexity began to be widely appreciated outside the kingdom. It is essentially based on chilli paste (*nam phrik*), a widely-used seasoning that has regional variations and distinctive flavours, especially when made with dried shrimp. The dull thump of the mortar and pestle resounds through the streets and lanes of Bangkok. By crushing the fibres of herbs the pores are opened to release essential oils and the process yields a richly aromatic paste in which the constituent parts are inseparable from the whole.

Although Thai cuisine yokes both eastern and western foods and cooking methods, the result is uniquely Thai. Take, for example, Indian curry. The Siamese substituted coconut oil for ghee and fresh herbs for spices. Portuguese traders, who had acquired a taste for South American peppers, brought the fresh red hot chilli peppers to Thailand in the sixteenth century. Watch out for the tiniest kind—*phrik khee noo*—barely a half an inch long. A surprise bite can taste like a spark from Vulcan's forge. It literally translates as "mouse shit chilli" since finely chopped bits hide unseen, like mice droppings, under tender pieces of young ginger, cilantro leaves and sweet garlic.

The American writer F. A. Neale's distaste for garlic, a key ingredient in almost every Thai dish, makes one wonder why he entitled his memoirs *Consul in Paradise* (1852). He found Siamese food "execrable and unwholesome; not from the want of the wherewithal to cook (for most certainly the pork and poultry were remarkably fine), but from want of *savoir faire*, and from the abominable practice they have of eating pickled garlic, and flavouring all their dishes with this unsavoury condiment."

Bishop Pallegoix, whose long sojourn in Bangkok overlapped with Neale's, was a true enthusiast of "strong and hot" Siamese cuisine. The good French prelate gave his European readers a traditional recipe for a fish curry that was both "very appetizing and favours the digestion." He also found traditional eating habits quite civilized and salubrious, from the custom of sitting on a mat or carpet on the ground to the avoidance of liquids until after the meal.

> The dishes are cut in small pieces and the rice is placed aside and to the right in a great, widening bowl. On the left side, there is a basin with water in which floats another small basin to drink. The diners have neither spoons, nor forks, nor knives. They use only a mother-of-pearl spoon to take from the plates. For all the rest fingers are sufficient. Only when they are satisfied do they drink pure water or a cup of tea... The Princes and the King are only different from their subjects by the richness of the cutlery and the variety of the dishes.

Thai cuisine, better described as four regional cooking styles, is based on blending different tastes to harmonious result. This balance of flavours—*phet* (spicy), *wan* (sweet), *kem* (salty) and *priaw* (sour)—as well as the fine contrasts in both taste and texture and the beautiful presentation are what gives Thai food its unique quality. Cooking is done in earthenware pots and woks and on grills. Thai cuisine has been greatly influenced by its neighbours, especially India, China, Laos and Malaysia. "Thai cooking is a paradox," writes Australian restaurateur David Thompson in his comprehensive cookbook *Thai Food*. "It uses robustly flavoured

ingredients—garlic, shrimp paste, chillies, lemongrass—and yet when they are melded during cooking they arrive at a sophisticated and often subtle elegance."

Cutting up all the vegetables, fresh herbs and spices is labour-intensive but since food is a national obsession and group eating emphasizes the communal nature of Thai society, this is quite acceptable. Thais seem to eat all day and the term for snacking is *khong gin len*—play eating. It is *sanuk* (fun), a philosophy of life consonant with Buddhist emphasis on living in the present.

A proper meal should consist of a soup, a curry dish with condiments or a spiced salad and a dip with accompanying fish and vegetables. Rice is the staple, and the colloquial expression for eating is *gin kao*—eat rice. All dishes are served simultaneously so that the complementary flavours may be fully enjoyed. Of the four condiments—chilli flakes, sugar, spicy vinegar, fish sauce (*nam pla*)—it is the last that has the most ancient western cousin. *Garum*, the pungent Roman fish sauce, was also made by fermenting fatty fish in brine.

Yam Yai, also known as the Siamese Princess Salad, is a perfect metaphor for the brilliantly assimilative habits of Thai cooking. The salad mixes shredded chicken breasts, lean pork, fresh shrimp and Chinese sausage, lacing these with a dressing of taste-bud awakening flavours—limes, vinegar, fish sauce, cilantro, chillies, garlic and palm sugar—to unforgettable gustatory effect. Another special dish is *kaeng kiaw wan* (green curry). The potent kick of the chilli peppers and spices is soothed by sweet, creamy coconut milk from the verdant plantations of the central plains. There is one soup which is positively erotic—*tom kha gai* (chicken coconut soup with lemon grass, kaffir lime leaves, fish sauce and galangal). As it arrives on the table the spicy and fragrant aromas and sweet coconut scent arise to tease the palate. The tip of the tongue first welcomes the sweet and salty tastes; then the spicy and slightly tart sensations ravish other taste buds providing exquisite bursts of intense pleasure.

Many of the Thai restaurants in Bangkok cook for *farangs* and temper the seasonings to the average tourist palate. This is not the case at the Sala Rim Naam Restaurant at the Oriental Hotel. For a lavish and authentically Thai meal, it is hard to beat the cuisine and the location. Like other fortunate writers in Bangkok I have been a guest at this beautiful riverfront restaurant housed in a richly decorated Thai pavilion almost directly across from the river wing on the Thonburi side of the river. Accessing it by the hotel's polished teak rice boat from a private dock reminds one that cooks in Old Bangkok drew upon the water for fish and hydroponic plants and herbs. Because of their Buddhist culture they eschewed large chunks of meat, instead shredding and marinating them with spices, herbs and thick sauces. Traditional Thai cooking methods were stewing and baking, or grilling and the Chinese methods of stir-frying and deep-frying were readily adopted.

A charming Victorian-style teak bungalow adjacent to the restaurant houses the acclaimed Thai Cooking School run by the hotel. Week-long "hands on" classes are structured according to the general cookbook categories: snacks and salads, soups and curries, stir fried, steamed and grilled dishes and desserts. Then it is *velaa thaan ahaan thieng*, time for lunch. Like the thousands of pampered graduates before me, I was awarded a certificate of accomplishment by the engaging chef as well as an Oriental Hotel apron, little sacks of spice and a pack of recipes. (But by that time I actually didn't want to cook any more.)

STREET FOOD

I had recently discovered street food. This informal economy is so vast that it must constitute the largest free-wheeling open-air cafeteria in the world and chefs from around the world routinely come to see what is new.

Many of the street chefs were puzzled by the $29,000-a-head gourmet dinner for forty well-heeled international guests hosted at a kitsch postmodern hotel in February 2007. Apart from the inappropriateness of such ultra-extravagance in a country where many people are still undernourished, locals on the ground thought that the foodies were unfortunate captives of the glass pleasure dome enclosing the restaurant. As a journalist who interviewed them accurately reported, "everybody knows the best food in Thailand costs just 30 baht and is cooked in a wok welded to a street cart and served at a fold-up metal table on the pavement."

One of my favourite eating streets is soi 38 off Sukhumvit, where superb *phad thai* and chicken *satay* are washed down with cold Singha beer. There are plastic stools and tables casually arranged, and finicky visitors can bring tissues to wipe off eating utensils, as some Thai do despite the fact that they have been washed. At Suda, a local restaurant off soi Asoke, you can keep your private bottle of Mekong whisky to mix with

soda, a meal accompaniment favoured by many Thai men.

Thai Hawker Food is the must-own pocket guide for anyone who really wants to eat well day and night either at the markets, the *raan aahan tii thanon* (street restaurants) or take-out eateries. Among other helpful features the authors identify the major areas where the vendors of push carts *(rot kehn)* congregate, a map of the best locations for particular food and a list of useful terms when pointing and smiling fail to work.

Anyone on a diet would be well-advised to stay inside as the aromas are irresistible, and locals tempt visitors by snacking all day long. There is an astonishing variety of street food in this hawkers' paradise, from the deadly hot *som tam* (papaya salad) to chewy *pla muk ping* (grilled dried squid) to unusual *takataen thord* (deep-fried locusts). Bangkok's street-fare has always attracted the fearless. An English journalist boasted in a newspaper report of 1899 that, "Crickets are said to be good roasted; they smell gamy and taste like the roasted bones of birds." Insects today are no longer just food for the poor but expensive delicacies like rare mushrooms. Philip Cornwel-Smith reports that the brown-tipped white caterpillars, called *rot duan* (express train) for their length and speed, can summon as much as 1,000 baht per kilo.

Although some weight-conscious people are not too keen on Thai desserts—mostly made with tapioca flour, coconut and sugared up for sweet-toothed customers—they have a host of fans (especially children) and vendors have always been beloved fixtures throughout the city. The compelling song of a waterborne sweet-meat vendor from 1925 returns us to the life of the floating city of Old Bangkok where this journey began.

Above the town the terrible sun
Burned all the hours, one by one;
The full-fed river marked them well;
And with the changing of the tide
A sampan slipped from the farther side,
Heavy with savoury things to sell;
And shrill the vendor's coaxing voice
Rose above the harbour's noise.

Ah, these cocoanuts of mine
Packed with meat and soaked with wine!

Sugar cane from Kanburee,
Fresh and succulent,—buy of me!
None has better store than I,—
Come and buy!
Come and buy!

The municipal government estimates that there are roughly 43,000 food vendors in Bangkok today. Most are women but more men joined their ranks following the dramatic 1997 collapse of the baht. Many established restaurants closed and the number of street food eateries and people preparing food at home for sale increased dramatically.

Then a few years later the "big box stores" came—Tesco, Carrefour and Big C—challenging the already well-established Makro mega-stores. The losers were *cho huay*, the countless small Chinese "dry goods" shops selling rice, oil and other staples.

Food vendors appear every day at the same time, at the same station, walking the same routes. No need for watches; just look and listen. At 11 a.m. sharp the Isaan lady appears across the street from me. Silence is golden. Then about a half hour later she begins to screech out like an alley cat in an echo chamber: *som tom* (spicy papaya salad), *kao nio* (sticky rice), *gai yang* (grilled chicken). Come and buy! It's hard to resist.

Part Five

CITY OF MODERNITY

Eighteen

MODERN CITYSCAPE

Bangkok is a fascinating mixture of rich Siamese heritage and startling modernity, often ugly at the macrocosmic level but abounding in fragments of intense beauty. It is packed with malls, department stores, restaurants and high-rise buildings and "probably the world's most cluttered streetscape," writes Philip Cornwel-Smith in his *Very Thai: Everyday Popular Culture.*

Back in 1970 when the 22-storey Dusit Thani Hotel first opened it was Bangkok's tallest skyscraper. Travel writer Paul Theroux, who looked down from its spanking new rooftop restaurant to the traffic-choked Rama IV Road, was bored by the "flattened anthill" that stretched out to the distant horizon.

I am looking out from the Revolving Skydeck on the 84th-floor of the Baiyoke II Tower in the Indian garment district of Pratunam. This soaring landmark dominates the urban landscape—a giant pencil with a flashing red tip for air safety. Skyscrapers extend in every direction. Flyovers on the expressway create inter-looping ribbons of movement. Whereas landmarks and identifiable areas often seem lost or hidden in the chaos on the ground, the Skydeck super-view gives the city the coherence of a seemingly well-planned, first-world megalopolis.

Spread out before me is a vast, shimmering plateau of light, like a starry sky flipped upside down. The 360-degree panoramic walk around the deck is utterly captivating. The city teems with life as millions of people, and even creatures of the jungle, make their presence known. A mahout leads his Surin elephant on a sidewalk, by-passing traffic-stalled high-end luxury cars.

Condos and office blocks, many offering world-class luxury, are rising up all over the city like concrete stalagmites. A moving forest of cranes at day makes way for the night shift. Workers from the north-east with portable lights look like puppets in old shadow plays (*nang talung*) through the green protective netting that enshrouds buildings under construction.

Linda Dusit, a character in Somtow Sucharitkul's horror novel *The Crow: the Temple of Night*, is down there somewhere driving to Chinatown. Dusit is a middle-aged weekend shaman. She owns a Thai restaurant in Los Angeles but rather improbably comes to Bangkok for a semester each year to teach at Chulalongkorn University, the "Harvard of Thailand". While en route to buy a coffin for a poor person—"an act that greases the wheel of karma"—she takes in the modern cityscape.

> Condominiums and apartment complexes towered above a congested expressway. Without zoning, building styles clashed: here a slab-like, primary colored building like a monstrous Mondrian, there a Greek colonnade athwart a deco skyscraper; there again an untouched temple, its pointed eaves and pastel pagodas drowning in a sea of architectural discord; and everywhere neon. Neon that screamed out world-class brands: Coke and Versace and Tag Heuer and Sony. Neon for massage parlors, transvestite clubs, live sex shows, gay bars, and fortune-tellers. The concrete support of an uncompleted L-train threading through the chaos, symbolizing both bureaucratic bungling and eternal optimism: all these things were Bangkok, a city both futuristic and feudalistic, a city where the first and third worlds were in endless collision.

The Skytrain mass transit project was initially met with great resistance, especially by locals who loathed living underneath the 36-feet-high concrete pylons and feared the invasion of their homes and shop houses by trapped exhaust emission, especially from four-stroke motorcycles. The *Bangkok Post* website published a series of pro and con haikus, one of which encapsulates the distress.

> pillars of concrete
> invading our consciousness
> driving us insane

The Skytrain was formally opened to the public in 1999 and is officially known as The Elevated Train in Commemoration of HM the King's 6th Cycle Birthday. The elevated system links 23 key places in the central and eastern part of the capital via two lines (Sukhumvit and Silom) along a fifteen-mile route. It usually moves faster than cars in the vehicular gridlock below. Siam Station, the largest and busiest Skytrain station, is the hub of the sister lines and links the city's main commercial and financial centres. Island platforms, rather than side platforms, facilitate transfer on two levels.

A single Skytrain ticket buys a fish-bowl tour of the city that can deliver Hitchcock-like shadows spotted through open windows, wide views over vast parking lots, an endless sea of white, generic buildings, rare glimpses of temple roofs and verdant tropical treetops. At some places you might spot Buddhist monks blessing "parvenu high-tech towers" that "thrust their way onto the skyline," notes local writer John Hoskin in *Bangkok: Subways, Skytrains and a City Redefined* (2000).

The Skytrain is a miasma of marketing, especially at the Siam Station. TV monitors hover overhead at most stops. Commuters eagerly watch a string of non-stop video clips on the train—for beauty products, hit action films, new condos, weight-loss miracles. A low-budget advertisement by Nestlé shows an animated cow jumping over a rope, seated in a sauna, and finally attached to a reducing machine that almost obscenely shakes its udders—all to convince the public that Bear Brand evaporated milk is low-fat.

Should you open a soft drink, light up a cigarette or step over the yellow safety line, a guard will blow a shrill whistle—the Billy stick of the vast ranks of Thai security men who guard offices and condominiums all over the city. It is a very effective method of public shame.

Many Bangkokians deeply grieved the loss of the stately Siam Intercontinental Hotel, even if they never went inside it. Until a few years ago the Siam Station gave views onto the landmark hotel, built in 1964, that shared a contiguous wall with Sri Paduma Palace (Lotus Pond Palace) dating from the Fourth Reign.

A photo taken during a quiet, off-hour at the Siam Station (2002) shows a few commuters against the striking backdrop of it peaked roof line, said to have been designed after a hat worn by King Rama II. It was one of the first international hotels in the city and a very popular one, both for foreigners and locals who socialized there. A gracious tree-lined driveway gave entrance to the 26-acre hotel-in-a-garden. It passed a colourful spirit house to the right and a little further up the spacious Siam and Saroja ballrooms. A charming triangular kiosk on the left housed the beauty salon, laundry and sweet shop. Following their drop-off at the limousine counter, guests entered a diamond-shaped building designed on the open-plan that was *à la mode* in the 1960s. Its great soaring roof harboured reception and concierge desks, a coffee shop, a gift store and other venues for amenities. It was easy to imagine vintage Hollywood stars of the period drinking Manhattans at the Terrace Bar. T-shaped garden wings flanked the pool, garden bar and barbeque lawn. Bedrooms looked out upon a mini-Central Park that offered such diversions as a children's playground, jogging trail, tennis, volleyballs and *pétanque* courts, putting green and driving range, as well as nurseries filled with brilliant flora, a charming tea garden and an exposition bird cage. Families of ducks nestled under the majestic old trees. In 1999 the lease was up. Despite an award from a government ministry for its environmental protection, this corner of paradise was lost.

MALLS AND MULTIPLEXES

Getting into Bangkok by expressway is relatively easy by taxi, bus, train, limousine, or special-order helicopter. Your map will be marked with the major shopping areas that are mainly centred on Siam Square, sometimes referred to as the Shinjuku of Thailand due to its similarities with the Tokyo shopping and entertainment area. The covered Skywalk leads pedestrians to the bevy of malls catering to wealthy budgets as well as backpackers.

MBK Center (Mah Boon Krong) is an enormous, eight-storey shopping centre with a gleaming spaceship-like façade imposed upon it. Pedestrian entrance from the Skytrain is through the four-storey department store (Tokyu) housed in the mall.

The jam-packed mall can be an overwhelming experience, especially on the upper floors where a bonanza of mobile phones makes for noisy, competitive business. Hard-to-find escalators lead tourists from all over the world (more than a 100,000 a day) as well as locals from one level to the next through a thicket of vendors. The view from the top, where the cinemas are located, is like imagining the tower of Babel inverted. Knock-off clothes and fashion items, electronics, the latest gizmo gadgets, costumes and fine jewellery and a dizzying array of trendy items are sold from over 200 market-style stalls. Bartering adds to the frenetic atmosphere. A traditional massage, beauty treatment or restaurant corner can offer some respite from the mercantile madness of the place. But after a few hours you might feel like screaming out William Klausner's pro-active response to the frenetic quality of contemporary urban life in Bangkok.

Stop the world
I just don't want to get off
I want to rearrange it.

A young Thai man refuses outright to go to Pantip Plaza (New Phetchaburi Road) in a recent song by the hot Thai rock group Loso. His current girlfriend is desperate to go to this Mecca for IT techies but he firmly resists because he cannot bear to see the girl who jilted him, now the owner of a shop there. The chorus reiterates his stubborn determination: *mai pai Pantip* ("I won't go to Pantip").

You have to experience it to believe it. The largest computer shopping mall in Thailand spills over from five plus jam-packed floors that contain hundred of shops selling computers, software, hardware, peripherals, gadgets, games and DVDs. Frequent raids by police try to halt piracy.

There is no chance of missing the Siam Paragon—the gleaming new mega-luxury shopping mall—built on the site of the old Siam Intercontinental Hotel. At is opening in 2005 it was billed with great fanfare and public relations savvy as "The Pride of Bangkok". Crowds now flock to the Siam station platforms for the "culture of spectacle"—fashion shows and other marketing promotions held in the large raised courtyard adjacent to the behemoth. Asian expert Marc Askew sees such shopping malls as "one of the conspicuous 'non-place' realms characteristic of late capitalism and its product, the so-called 'post-modern city.' They are invented commercialized fantasy land divorced from older locality-based identities generated by history and memory."

One enters the opulent mall like a wannabe millionaire in *Second Life*. It is so excessive that it seems virtual. The mall is one of the largest shopping centres in Asia with a retail floor area of some three million square feet. After a meal at one of the eighty restaurants, you can shop at the 80,000 square-foot Gourmet Market on the ground floor adjacent to the Food Halls or pull out the plastic at the international fashion and designer's boutiques. For metrosexuals there is a California fitness centre, for moneyed men flashy sports car showrooms (Ferrari, Maserati, Lamborghini, Porsche) and for the old-timers a computerized thirty-lane Blu-o Rhythm Bowling alley. Hollywood and Asian blockbusters are featured at the fourteen multiplex cinemas. These are preceded by the mandatory tribute to the king during which the entire audience stands at obligatory attention. At the Ultra Screen cinemas the seats recline into chaises longues. Pillows, blankets and comfort socks are provided. Food and beverages may be ordered. The 12,000-watt sub woofer of the IMAX Krungsri theatre makes 3D animated films and tinsel town hits like *Superman Returns* 3D and *Ant Bully* 3D like being in a reality show.

Thai masked dramas based on the *Ramakien* are regularly performed on weekends for tourists and traditionalists. Well-heeled *hi-so* (Thai slang for socialites) women can applaud without bags to hold. Immaculately groomed young Siam Paragon Ambassadors in smart uniforms provide varied customer services, including Hands-Free Shopping with a one-stop payment for the entire spree.

The under-thirties mantra—"cash was so last millennium"—probably means that the Monterey Aquarium in California looks old-fashioned by comparison to the extraordinary new oceanarium, Siam Ocean World, on the subterranean level of the mall. "The Largest Aquarium in the Southern Hemisphere" takes you through different eco-zones: Weird and Wonderful, Living Ocean, Rainforest, Rocky Shore, Open Ocean, Sea Jellies. A giant bow-fronted tank contains a full coral reef stocked with schools of exotic fish. You can visit haunted lighthouses, "dive" with the sharks and walk through a glass tunnel surrounded by marine life. All this aqua-fun while your car is pampered at the Auto Spa below.

Siam Paragon, "The Shopping Paradise of Asia", aims to become a major art centre with regular exhibitions and sales of contemporary art. While the art-gallery-in-a-mall concept has caught on in Bangkok, local artists have long sought a radically different, non-commercial space. The Warehouse (Ekkmai BTS stop, near soi 17) modelled on Bergamot Station in Santa Monica, the largest art gallery complex and cultural centre in southern California, is an emerging new landmark on the cultural scene for innovative contemporary art that is often controversial.

THE DARKER SIDE

As art critic Michael Wright has observed, much contemporary Thai art "reflects the darker side of the Thai personality and society. It sheds light upon the pain of the individual, and upon the pain of a changing society full of unresolved contradictions."

Adjacent to the Siam Paragon, and hidden from its shoppers, is one of Bangkok's oldest and most historic slums near Wat Pathumwan. There

is an entrance to the slum behind the temple and another near the Isetan department store. One feels like Alice entering a tunnel. This authentic old neighbourhood with a long serpentine lane running through it splinters off into short, narrow small alleys. Compared to the swanky mall it is real, rumble-tumble, full of make-shift corrugated structures, of glimpses of other centuries. It resembles a medley of film clips in random order: children in school uniforms buying sweets from vendors, a jumble of pots and pans, a Thai variant of Van Gogh's famous image of worn boots, cockerels in covered cages until the next fight, stray dogs, a fish tank guarded by a spirit house, gracious residents. But there is also evident economic hardship and the conditions of hygiene are poor. Amphetamine addiction in slums takes a huge toll, especially in Klong Toey, the largest and poorest community near the Bangkok port.

Over a million people in Bangkok live in slums, though most are officially and more accurately designated as "congested communities," reports James Ockey in an article in the *Bulletin of Concerned Asian Scholars* (1996). Many slum communities have been in existence for decades. Some were once semi-rural communities until they were gobbled up by the city.

Although the majority of residents were born in the capital, most heads of households have migrated from rural areas up-country. "There is tremendous variety in this official category of congested communities," Ockey writes, "while some communities are small, temporary, new, and built under bridges or overpasses, some are large old homes built of permanent materials, and occupy blocks of valuable land. Many of the houses in older slum communities are well-constructed, although crowded homes complete with electricity."

Out of these slums have come the authentic voices of writers whose disillusions are profound. Preechapul Booonchuay writes in "A Mote of Dust on the Face of the Earth" (1980):

> I want to tell you about my Bangkok: it is a splendid city. I have been here for a long time. Of course, it is not the city my parents believed in, the gold mine that held nothing but prosperity, nothing but money. Not that is doesn't have those things. It has them—but not for people like my mother and father, or for the child that I was. My Bangkok is a prosperous, glittering city and a lonely one. But don't think that I feel sorry for myself, because I don't.

In "Light after Dark" (1980), a gifted social-realist writer known as Sidaoru'ong describes the deep-seated alienation of a working-class woman whom she knew at first-hand. After being sent from her childhood home in a market town in Phitsanulok province to the capital she had a succession of jobs, among them maid, seamstress, factory worker, cook and cashier. She eventually became one of the best-respected writers of modern Thai prose fiction but her long dislocation from her roots and sense of anomie in a rapidly-changing capital left her feeling at mid-life like the "empty space on a sheet of paper, blank, white, devoid of letters."

Film critic Robert Williams suggests that the gritty urban dimensions of Bangkok are not featured in Thai films because the industry depicts the city as people would like it to be, as a fairytale metropolis, using visual techniques of advertising. "Films here need not appeal to the viewer's sense of self," he writes, "and consequently the way in which Bangkok's physical landscape may reflect something more internal."

Witness *Paksa wayu*, a monster film made by Monthon Arangkoon (2004). A nightmare occurs when the subway construction workers discover that they have awoken a huge part-mythical, part pre-historic beast. The army sends in Special Forces but their high-tech military hardware cannot stop the monster-on-the-loose. He escapes from the tunnel and terrorizes Bangkok just like King Kong did in New York. Given the poor pacing and acting, a reviewer on the *Internet Movie Database* was quite generous in awarding the "first Thai monster movie goodwill points for coming up with a new beast, even if he does look like a mutant parrot and is given nothing to do except scream and stomp about."

Many older city residents of every income class were deathly afraid of the new subway system that opened in July 2004, and a subsequent accident contributed to anxieties. Given that Bangkok rests on an alluvial plain that is prone to flooding, many precautions had to be taken, including floodgates, to avoid water inundating the system.

The subway currently consists of a single line connecting 18 stations over twelve miles. It has proven to be a great success and plans are underway to extend it to other key areas as well as to the new Suvaranabhumi (The Golden Land) International Airport (2006) located in nearby Samut Prakan province about fifteen miles to the east of Bangkok. Suvarnabhumi (pronounced *su-wan-na-poom*) has one enormous (six million square feet) terminal for all international and domestic flights that is decorated with mural paintings and contemporary works by Thai artists.

Soi Thong Lor (soi 55)

Many of these artists have grown up in the *sois*, the backstreets of Bangkok, where there is plenty of visual stimulus. Daily life is lived out in the open where random objects appear in heterogeneous confusion, like a giant schoolboy's pocket turned inside out: a vintage mannequin's bust surmounting the clutter of an office supplies display window, bottles of the local (and original) Red Bull in a dark corner, yellow cigarette cards tiling a window sill. To the foreigner it is a city full of *bricolage*—unrelated objects and events that invite imaginative narrative.

Yet some streets are full of dreams. Take Soi Thong Lor (soi 55), formerly a path to and from the San Saep canal. Now a wide thoroughfare, it takes its name from the gold shops at the interesection with Sukhumvit Road. It is paved with the new wealth of the aspirational who cross paths with people who try to eke out a living on the street—among them food vendors, mobile balloon sellers and cardboard recyclers. Owners of some of the most expensive real-estate in the city co-exist with others who may be lucky to earn a few hundred baht a day.

This newly hip street, which used to be known as Wedding Shop Lane after all the western-style bridal shops, is chock full of eccentricities and fusion culture: wildly eclectic architecture and simple vernacular buildings, theatrical gestures and a mixed bag of advertising messages. There are multiple points of view in this complex, ambiguous, post-modern jumble of high and low: it teems with paradox and seems to reflect a contemporary taste for a rootless cosmopolitanism.

Certain places impose themselves. It is hard to miss the the silo-like 55th tower in Christmas colours, Thong Lor Town Center complex with western fast-food joints and yet another Starbucks, Witch's Tavern, an ersatz British Town development, the Feng Shui Dragon Building, Camillian Hospital with its Catholic iconography and Log Home Dining Complex.

Young designers, photographers and stylists gather at the Au Bon Pain in a small strip mall on J-Avenue and at H1—a cluster of up-scale businesses near the Accademia Italiana, a fashion and design institute sponsored by the University of Wales. Thai advertising wins awards for innovation and a vibrant interior-design culture supports half a dozen magazines.

Playground is a new three-storey urban lifestyle venue for the must-haves in a black-slate mini-mall store with a huge Disney-like rabbit mascot in front. Modelled on the Colette concept store on the Rue Saint-Honoré in Paris, Playground's products reek of cool: foreign and Thai fashion magazines, CDs, designer jewellery, cutting-edge clothing, Japanese futons and housewares for the hip, cosmopolitan set. You can book a trip, buy a tennis racket or get the latest graphic design books. Trend setters have a choice of two restaurants, a cooking school and another *latte* at the third Starbucks on the street. Play Gallery on the top floor displays works by top Bangkok artists.

The Thailand Creative & Design Center on the sixth floor of the Emporium Shopping Mall is a nationally funded creative space for new designers built with the aim of helping them gain local and global visibility. Asia's first design learning and resource centre offers state-of-the-art facilities, including a comprehensive design library and multi-media resources as well as a trendy restaurant and café.

Wat Dammamonkol in the Phrakanong district houses the world's largest jade Buddha and the Chanapatana International Design Institute (CIDI), founded in 2000 by an octogenarian Buddhist monk. A school in a temple is not as improbable as it sounds as temples functioned for centuries as educational and community centres. CIDI offers a two-year Thai/Italian diploma but is dedicated to promoting unique contemporary Thai design sense by drawing on its rich cultural heritage. The atmosphere of Buddhist serenity is a far cry from the fast-paced world of international fashion outside the temple gates but the curriculum includes marketing.

For a brief escape to Old Bangkok from Soi Thong Lor, walk to the end opposite Sukhmvit Road and under the bridge to the San Saep Canal. The old canalside promenade is a kaleidocope of local colour and contrast—ramshackle wooden homes and fine mansions, local convenience shops and towering office blocks, temples and mosques, 1960s night club signs and laundry hanging on the line in the late afternoon sunlight. As François Henri Turpin observed in his *Histoire de Siam* (1771), "The character of the Siamese partakes much of the nature of their climate."

Nineteen

Siamese "Soul" Music and the Culture of the Second Xylophone

There are no sounds of silence in Bangkok. Although car horns are rarely heard and tinkling temple bells enchant, popular music is just that. Driving into the city from the airport your cabbie is likely to be listening to FM 90, the first 24-hour *luk thung*, ("child of the field") music.

One result of the 1997 economic bust was a return to traditional crafts and a new appreciation of authentic musical forms associated with the rural and urban poor. The two most popular styles of modern Thai music, *luk thung* and *mor lam*, have absorbed important influences from Laos and other neighbouring nations. During the 1980s *mor lam* emerged and had wide appeal among the marginalized in Bangkok, especially immigrants from the north-east. It is hard-driving, with bluesy vocals, electric instruments, a funk feel to the percussion and a lot of bawdiness. Some call it "Siamese Soul" but it is broader than that as contemporary eclectic fusion sounds draw from other Asian musical expressions.

Amateur urban crooners can de-stress by singing pop billboard hits in a Karaoke Cab driven by Khun Suwit Thongthim. It is equipped with a five-inch mini-television monitor installed on the ceiling, two wired microphones, a video karaoke player and flashing lights for that groovy disco party atmosphere. It is free fun and the passenger only pays the price on the meter. Khun Suwit is never without a fare.

Blind street musicians on Bangkok's sidewalks play a wide gamut of instruments, from flute, guitar and harmonica to traditional Thai instruments like *kaen* (a bamboo reed-organ) from the north-east. Some are wired to microphone and amps and are accompanied by a sighted person who usually holds the tin cup. Philip Cornwel-Smith cites Thai writer Veera Somboon's novel about a blind busker that "celebrates music as an effective means to understand human existence and to grasp compassion" through the often painful experiences of people who see with other eyes.

An escape from these harsher realities is just a button away. Through open doors and windows, whether from small box or a wide screen TV, the flickering images of soap operas show their strong hold on the public imagination. Archetypal tales of romance are often repeated and rehashed but there is an unusual twist in Thailand, as Cornwel- Smith notes: "Most of the public see soap operas for what they are, calling them *nam nao* (murky waters) due to their stagnant plots and unsavoury behaviour." Strict censorship rules out love scenes, even kissing. While they "wring every last drop of emotion from envy to infidelity, they avoid social controversy," he writes.

Behind the discretion and omnipresent human warmth of the so-called "Land of Smiles" is an extraordinarily complex culture that has ingeniously absorbed Chinese, Indian, Japanese, Khmer, Burmese, Malay and western influences. This hybrid cloning has resulted in a cultural fusion that is authentically Thai. "Thainess" is on the one hand obvious and on the other very difficult to define. As a result, Thailand remains "one of the most elusive countries in Asia," affirms writer Ian Buruma.

It is nearly impossible to do justice to the extraordinary richness of Thai culture in a few pages, but Ajarn Chetana Nagavaraja provides precious insights in *Criticism as an Intellectual Force in Contemporary Society* (2003). Buddhist philosophy permeates all aspects of culture, and the spontaneous qualities of "human experience and contact" take precedence over the written text. As Buddhism posits the impermanence of human life, it also affirms that the "aspiration of art towards permanence is but illusory." Good Buddhists have "always been wary of the theatre of illusion," the Thai scholar observes. The same is true for celebrity culture, as Cornwel-Smith writes: "Despite all the cooing, Thais recognize the flimsiness of showbiz, calling it *maya*—Sanskrit for 'illusion'."

Illusion is also shunned in the performing arts, the pre-eminent cultural form in Thailand. Popular theatre always begins by setting out the rules and the highest value is accorded to improvisation. Thus there is no clear dividing line between performers and spectators. Actors quite intentionally interrupt and the audience makes spontaneous interventions (shouting out rhymes if the actor's memory fails and presenting floral garlands or money to favourites). Improvisational skills of spectators frequently rival those of the actors, Ajarn Chetana reports: "It is no rare sight to see a member of the audience step into an orchestra and take over (and surely not usurping) the place of a performer who steps out to assume the role of listener."

In the improvised folk theatre known as *likay* music, dance, song, and spoken words elaborate upon one another like a Baroque musical composition where tempo, drama, ornamentation and phrasing create a complex and life-like interpretation. The process of improvisation favours flexibility and freedom of expression over concision, leading Ajarn Chetana to identify verbal ingenuity as the "root of the incomparable richness of our popular culture." The oral tradition recognizes the power of language as true aesthetic experience.

> Our traditional songs take the form of improvised verse repartee between male and female protagonists, in which the two opposing parties spend the whole night fighting each other verbally, each doing his or her utmost to outmanoeuvre the opposite sex. It is a verbal art bordering on verbosity, but this is contained within the rules of the game. The public enjoy this verbal belligerence, which is at the same time a contest of intelligence, because they are fully conscious (as much as the singers themselves) that they are engaged in a game, which is not real life.

Perhaps ironically, cultural decorum in Thailand seeks to contain expression of personal feelings in real life. As a result of this reticence towards giving free rein to emotion, hundreds of Thai phrases have been created to express the language of the heart—*jai*—metaphorically. Among them are expressions for panic heart, stunned heart, astringent and bitter heart and black heart.

The expressive urge of Thai people prioritizes multi-dimensional, multi-faceted, highly-decorative forms be they floral pieces, altars in taxi windows or Thai boxing matches. In temple murals both simultaneous and diverse actions take place in the same time frame at different levels, as in a medieval stained glass. Angels, monks, mythological figures and everyday people inhabit a highly stylized world at top. Its illusory nature is intentionally made evident by the often fascinating anecdotal life of commoners at bottom. This disinterest in the three unities that have dominated western cultural thought since antiquity is evident all over Bangkok. The Thai Tourist Authority cleverly markets the "charm of chaos" to promote the city to westerners. It might do better to focus on the fact that

the majority of people really seem to be having fun—*sanuk*—no matter what they are doing.

Just watch a performance of traditional Siamese music. It may seem random but actually has highly sophisticated rules. The most common traditional Central Thai ensemble, the *piphat,* can be traced back to the first capital at Sukhothai. It combines fiddles, oboe-like wind instruments, xylophones, cymbals and a circular set of tuned gong-chimes. Eminent British musician Hans Keller found the classical Thai orchestra concert that he attended in London both dissonant and chaotic: it was "pre-music". He completely overlooked the essence of Thai classical music: based on memory rather than written notation, it gives freedom to individual musicians to go their different ways, while adhering to the common framework. A master musician named Khun Bunyong Ketkhong has a repertoire of roughly 20,000 tunes.

Appearances can be deceptive, Ajarn Chetana reminds us. This is especially true with respect to the artistic functions of the two xylophones placed in front of the orchestra. The musician at the first instrument (*ranak ek*) carries the main melody. The second player of the *ranak thum* hits keys that produce a softer resonance. We may interpret his position as "second fiddle" whereas he actually has the authority of the conductor. He syncopates, accentuates and sometimes "comments" on the main melody. With rare creative freedom he may improvise, relaxing or speeding up the pace, on the condition that the dominant theme is kept. Virtuosity is sacrificed for collective music-making to the pleasure and pride of all.

The contemporary creative community in Bangkok has been collectively enriched by the significant contributions of King Bhumibol Adulyadej both as a munificent patron of the arts during his long reign and as an active participant. As jazz musician, painter, photographer and composer, he lends highly visible royal encouragement to the imaginative. *Song Phra Charoen!* Long live the King!

Glossary

Ajarn	Professor
Bang	Village on water
Chedi	Tapering spire normally containing relics
Devaraja	God-king
Garuda	A mythical half-man-half-bird, carrier of Lord Vishnu
Kinaree	A mythical bird in female form
Kinnon	A mythical bird in male form
Klong	Canal
Krung Thep	City of angels, the official Thai name for Bangkok
Mondop	Multi-tiered roof on a square plan
Muang	City
Naga	Mythical serpent; symbol of water, immortality and wisdom, of renewed births, of secret knowledge and, when the tail is in the mouth, of eternity. Protective snake of the Buddha
Nirat	Descriptive travel poem
Panung	A wrap-around cloth in the form of breech clout; folded around the body from one long sheet of silk or cotton
Pom	Fort
Prang	Khmer-style square spire
Sanuk	Enjoyment, fun
Siam	A geographic entity that roughly corresponds to present-day Thailand and included, in former times, adjacent areas such as the Shan States (Shan being the Anglo-Burmese corruption of Siam)
Soi	Lane; not originally a through road
Stupa	Bell-shaped spire
Thai	Ethnic name or language, also spelt Tai, T'ai and Dai. The Thais spread from Assam, the Shan States, south and

south-east China, Laos and North Vietnam down to present-day Thailand as well as in the Malay Peninsula where they form a minority. The notion that the name means "free" is of a recent nationalistic vintage

Thanon   Street

Trok   Path that formerly led off from riverbanks and canals: alleyway

Ubosto (*bot*)   Preaching and ordination hall in a temple

Vihara (*viharn*)Large building in a temple where sacred objects are housed

Wai   A prayer-like gesture of greeting and respect in which men and women bring their palms together at chest level with a soft bow of the head

Wat   Temple, monastery

Chronology of Bangkok Kings

1767-1782	Taksin	(King of Thonburi)
1782-1809	Rama I	Phra Phutthayotfa (Phraya Chakri)
1809-1824	Rama II	Phra Phutthalaetla Naphalai: son of Rama I
1824-1851	Rama III	Phra Nangklao: son of Rama II
1851-1868	Rama IV	Mongkut: son of Rama II
1868-1910	Rama V	Chulalongkorn: son of Rama IV
1910-1925	Rama VI	Vachiravudh: son of Rama V
1925-1935	Rama VII	Prajadipok (abdicated): son of Rama V
1935-1946	Rama VIII	Ananda Mahidol: grandson of Rama V
1946-	Rama IX	Bhumibol Adulyedej: grandson of Rama V

Kings had different names before assuming the throne, during their reign, and sometimes after their demise. For example, Rama I reigned as King Ramathibodi, and Phra Phutthayotfa was a posthumous title. The kings of the Chakri Dynasty were renamed in the early twentieth century adopting Rama, hero of the Indian epic, as the royal patronymic.

Further Reading

Anderson, Benedict R. O'G. and Ruchira Mendiones (eds. and trans.), *In the Mirror: Literature and Politics in Siam in the American Era*. Ithaca: Cornell University Press, 1985.

Askew, Marc, *Bangkok: Place, Practice and Representation*. London and New York: Routledge, 2002.

Augustin, Andreas and Andreas Williamson, *The Oriental Bangkok*. Vienna: 2000.

Baker, Chris and Pasuk Phongpaichit, *A History of Thailand*. Cambridge: Cambridge University Press, 2005.

Bangkok. Text by John Hoskin. Photographs by Luca Invernizzi Tettoni. Singapore: 1986.

Barang, Marcel (ed. and trans.), *The 20 Best Novels of Thailand*. Bangkok: TMC, 1994.

Barmé, Scot, *Woman, Man, Bangkok: Love, Sex, and Popular Culture in Thailand*. Lanham MD: Rowman and Littlefield, 2002.

Batson, A. B., *The End of the Absolute Monarchy in Asia*. Singapore: Oxford University Press, 1984.

Beauvoir, Marquis de, *A Week in Siam* (1870). Bangkok: Siam Society, 1981.

Bock, Carl, *Temples and Elephants* (1884). Bangkok: Orchid Press, 1985.

Boisselier, Jean, *La Peinture en Thailande*. Fribourg: Office du Livre, 1976.

Botan (Supa Sirising), *Letters from Thailand* (1969). Trans. Susan Fulop Kepner. Bangkok: DK Book House, 2003.

Bradley, William L., *Siam Then: the Foreign Colony in Bangkok Before and After Anna*. Pasadena CA: William Carey Library, 1981.

Buls, Charles, *Siamese Sketches* (1901). Translated, illustrated and introduced by Walter E. J. Tips. Bangkok: White Lotus, 1994.

Campbell, J. G. D., *Siam in the Twentieth Century*. London: Edward Arnold, 1904.

Carter, A. C., *The Kingdom of Siam*. New York: Putnam, 1904.

Chakrabongse, Prince Chula, *Lords of Life: a History of the Kings of Thailand*. London: Alvin Redman, 1967.

Conrad, Joseph, *Lord Jim* (1900). London: Penguin, 1988.

—, *The Shadow Line* (1917). London: Penguin, 1993.

Cornwel-Smith, Philip, *Very Thai: Everyday Popular Culture*. Bangkok: River Books, 2005.

Cruysse, Dirk van der, *Siam and the West 1500-1700*. Bangkok: Siam Society, 2002.

Exell, F. K., *Siamese Tapestry*. London: Hale, 1963.

Finlayson, G., *The Mission to Siam and Hué the Capital of Cochin China in the Years 1821-22*. London: 1826.

Flood, T, and C., *The Dynastic Chronicles. Bangkok Era, First Reign*. Tokyo: Centre for East Asian Cultural Studies, 1978.

Fournereau, Lucien, *Bangkok in 1892*. Trans. Walter E. J. Tips. Bangkok: White Lotus Press, 1998.

Garnier, Derick, *Ayutthaya: Venice of the East*. London: Thames & Hudson, 2004.

Girling, John L. S., *Thailand: Society and Politics*. Ithaca and London: Cornell University Press, 1981.

Guelden, Marlane, *Thailand: Into the Spirit World*. Singapore: Times, 1993.

Gutzlaff, C., *Journal of Three Voyages along the Coast of China in 1831, 1832, and 1833, with notices of Siam, Corea, and the Loo-Choo Island*. London: 1834.

Jottrand Emile, Mr. and Mrs., *In Siam. The Diary of a Legal Adviser of King Chulalongkorn's Government* (1905). Trans. Walter E. J. Tips. Bangkok: White Lotus, 1996.

Jumsai, M. L. Manich, *King Mongkut and Sir John Bowring*. Bangkok: Chalermnit, 1970.

—, *Understanding Thai Buddhism*. 5th rev. ed. Bangkok: Chalermnit, 2000.

—, *History of Thai Literature: Including Laos, Shans, Khamti, Ahome, and Yunnan-Nanchao*. 3rd rev. ed. Bangkok: Chalermnit, 2000.

Jumsai, Sumet, *Cultural Origins in Siam and the West Pacific*. Singapore: Oxford University Press, 1990.

—, *Let's Have a Coup Once a Year and Sundry Musings*. Bangkok: 1999.

Kaewsuriya, Rumphaipun, *Guidebook Wat Pho*. Bangkok: 2004.

Kepner, Susan Fulop (ed.), *The Lioness in Bloom: Modern Thai Fiction about Women*. Berkeley and Los Angeles: University of California Press, 1996.

Knight, Ruth Adams, *The Treasured One: the Story of Rudivoravan Princess of Siam*. New York: E. P. Dutton, 1957.

Kornerup, Ebbe, *Friendly Siam: Thailand in the 1920s* (n.d.). Bangkok: White Lotus, 1999.

Kruger, Rayne, *The Devil's Discus*. London: Cassell, 1964.

Krull, Germaine with Dorothy Melchers, *Bangkok: Siam's City of Angels*. London: Hale 1964.

Kukrit Pramoj: His Wit and Wisdom. Writings, Speeches and Interviews. Velas Mamuat and Steve van Beek (eds.). Bangkok, Duang Kamol, 1983.

La Loubère, Simon, *A New Historical Relation of the Kingdom of Siam* (1693). Singapore: 1986.

Landon, Margaret, *Never Dies the Dream*. Garden City NY: Doubleday, 1949.

Leonowens, Anna, *The English Governess at the Siamese Court*. London: Trubner & Co., 1870.

Malcolm, H., *Travels in South-Eastern Asia, embracing Hindustan, Malaya, Siam, and China; with Notices of Numerous Missionary Stations, and a Full Account of the Burman Empire*. Boston: 1838.

Matics, Kathleen A., *A History of Wat Phra Chetuphon and Its Buddha Images*.

Bangkok: 1979.

Maugham W. Somerset, *A Gentleman in the Parlour*. London: Heinemann, 1930.

—, *A Siamese Fairytale* (1922). Bangkok: 2002.

McDonald, Rev. N.A., *A Missionary in Siam (1860-1870)*. Bangkok: White Lotus, 1999.

Mouhot, Henri, *Travels in the Central Parts of Indo-China (Siam), Cambodia, and Laos, during the Years 1858, 1859, and 1860*. London: John Murray, 1864.

Nagavaraja, Ajarn Chetana, "In Search of Indigenous Theories," *Criticism as an Intellectual Force in Contemporary Thai Society. Summary Report of a Research Project by Chetana Nagavaraja*. Under the Aegis of the Thailand Research Fund (THF). Bangkok: 2003, pp.197-220.

Neale, Frederick A., *Narrative of a Residence in Siam*. London: 1852.

Nicholl, Charles, *Borderlines: A Journey in Thailand and Burma*. London: Secker & Warburg, 1988.

O'Connor, Richard, "Place, Power and Discourse in the Thai Image of Bangkok", *Journal of the Siam Society*, Vol 78, Part 2, 1990, pp. 61-74

O'Neil, Maryvelma Smith, "Corrado Feroci a.k.a. Silpa Bhirasri (1892-1962) and Modern Art in Thailand" in *La Cultura Thailandese et le Relazioni Italo-Thai*. Turin: Cesmeo, 2005, pp.247-72.

An Oriental Album. A Collection of Pictures and Stories about the Oldest Hotel in Thailand Presented by Giorgio Berlinghieri. Bangkok: n.d.

Pallegoix, Mgr. J.-B., *Description du Royaume Thai au Siam*. Paris: 1854.

Peleggi, Maurizio, *Lord of Things: the Fashioning of the Siamese Monarchy's Modern Image*. Honolulu: University of Hawaii Press, 2002.

Phillips, Herbert. P., *Modern Thai Literature: with an Ethnographic Interpretation*. Honolulu: University of Hawaii Press, 1987.

Poshyananda, Apinan, *Modern Art in Thailand*. Singapore: Oxford University Press, 1992.

Pramoj, M. R. Kukrit, *The Four Reigns*. Chiang Mai: Silkworm Books, 1999.

—, *Many Lives*. Chiang Mai: Silkworm Books, 2000.

Pramoj, M. R. Seni and M. R. Kukrit Pramoj, *A King of Siam Speaks*. Bangkok: Siam Society, 1989.

Reynolds, Jack, *A Woman of Bangkok*. Bangkok: 1992.

Ringis, Rita, *Thai Temples and Murals*. Kuala Lumpur: Oxford University Press, 1999.

Roberts, Edmund, *Embassy to the Eastern Courts of Cochin-China, Siam and Muscat; in the U.S. Sloop-of-War Peacock during the Years 1832-3-4*. New York: 1837.

Seidenfaden, Erik, *Guide to Bangkok with Notes on Siam* (1938). Singapore: 1984.

Siburapha, *Behind the Painting*. Trans. David Smyth. Chiang Mai: Silkworm Books, 1995.

Sioris, George, Phaulkon. *The First Greek Counselor at the Court of Siam: an*

Appraisal. Bangkok: Siam Society, 1998.

Sivaraksa, Sulak, *Siam in Crisis: Collected Articles by Sulak Sivaraksa.* Bangkok: Thai Inter-Religious Commission fore Development, 1980.

Smith, Malcolm, *A Physician at the Court of Siam.* London: Country Life, 1946.

Smithies, Michael, *Old Bangkok.* Singapore: Oxford University Press, 1986.

—, *Bight of Bangkok: a Collection of Short Stories.* Singapore: Heinemann, 1993.

—, *Descriptions of Old Siam.* New York: Oxford University Press, 1995.

Smyth, H. Warington, *Five Years in Siam from 1891 to 1896.* New York: 1898.

Sparrow, Gerald, *Land of the Moonflower.* London: Elek, 1955.

—, *The Star Sapphires.* London: Jarrold, 1950.

Sternstein, Larry, *Portrait of Bangkok.* Bangkok: Bangkok Metropolitan Association, 1982.

Stevenson, William, *The Revolutionary King: the True-Life Sequel to The King and I.* London: Constable, 1999.

Stowe, Judith A. *Siam Becomes Thailand: a Story of Intrigue.* London: Hurst, 1991.

Suksri, Naengnoi, *The Grand Palace Bangkok.* London: Thames & Hudson, 1999.

Terwiel, B. J., *Monks and Magic: an Analysis of Religious Ceremonies in Central Thailand.* Bangkok: White Lotus, 1994.

Three Worlds According to King Ruang: a Thai Buddhist Cosmology. Trans. Frank E. Reynolds & Mani B. Reynolds. Berkeley CA, University of California Press, 1982.

Tomlim, J., *Journal of a Nine Months' Residency in Siam.* London: 1831.

Umavijani, Montri, *Facets of Thai Cultural Life.* Bangkok: Foreign News Division, 1984.

Van Beek, Steve, *Bangkok Then and Now.* Bangkok: AB Publications, 2001.

Vella, Walter F., *Siam under Rama III 1824-1851.* New York: Augustin, 1957.

Warren, William, *Jim Thompson: the Unsolved Mystery.* Singapore: Archipelago Press, 1998.

—, *The Truth About Anna and other Stories.* Singapore: Archipelago Press, 2000.

Waugh, Alec, *Bangkok: the Story of a City.* New York: W. H. Allen, 1971.

Wenk, Klaus, *The Restoration of Thailand Under Rama I, 1782,-1809.* Tucson: University of Arizona Press, 1968.

—, *Thai Literature: an Introduction.* Trans. Erich W. Reinhold. Bangkok: 1995.

Wood, W. A. R., *A Consul in Paradise.* London: Souvenir Press, 1965.

Wright, Arnold and Oliver T. Breakspear, *Twentieth Century Impressions of Siam* (1908). Bangkok: White Lotus, 1994.

Wright, Joseph J. Jr., *The Balancing Act: a History of Modern Thailand.* Oakland CA: Pacific Rim Press, 1991.

Wyatt, David. *Thailand: a Short History.* New Haven CT and London: Yale University Press, 1984.

Young, Ernest, *The Kingdom of the Yellow Robe* (1898). Kuala Lumpur: 1986.

Index of Literary & Historical Names
(Thai names listed by given name)

Index of Places & Landmarks